Insider Threat Prevention Cyber Security
Part 5
Mastering the Components and Systems of Insider Threat Prevention Cyber Security

by

Dr. Raymod Leslie Newkirk

Also by Dr. Raymond Leslie Newkirk

21st Century Executive Life
21st Century Executive Life

Cosmic Truth God, Us and Them
Cosmic Truth: God, Us, and Them

Paleo-Leadership
Reconstructed Leadership

Systems Thinking in Requirements Analysis
Systems Thinking in Requirements Analysis

The Psychology of Insider Threat Prevention
The Psychology of Insider Threat Prevention Part 2
Psychology of Insider Threat Prevention Part 4
Insider Threat Prevention Part 5

Standalone

A Person Passing By

Sociopaths at Work

From Confusion to Clarity

Table of Contents

Human Beings are very creative. We are experts at finding solutions to the bigger problems that emerge from the previous solutions.

Systems Management Institute, Orlando, Florida 32835.

This book is available at a special discount when ordered in bulk quantities. For more information, contact Publications Sales Department, SMI Press, Orlando, Florida 32835, Tel: (407) 864 7756

www.drraynewkirk.com

www.smirsp.com

For

Felicisima Calma Newkirk

&

Maria Calma Dorothy Newkirk

Very Wonderful, Very Wonderful Indeed!

Something Worth Remembering

Cyber Security, or Cybersecurity, is a huge topic. It is bigger than the Empire State Building. It covers the globe. More people are concerned about Cyber Security than they are their own diets. Perhaps for good reason. If you are a senior executive or a high-level government official, you have probably lost some sleep over it, and it is just getting started. Believe it or not. Insider Threats are a very complicated situation simply because some of the "Insider Threats" do not intent to be threatening anyone or any system or any data. They are Insider Threats because they are ignorant about their environments and through their ignorance they create "big messes" that can deliver significant harm to organizations and teams.

Then there are the people who "cry havoc and let slip the dogs of war," Mark Antony got that right. These are the Cyber Terrorist. These are the people who will experience some sort of satisfaction by your Cyber destruction. These are the actual terrorists and malicious insiders who have something to gain by your data and systems destruction. They do this for a range of reasons that all come down to some kind of intrinsic motivation. They work alone or with a team from somewhere else. Billion Dollar companies have been destroyed because of these people and their complex behaviors. Some of these people are state actors who have been trained and motivated to succeed. For them, the stakes are indeed high. Some of them have even based their personal futures on the success of these Malicious Cyber Operations. You would not be the first person to be fooled by these "Guys and Dolls". They are indeed "Smooth Operators".

ITP Psychological Factors

We store memories differently based on how they were experienced.

- Tip of the tongue effect
- Google effect
- Next-in-line effect
- Testing effect
- Absent-mindedness effect
- Levels of processing effect

We reduce events and list of effects to document their key elements:

- Suffix effect
- Serial position effect
- Part-list cueing effect
- Recency effect
- Primacy effect
- Memory Inhibition
- Modality effect
- Duration Neglect
- List-length effect
- Serial recall effect
- Misinformation effect
- Leveling and Sharpening
- Peal-end rule

We discard specifics to form generalities:

- Fading affect bias
- Negativity bias
- Prejudice
- Stereotypical bias
- Implicit Stereotypes
- Implicit associations

We edit and reinforce some memories after the fact:

- Spacing effect
- Suggestable
- False Memory
- Cryptomnesia
- Source Confusion
- Misattribution of memory
- Too Much Information

We notice things already primed in memory or repeated often:

- Availability heuristic
- Attention bias
- Illusory truth effect
- Mere exposure effect
- Context effect
- Cue dependent forgetting
- Mood congruent memory bias
- Frequency Illusion
- Baader-Meinof Phenomenon
- Empathy gap
- Omission bias
- Base rate fallacy

Bizarre, funny, visually-striking, or anthropomorphic things stick out more than non-bizarre and unfunny things:

- Bizarreness effect
- Humor effect
- Von Restorff effect
- Picture Superiority effect
- Self-relevance effect
- Negativity bias

We notice when something has changed:

- Anchoring

- Conservatism
- Contrast effect
- Distinction bias
- Focusing effect
- Framing effect
- Money illusion
- Weber-Fechner Law

We are drawn to details that confirm our own existing beliefs:

- Confirmation bias
- Congruence bias
- Post-purchase rationalization
- Choice-supportive bias
- Selective perception
- Observer-expectancy effect
- Experimenter's bias
- Observer effect
- Expectation bias
- Ostrich effect
- Subjective validation
- Continued influence effect

We notice flaws in others more easily than we notice flaws in ourselves:

- Bias blind spot
- Naïve cynicism & Naïve realism
- Not Enough Meaning
- Semmelweis reflex

We tend to find stories and patterns even when looking at sparse data:

- Confabulation
- Clustering illusion
- Insensitivity to sample size
- Neglect of probability

- Anecdotal fallacy
- Illusion of validity
- Masked man fallacy
- Recency illusion
- Gambler's fallacy
- Hot-hand fallacy
- Illusory correlation
- Pareididolia
- Anthropomorphism

We fill in characteristics from stereotypes, generalities, and prior histories:

- Group attribution error
- Ultimate attribution error
- Stereotyping
- Essentialism
- Functional fixedness
- Moral credential effect
- Just-world hypothesis
- Argument from fallacy
- Authority bias
- Automation bias
- Bandwagon effect

We imagine things and people we are familiar with or found of as better:

- Out-group homogeneity bias
- Cross-race effect
- In-group bias
- Halo effect
- Placebo effect
- Cheerleader effect
- Positivity effect
- Not invented here
- Reactive devaluation
- Well-traveled road effect.

We simplify probabilities and numbers to make them easier to think about:

- Mental accounting
- Appeal to probability fallacy
- Normalcy bias
- Murphy's law
- Zero sum bias
- Survivorship bias
- Subadditivity effect
- Denomination effect
- Magic number 7+2

We think we know what other people are thinking:

- Illusion of Transparency
- Curse of knowledge
- Spotlight effect
- Intrinsic incentive error
- Illusion of external agency
- Illusion of asymmetric insight

We project our current mindset and assumptions onto the past and future:

- Consistency bias
- Restraint bias
- Projection bias
- Pro-innovation basis
- Time-saving basis
- Planning fallacy
- Pessimism Bias
- Impact bias
- Declinism
- Moral luck
- Outcome bias
- Hindsight bias
- Rosy Retrospection

- Telescoping effect

We Need to Act Fast and favor simple looking options and complete information over complex, ambiguous options.

- Less-is-better effect
- Occam's Razor
- Conjunction fallacy
- Delmore effect
- Law of Triviality
- Bike-shedding effect
- Rhyme as reason effect
- Belief bias
- Information Bias
- Ambiguity Bias

To avoid mistakes, we preserve autonomy, group status, and avoid irreversible decisions:

- Status quo bias
- Social comparison bias
- Decoy effect
- Reactance
- Reverse Psychology
- System justification

To get things done, we tend to complete things we have invested time & energy in:

- Backfire effect
- Endowment effect
- Processing difficulty effect
- Pseudocertainty effect
- Disposition effect
- Zero-risk bias
- Unit bias

- IKEA effect
- Loss aversion
- Generation effect
- Escalation of commitment
- Irrational escalation

To stay focused, we favor the immediate, relatable thing in front of us:

- Identifiable victim effect
- Appeal to novelty
- Hyperbolic discounting
- Sunk Cost Fallacy

To act, we must be confident we can make an impact and feel what we do is important.

- Peltzman effect
- Risk compensation
- Effort justification
- Trait ascription bias
- Defensive attribution
- Fundamental attribution error
- Illusory superiority
- Illusion of control
- Actor-observer bias
- Self-serving bias
- Barnum effect
- Forer effect
- Optimism bias
- Egocentric bias
- Dunning Kruger effect
- Lake Wobegone effect
- Hard-easy effect
- False consensus effect
- Third person effect
- Social desirability bias

- Overconfidence effect

Acknowledgement

This Five Part Work emerged from a lifetime of experience assisting organizations, teams, and individuals with finding inventive ways to solve problems more rapidly. As you move from country to country and culture to culture in search of inventive solutions to problems that are more common than one would ever imagine, you begin to notice several patterns emerge that reduce some of the mystery that shrouds the nature and character of human relationships including: How we form them; how we manage them; how we end them, and how we overcome them?

> This is the stuff of life. Life is relationship living. In Christianity, we believe in God as Relationship

If you ask how I describe human life, I would answer you this way: Life is Relationship. For good or bad, from hope to hopelessness, from self-doubt to confidence, from Ego to Self-Esteem, and from life to death, I would tell you that human life is formed, nourished, developed, enjoyed, and even made miserable through relationship, from birth to death. From the day you meet your mother to the day you meet your dreaded undertaker you pass through life in relationship.

How you manage your relationships says everything about how you will become a fully human person imbued with the capacity for living a life of significance. We are creatures with the capacity to reason well, true; but human life is considerably more emotional than rational. Rationality is a power we possess to navigate life on a material planet. However, we feel more than we think. We use reason occasionally to assist in decision-making, but use our emotions most often to navigate the experiences of our lives.

Think about this: Reason concerns the rules of logic, but emotion flows from the values we hold dear. Emotions represent value judgments, and reason represents logical conclusions, if-then-else. The decisions we make based on value judgements we render often conflict with the decisions we conclude from deduction or induction. This is how we live human life on planet earth. Other places, I am not so sure.

All my life, wise people have told me that the power of reason makes us human. We are the "rational animal". I guess, then, some people are more human than others. Does this make the artist less human than the scientist? Or, are we speaking about the human potential for rational thought so that the scientist is actually a human being and the artist is potentially a human being?

Moreover, the claim that human beings are "rational animals" is rather simplistic because human beings are more than animals, as Aristotle suggested. Although we do have the powers that animals share such as reproduction, self-mobility, growth, and so forth, we enjoy powers beyond those of brute animals like spiritual development, cultivation of virtue, and creative powers of the imagination.

An animal has body, like a rock has material volume occupying space, but an animal is not a rock. A rock requires transitive motion through an external agent to move it, while an animal enjoys imminent motion from within to move itself. So an animal enjoys the powers of a rock in having existence and a body, but exceeds rocks with its own many powers not enjoyed by rocks. In like manner, human beings possess powers not enjoyed by animals.

Human beings are, in fact, beings governed by conscience and the Cardinal Virtues. While we do not call animals "self-moving rocks", we really ought not to call human beings "rational animals". We are considerably more than that.

The problem for human beings here is one of reconciling our emotional powers with our rational powers. It is more than a matter of being "rational animals or "emotional animals". Being more than rational animals who enjoy the power of emotional judgment, the question persists: What kind of creature are we if not a rational animal? What is the influence of virtue in all of this?

Throughout their lifetimes, human beings experience multiple environments concurrently. As self-directed evolutionary beings, we share many of these environments in common with people around the world. We also experience these environments uniquely in ways that reflect our personal interests, commitments, beliefs, and aspirations as social beings. The three environments that most impact the development of this book and Parts Two and Three that follow it are the:

- Via Virtutis, the Way of Virtue
- Via Inventio, the Way of Invention, Creativity, or Problem Solving

- Via Rationis, the Way of Reason, Structured Thinking, or Logic

About this Series

This Insider Threat Prevention series spans five volumes. Book One identifies the pieces to the Insider Threat Prevention Cyber Security puzzle. Book Two defines the environment for putting the pieces together. Book Three examines the strategies of the Insider Threat Prevention Cyber Security Unification Program. Book Four assists readers with mastering the components and systems of Insider Threat Prevention Cyber Security. Book Five talks about the path forward for the Cyber Security enterprise architects. Although each book presents an independent look at a specific segment of the entire architecture unification program, mastery of the Framework requires readers to create a model as a roadmap of the entire Insider Threat Prevention Cyber Security-Enterprise Architecture.

This series differs from the more customary presentations on Insider Threat Prevention Cyber Security. Rather than drilling down into the usual technical presentations of Cyber Security within a Zero Trust environment, I have focused on the design of a behavioral and psychological solution to the challenge of building a unified ITPCS-Enterprise Architecture. Naturally, this focus tremendously increases the volume of material that could be included in each book. So, I o made several choices about the design paths I had to select. This series reflects my design decisions. As you will see, I highlighted the strategic vision rather than the operational. In this regard, I focused more on the possible strategies for unification rather than on the number of workflows involved in technical Insider Threat Prevention Cyber Security.

Our World Today

The following four environments, and the people who inform them, have contributed to building the world we live in today. Their efforts will form the future even more than they do now as Artificial Intelligence begins to impact society in even more potent ways.

First Order Cybernetics

- Mathematics: Ashby & Weiner
- Physiology: Shannon
- Information Theory: Weaver
- Computing: McCulloch
- Engineering: Prigogine
- Control Theory: Bateson
- Anthropology: Mead

Second Order Cybernetics

- Biology of Cognition: Pask
- Experimental Epistemology: Maturana
- Family Therapy: Bowen

The Systems Sciences

- Interdisciplinary Movements:
- First-Order Cybernetics
- Science Studies

Systems Approaches

- Management Cybernetics: Beer, Espejo
- Critical Systems: Jackson & Flood
- Critical Systems Heuristics: Ulrich
- Systemic Inquiry: Checkland
- Applied Systems: Checkland
- Systems Failure: Checkland
- Applied Systems: Checkland
- Information Systems: Stowell, Wood-Harper

- Systems Agriculture: Spedding, Badwen
- Social Systems: Buckley, Vickers
- Management Science: Ackoff
- Soft OR: Management Sciences, Ackoff
- Systems Analysis: RAND Corp.
- Management Learning: Schon, Argyris
- Systems Dynamics: Forrester, Meadows, Senge
- Whole Earth SD: Macy
- Systemic Complexity: Capra
- General Systems Theory: Bertalanffy
- Second-Order Cybernetics: Von Foerster
- Operations Research: Beer, Churchman, Ackoff
- Complexity Science: Ashby

Dedication

"I t's Not Very Often You Get to See Into
The Development of a Cyber Terrorist"

Welcome to a newer, simpler, and more effective way of navigating the professional minefield you call work. I dedicate this series to everyone who suffers from the assault of painful and ineffective colleagues. Whether you are a member of the Board of Directors or a new hire beginning your career, no one wants to work with colleagues who characteristically produce more turmoil than satisfaction and disaster than productivity.

I wrote this book for all of us who at some time or another had to snatch victory out of the jaws of defeat and overcome the "strangeness" of colleagues we could rarely understand. If you are a Millennial, this book is especially for you. If you cannot relate to such a situation, this book is really for you. I wrote this book for everyone who looks at their organization and murmurs: "This place really doesn't make any sense. I just don't get it."

Well guess what? A lot of people just don't get it, especially the ones who think they do. If you get it, answer me this: Are you the kind of person who should recruit other people to work with you? Are you good for others? Are you really a good person who should be invited onto a team responsible for producing critical deliverables? Simply put: Should people want you as a colleague? Will you be good for them, or only good for yourself? What do you think? Have you ever thought about it? If not, you probably already have your answer. Some people are not even good for themselves.

I wrote this book for all of us who are currently building our careers and for the generations who will follow in our footsteps. This book emerged to assist you with navigating the hidden influencers that energize the workplace. These are the sparks that make-or-break effective performance. These are the sparks that produce the painful or joyful lives we live. I tip my hat to all of us. Now let us get busy and achieve something great with our careers. Why settle for less?

Preface

Insider Threat Prevention Cyber Security (ITPCS) is scary. In the first place, ITPCS challenges the most knowledgeable people in the organization. In the second, ITPCS is disastrous when it fails. A single criminal incident can completely ruin a company and render the company completely out of business (OOB). As far as I can remember, we have always faced the challenge of Insider Threat Prevention. Cyber Security, however, is the complicating factor today.

Today, ITPCS has become a chronic problem for executives and the organizations they lead. You would probably be correct to guess that about forty percent of all Cyber Security incidents result from malicious insider attacks. Insider cyber-attacks are more expensive than the attacks of external hackers. While "credentialed" Insider attacks leave the most damage behind, the malicious insider attacks perpetrated by malicious outsiders through coercion often cause the most damage.

Here is a perennial fact: Insider Threat Prevention is fundamentally behavioral and psychological. Highly secure technology assists ITPCS, but it is not enough. ITP begins with people, moves to process, and terminates with technology, always facilitated by people. ITP is a direct attack on an organization's information resources.

Anything can be a target such as data, Intellectual Property, Trade Secrets, and Knowledge Applications. Malicious success requires Cyber Terrorists to discover where the organization's targeted information resources are located as well as the rules governing access and usage. These rules enable teams to manage data classification, access governance, data sharing, monitoring, procedures and controls, legal and cultural considerations.

The missing key to stopping malicious insiders is, of course, not hiring them and selecting them out early during the customary probationary period. Since malicious insiders can operate more silently and inflict more damage than outsiders, designated managers have to pay attention to the "lateral movement" activities of their employees as they access the information systems internally and externally.

While everyone relies on technology to assist with ITP CS, the Cyber Terror threat still exists. SIEM, Data Loss Prevention, User Behavior Analytics, Privileged Access Management, and User Activity Monitoring all fall short and are defeated by smart criminals. There is no doubt that these approaches can be helpful in reducing the severity of attacks. However, they are often helpful only after the attacks have occurred. Nevertheless, they can help management reduce the success rate of future attacks by preempting, detecting, and responding to the lateral movements of trusted insiders.

Although this "Suppression Approach" has become customary when insiders reach beyond their credentials to capture or disrupt an information stream, an innovative insider can defeat it, especially if he or she is knowledgeable about the embedded exposures hidden in the targeted systems such as "temporary" connections and credentials that by default have become permanent.

These careless mistakes increase the pressure on organizations to employ an expanded range of Cyber Security practices such as the use of data deceptions that mimic targeted data and files. Additionally, Cyber Security specialists may employ systems that collect highly accurate forensic evidence that arm first responders to resolve exfiltration more rapidly.

Companies adopt Continuous Performance Management to build and maintain cultures of trust, collaboration, and cooperation. Although trust is important among teams, it has to be earned. Blind trust fails the test of reasoned action. Senior management of CPM-designed organizations, above and beyond most other organizations, must continuously enhance their organizations' Insider Threat Prevention Cyber Security defenses.

Executives expect CPM organizations to remain consistently vigilant about the threat of Cyber Terrorism. Managers expect their team leaders to protect their systems, networks, and people against the constantly emerging attack techniques perfected by the malicious Cyber Terrorists inside and outside the company.

Insider Threat Prevention Cyber Security teams succeed whenever they prioritize, investigate, and respond to malicious insider attacks well enough to both reduce the risk of insider threats and prevent the occurrence of every targeted attack.

The Formative Questions, Revisited

Let me ask you several important questions that I previously asked you in an earlier volume. They will be a little different this time.

What Do You Deserve with Your ITP Program?

Your ITP career can be a rewarding life-long experience. It can be an enduring and wonderful gift of great success. Or, it can become a dismal punishment whenever you ignore the Moral Wisdom aspect of your ITP Program. ITP success, however, is a lot like the weather: Everyone talks about it, but no one does anything about it. Sound familiar? So, what kind of ITP outcome do you want, a barely acceptable one, a good one, or an excellent one that actively ensures a safer operation for your organization? If you choose to accept a mediocre and perhaps a miserable ITP situation, you have become an Insider Threat by default and thus the cause of your own misery.

Where Do You Belong in the ITP Threat Environment?

You do realize, don't you, that developing effective ITP competence in Cyber Sensitive Environments requires a combination of soft-skills, hard-skills, and personal qualities hardly imagined only a decade ago. University did not prepare you for this, but Moral Wisdom does. It prepares you to care more deeply about what happens to your organizations, generally, and your Teammates, specifically, if your organization's ITP efforts fail.

Do You Know These Few Relevant Terms?

Insider Threat, Threat Attack, Threat Strategy, Psychological Manifestations, Emotional Disorder, Stereotype, Pervasive Manipulation, Moral Wisdom; Continuous Performance Management; Cyber Security; Insider Threat Prevention; Archetypes; Workplace Relationships; Resilience; Excellence; Existential Hunger; Applied Intuitive Solutions; Knowledge Base Systems; Mobility; Human Activity Systems; Evolutionary Guidance; Design Inquiry; Coaching; Trust; Zero Tolerance; Invincible Ignorance; Cardinal Virtues; Sociopathology; Problem-Based Learning; Case-Based Reasoning; Evidence-Based Solutions; Traces-Based Reasoning; Unified Problem Solving Method; Unified Problem Solving Method Description Language.

Agony, If Nothing Else, Is Life's Faithful Retribution for
Entering an Ill-Advised Workplace Relationship

Introduction to the Series

I wrote this series to address the dramatic challenge of Insider Threat Prevention Cyber Security, a much-ignored urgency in this time of Cyber Terror. The work began as a single paper about the dangers of Insider Cyber Threats, but the incessant questions of colleagues led me to see the need for a more detailed and expansive evidence-based work that can guide workplace practice.

This series addresses The Psychology of Insider Threat Prevention in a practical sense by discussing the need to "Unify", not integrate, the Continuous Performance Management organization and Insider Threat Prevention discipline.

I chose Continuous Performance Management (CPM) as a model of discussion for two reasons. First CPM is an extremely popular Human Resource Management model for engaging in Organization Design. Secondly, CPM vastly increases the danger of an Insider-generated Cyber Attack that can rapidly destroy an entire enterprise, and few seem to note this. I chose the Problem of Workplace Psychology as the overarching theme to coherently tie the components of the "CPM-ITPCS Unification" Program together.

I have studied the problem of Insider Threat Prevention Cyber Security in the USA, Europe, Asia, the Middle East, Australia, and all points south for more than 50 years. In the beginning, no one called it Insider Threat Prevention Cyber Security. People used novel expressions I will not dare to repeat. When I speak of "prevention", I mean A Priori Prevention, prevention before a threat even requires mitigation. This is challenging.

Part One identifies the pieces to the puzzle, Part Two discusses what to do what all the pieces after you identify them, and Part Three presents a Unified Model of CPM and ITP Cyber Security. Part Four delivers an approach that assists readers with mastering the components and systems of a unified CPM-ITPCS enterprise architecture. Part Five integrates the first four volumes. Here, I use Behavioral Science, Psychology, and Systems Thinking to clarify the depth of the problems and the range of the strategies available for delivering successful ITP CS.

I hope you find each Part of this series stimulating. I write this series to remove the intellectual cobwebs that are so common today. Success with this Insider Threat Prevention Cyber Security requires curiosity, interest, dedication, abundant study, and practice.

Insider Threat Prevention Cyber Security emerges as a Human Activity System in which the components of the Has are indeed human beings. You know what this means right? Human Beings can be incredibly creative and unbelievably destructive. We have to be more creative and better enterprise designers. You will never have time to be bored.

1: Systems of ITP Cyber Security

Management Challenge

Continuous Performance Management (CPM) has emerged as the dominant organization model for building high performance teams. Challenged by the necessity to implement new models of workplace relationships, mangers have become coaches as their employees learn to collaborate as members of self-directed teams. Common employee assessments have become uncommon as employees more often assess the skill of their coaches in real time.

Beyond these common hallmarks of Continuous Performance Management, however, a new spirit of openness has emerged that grants even unqualified Employees access to data, systems, and business information in unprecedented ways. Skills assessment and performance evaluation has given way to a new corporate spirit of trust and openness. In a world characterized by Cyber Terror and Insider Threat Prevention Cyber Security, Continuous Performance Management may well become the 21st Century "formula for failure".

The Fourth Option

Management has several choices. It can do nothing and let Continuous Performance Management continue unabridged and hope for the best, while knowing that hope is never a strategy. It can abandon Continuous Performance Management altogether and look for a different model that replaces Continuous Performance Management as the next great hope of raw optimism. Or, management may simply attempt to integrate Continuous Performance Management with Insider Threat Prevention Cyber Security to contrive a solution in record time. However, there is a fourth option. Management can build a robust enterprise by unifying, not integrating, Continuous Performance Management and Insider Threat Prevention Cyber Security.

Through Option Four, management designs an enterprise that intimately unifies Continuous Performance Management and ITP Cyber Security to form a novel, productive, robust, and secure enterprise architecture. Although ITP Cyber Security conflicts with Continuous Performance Management in several fundamental ways, we can design a solution that transforms ITP Cyber Security into an essential component of Continuous Performance Management and Continuous Performance Management as an essential component of enterprise design.

I recommend Option Four. True, it is more difficult than implementing Continuous Performance Management alone or Insider Threat Prevention Cyber Security alone. Option Four, however, delivers the best choice for gaining control of your enterprise as it sails its way through the stormy seas of a high-risk future. Option Four begins with the design of the meta-methodology that you will use to design an appropriate Continuous Performance Management-Insider Threat Prevention Cyber Security Unification Methodology.

Unification Meta-Methodology

If you could go back to the mid 1970's and early 1980's, you would discover that the idea of using a methodology to develop and deliver Management Information Systems was the norm. Input and output-based methodologies and data-driven development methodologies were common. So were rule-based design methodologies and, of course, the relational design methodologies.

Phased Development Process-based methodologies, referred to as the Waterfall Model, started the ball rolling. Today, Agile Methodologies needlessly rule everything. Names like Ken Orr and Ed Yourdan were legendary. Even Fran Tarkenton. The Great NFL Quarterback, had a software development company with a common methodology. That was Tarkenton Software.

The problem was, and still is, that people generally do not get it. People, indeed, and entire organizations, generally mandated a preferred methodology as a standard for software systems development, and that was it. Technical managers thought that "one size fits all". They failed to grasp the meaning of methodology. They did not quite grasp the science behind it: A methodology to be valid must be appropriate to its subject. Methodologies are problem, and perhaps, environment specific. It is not a good idea to use the same methodology for every problem. It simply will not work.

A methodology is not the solution of an ultimate problem; it is a way to get to the solution. The first step in solving a non-casual problem is to design the methodology that will assist you in solving the problem. This means that a person has to step back and design a meta-methodology to do this. An authentic methodologist must first become a master meta-methodologist before he or she learns how to skillfully design a methodology appropriate to a problem. People require skills in methodology design to determine the most appropriate methodology that assists with resolving a problem situation. Understanding this, we can now design our meta-methodology to Unify Continuous Performance Management and Insider Threat Prevention Cyber Security.

Systems Science

Systems Science is the scientific inquiry into systems. We can describe a system as a set of related components that function as an organized whole by employing the core processes of input, transformation, output, and feedback and adjustment within a specific environment. The components share interactive relationships. Collectively these components and their interactions form the whole system. At the base system level, the components cannot be divided into independent elements. Every system's element enjoys properties that are lost when separated from the system. Moreover, every system consists of essential properties that no component of the system enjoys individually. A system is whole because it is greater than the sums of its parts. Emergence is the characteristic system's process that enables the system to become whole. Systems science, therefore, studies whole systems. This means that systems theory employs a holistic approach during systems inquiry, or when studying systems.

Holistic Approach

A holistic approach is an expanded approach of scientific investigation. Here, the investigator examines, the system at hand, other systems sharing the same environment, and the mutual impact these systems have on each other. These systems are open systems because they interact with their surroundings and exchange matter, energy, and information with their environments across a boundary

Spaces of Meta-Methodology Design

The effort to unify Continuous Performance Management and Insider Threat Prevention Cyber Security occurs in several spaces including the Design Solution, Knowledge, Problem or Contextual, and Experience Spaces. These four spaces define the environment in which the meta-methodology designs the Methodology that unifies Continuous Performance Management and Insider Threat Prevention Cyber Security.

Design Solution Space

This is the conceptual space where the design team establishes the purposes and goals of the Continuous Performance Management and Insider Threat Prevention Cyber Security Unification. The interactive dynamics of design occur in this space. While the definition of the purpose of the unified system initiates the design process, the attainment of the goals terminates the process. The Reproducer Subsystem functions in this space.

Reproducer Subsystem

The Subsystem functions as a self-design model for the production of other systems similar to itself. It accepts appropriate matter-energy and information to produce systems with components and functions similar to itself.

Knowledge Space

The Space contains all the knowledge explored and gathered during design. This space is comprehensive and consists of specific, generic and general design knowledge.

Problem or Contextual Space

This Space contains all the sources for defining, studying, and characterizing all the problems, values, and subsystems relevant to the design project (Banathy, 1984). The Problem or Contextual Space includes the environments and systems of design specific to the problem context, the Continuous Performance Management and Insider Threat Prevention Cyber Security unified system, and the existing Continuous Performance Management Human Activity System. Metasystems design and hypersystem definition occur in this design space.

Experience Space

This is the conceptual space where designers test alternative models of Continuous Performance Management and Insider Threat Prevention Cyber Security unification against reality. This space consists of the environments and systems of design specific to the knowledge base systems, the existing Human Activity System, the support systems, and the design inquiry system. Value systems design occurs in the experience space.

Systems of Design

The design team, as the design Human Activity System (HAS), executes all design tasks and activities. At the macro-level, a project architecture or project organization Human Activity System exists as an embedded suprasystem consisting of several subsystems that include the systems and environments of design. Specifically, the subsystems vary with each project but generically they include a System of Problems, Ideas or Intention, System to be Designed, Design System, System of Operations, Knowledge System, and the Design Support System. Systems of Design are not the same as the Spaces of Design.

System of Problems, Ideas or Intention

This system focuses on the problem context, including the existing problems in the current Continuous Performance Management Human Activity System such as the failure to define normative categories for Insider Threat Prevention Cyber Security system development.

System to be Designed

This system focuses on the "Ideal System" that is to be designed as the future Unified Insider Threat Prevention Cyber Security Human Activity System.

Design System

This system produces the new Unified Insider Threat Prevention Cyber Security Human Activity System in respect to the "Ideal System" models developed by the value system as a product of the metasystem. The Design System conducts the design inquiry.

Knowledge System & System of Operations

The Knowledge System comprehensively delivers the knowledge relevant to the design project. This System delivers input to the Design System to energize the System of Operations within the Problem Solution Space. The System of Operations consists of the operations required to initiate the systems methodology and energize the component systems in the Problem Solution Space.

Design Support System

The design Support System energizes the Design System through management and maintenance functions. This System empowers the Design System to manage the design inquiry and maintain itself as it designs the "Ideal System".

Environments of Design

The Systems of Design function in the Spaces of Design which form the interfaces between the Environments of Design and the Systems of Design. The Environments of Design surround each Design System and consist of the environments of the Systems of Ideals, Aspirations, and Intentions, Problems, Future System, Design System, and the large Knowledge Environments.

Environment of the Dynamic System of Organizing Perspective

This environment consists of the ideas, aspirations, intentions, and problems that form the Unified Insider Threat Prevention Cyber Security Human Activity System. This environment serves as the conceptual space of the System of Problems. This environment consists of the concrete, currently existing Continuous Performance Management Human Activity System and the Model of the Unified Insider Threat Prevention Cyber Security Human Activity System.

It also includes the models of the objectives and goals of the Unified Insider Threat Prevention Cyber Security Human Activity System in the form of structural models and the System of Intentions or Values which ignited the vision to redesign the current Continuous Performance Management Human Activity System to implement a Unified Insider Threat Prevention Cyber Security environment that improves employee performance while securing the enterprise against insider threats.

Environment of the Future System

This environment serves as a conceptual source of inputs for the Unified Insider Threat Prevention Cyber Security Human Activity System to be designed. This Environment contains the models of the future system and is the environment in which the Unified Insider Threat Prevention Cyber Security Human Activity System emerges.

Environment of the Design System

This environment delivers the matter, energy and information required for design. It contains the design Human Activity System and the models of the design system that becomes a concrete system during design.

Knowledge Environment

This environment delivers the inputs that form the Knowledge Base System as an abstract system. This Environment is an abstract environment that contains the entire knowledge repository relevant to design as a disciplined inquiry (Banathy, 1984).

Metasystems of Design

Prior to design initiation, system designers engage in design inquiry to design the design project. Design inquiry is the design of design (Banathy, 1984) and as such is metadesign. At the level of meta-design, the design inquiry identifies, defines and establishes the metasystems issues of design. Hall (1989) argues that a specific system designed during problem definition and value system design is the metasystem.

Metasystems are decision oriented. They are based on value judgements about the system to be designed. In the case examined in this book, the metasystem is based on value judgements about the design of the Unified Continuous Performance Management-Insider Threat Prevention Cyber Security Human Activity System. Designers use the facts and impressions about the problem situation in the environment to frame the problem.

In the case of Continuous Performance Management-Insider Threat Prevention Cyber Security Unification, designers use the facts and impressions about the Continuous Performance Management Hallmarks to frame the Insider Threat Prevention Cyber Security compromise problem. The frames enable designers to produce the first version of the metasystem. Hall (1989) reasoned that a metasystem establishes a set of value sentences that describe a desired physical system and imply or comprise the parts and relationships of the metasystem.

Value System Design

Value System Design is normative design. Problem solvers employ Value System Design to evaluate design alternatives in arriving at the Ideal System Design. During Ideal System Design, designers examine questions regarding formal, factual, and value truth. Through Value Systems Design, designers construct metasystem models that eventually become hyper-statements about the value and criteria for system selection from among the alternatives explored during design inquiry.

Value System Design focuses on questions of Information Systems-OUGHT and the relationships among different descriptive and normative (Information Systems-OUGHT) system categories relating to the perspectives and attitudes of specific social actors, groups and individuals. Designers construct a hyper-system (Ivanov, 1990) to define, organize and track the relations examined during value system, or metasystems, design.

Hypersystem Design

Hypersystem Design assist in Value System Design by framing the propositional categories requiring metasystem evaluation. Ivanov (1990) defines the categorical relations in respect to Information Systems or OUGHT judgements, as Designer's System; Decision Maker's System; Client's System; System Philosopher's System, and Witness' System.

Interaction Dynamics in Design

As design proceeds among the environments, systems and spaces outlined above, designers engage in specialized interactions and dynamics that form the flow of the design process (Banathy, 1984). Design occurs as a non-linear activity consisting of discrete stages of analysis-synthesis and evaluation (Jones, 1963). As Banathy (1984) reminds us, design occurs as a process of interactive cycles consisting of the integration of the following dynamics:

Dynamics of Interactive and Spiralic Design

Here, designers visit and revisit the conceptual design spaces until the new design emerges.

Dynamics of Feedback and Feedforward

Here, designers discern the iterative requirements of design using qualitative progression as a concurrent validation, verification and testing approach.

Dynamics of Divergence and Convergence

Here, designers search for alternative designs while settling on the most appropriate design according to the goals and objectives of the design project. Bogdanov (1984) wrote that systemic divergence contains a tendency for evolution directed toward complementary connections.

Further we learn that contra-differentiation through conjunction leads to quantitative equalization which reduces systemic contradictions so that the system evolves. Bogdanov (1984) reasoned that convergence results from similarly directed selections by agents within similar environments.

Dynamics of Multi-Systemic Thrust in Design

Here, designers coordinate and refine preliminary designs, at all levels of the design hierarchy, so that designers do not ignore any of the expediencies of design.

Dynamics of Participative Design

Here, designers navigate the exploratory and issues resolution cycles of design. These Dynamics ensure that designers examine the relevant information and hear all voices. The underlying assumption here: Design occurs as an iterative human activity.

Design Models

Through the Systems Models Approach (Banathy, 1973), designers construct environment, structure and behavioral models to describe any system (Banathy, 1984). Collectively, designers build these models to perform a macro-analysis of the system (Collen, 1988).

Environment Model

Environmental Models describe the relationship of the Human Activity System to its environment in respect to boundaries, inputs, outputs, and system's space. This model describes the system entities and their functions; relationships of the system to environment systems, and system control.

The Structural Model

Structural Models present a picture of the Human Activity System at any given point in time. Banathy (1973) referred to this Model as the "still picture model." The Structural Model describes the goals, functions, and components of the Human Activity System and the connections among them. The goals establish the linking-pin function between the Environmental and Structural Models (Banathy, 1973). In the object-oriented paradigm, Structural Models describe important constraints that enable information hiding or encapsulation.

The Process Model

The Human Activity System performs four fundamental systems operations: (1) input, (2) transformation, (3) output, and (4) feedback and adjustment. The Process Model describes these operations for any Human Activity System. The flow of these operations forms the processes of the Human Activity System.

Fundamentally, this Model transforms inputs into outputs. Using Living Systems Theory, designers model the four operations whenever they describe the input, transformation, output, and feedback and adjustment operations within the subsystems described in the Structural Model of the Human Activity System and the inputs of Matter, Energy, and Information.

2: Describing Living Systems

Human Activity System

A Human Activity System is a goal-directed or purposiveful system in which the human beings forming the system share a common purpose. Checkland (1981) argues that Human Activity Systems function as notional purposive systems. They express some purposeful human activity which in principle can be found in the real world. Banathy (1986a) wrote that Human Activity Systems employ design to direct their evolution. Bogdanov (1984) wrote that in conceptual design, Human Activity Systems evolve through the unity of experience rather than by discovery alone (Bogdanov, 1984). The components of Human Activity Systems (HAS) are human beings.

Hypersystem

As we extend the work of Ivanov (1990), Forsgren and Ivanov (1990) to support the design of Workflow Human Activity Systems, we see that a Hypersystem becomes the locus of categories for all subsystems composing the workflow system and the relevant subsystems of the narrow-environment-of-interest such as the client. During design inquiry, the Hypersystem clarifies the categories established during metasystem design as an examination and acceptance of Workflow Human Activity System project values. Ivanov (1990) wrote:

> Systems structuring, considering ends-means hierarchies in the physical artifact and the human-purposeful dimension is attained as, not only morphological-structural (physical) categories that were implicit in most ideas of information about the physical world, but also in terms of functional and teleological classes which take into consideration more complex relations, including the human striving for goals and values.

Design Inquiry

Design Inquiry examines the design of methodologies. It explores the Characteristics of the design problem situation, Competence of the designers, and the Capacity of the Human Activity System that initiates design including the resources available to support design (Banathy, 1986a).

Evolutionary Competence

We attain evolutionary competence through evolutionary learning by nurturing evolutionary values and attaining competence in cooperative group interaction consisting of Systems Thinking and Action; Anticipatory Thinking, Problem Management, and System Design (Banathy, 1987).

Evolutionary Guidance System (EGS)

An Evolutionary Guidance System is a HAS in which the components continually evolve toward evolutionary consciousness. Evolutionary Guidance belongs at the very center of our societal systems. If they are to become a viable force of change, Evolutionary Guidance has to be mapped into all systems, from the family to the global human community. The Evolutionary Guidance System has to be unified with each and every dimension of human life.

Conceptual Framework of Organization Change

Change Content and Change Process impact the Continuous Performance Management –Insider Threat Prevention Cyber Security Unification Framework. Here, we focus on the two content challenges of clarity of the unification vision and the appropriateness of the change delivered through the unification vision. The enterprise further establishes a continuous assessment of the change process and qualifies the execution of the unification program.

Change Attitudes

Attitudes about Insider Threat Prevention Cyber Security Unification directly influence the organization's readiness for change and its institutionalization. The clarity of the unification vision, and its effective communication, justifies such a sentiment. A well-articulated vision, when adequately presented, ignites radical transformation. The creation and communication of such a vision prepares the way for the acceptance of the Insider Threat Prevention Cyber Security Unification Program whenever it is sensible, clear, and understood throughout the enterprise.

Who can doubt that Vision Effectiveness is an important goal of any organization's transformation program? The Insider Threat Prevention Cyber Security Unification Program requires a Framework built upon an effective vision as the impetus for defining a potent program mission. Who can argue that content without clarity is ineffective?

Organizations need to clearly see how they will be structured as they achieve their Insider Threat Prevention Cyber Security Unification goals. Changes supported by clear visions deliver positive affective outcomes when organizations accept their change program as the appropriate reaction to the need for change and vision.

The test for appropriateness never ends. It remains a concern throughout the program because while teams may accept the vision, they may resist the change. Teams may see the change as an insufficient attempt to realize the vision. Here, one or more teams may become unwilling to initiate the changes implicit in the ITP Cyber Security Unification Program.

In this case, management may suggest several paths to Insider Threat Prevention Cyber Security Unification. These paths possibility could lead to multiple changes in the environment to realize a single vision. Since teams become more acceptable of change whenever they feel that the change is appropriate, appropriateness remains a critical measure throughout the execution of the unification program.

Program Execution

Vision clarity and change appropriateness reflect the thinking of teams about the change initiated through the ITP Cyber Security Unification Program. However, the perception of change execution by individuals throughout the enterprise reflects the introduction and unfolding of the changes within the organization. Therefore, as an evaluative sentiment, change execution reflects an individual's personal experiences with the implementation of the organizational change characteristics of the Insider Threat Prevention Cyber Security Unification Program. Briefly, from a Program Manager's perspective, we can define a short but potent Change Implementation process:

First, form a potent guiding coalition to deliver the guiding vision. Second, build and empower teams to implement change. Next, create abundant opportunities for rapid "wins" that generate incremental changes. Then, consolidate improvements by linking requirements. Finally, institutionalize new behaviors to change the enterprise culture.

A change, when viewed positively from a content-oriented perspective, may be seen by the target of change as executed successfully or poorly. Although we may view effective change implementation as positive, teams may view effective change implementation negatively if they view the change itself as inappropriate. The guiding vision for ITP Cyber Security Unification serves as an action lever that energizes the rationale and values behind the program.

Defining the management and technical perspectives, the vision progresses from planning and design to implementation and operations. Success emerges as the unification program resolves the organization and staff issues that impact the management of a high-performance environment now operating at appropriately defined levels of Insider Threat Prevention Cyber Security. The activities involved in defining and realizing the guiding vision of the ITP Cyber Security Unification Program begin with igniting a Sense of Urgency when assisting others with seeing the need for change and the importance of acting immediately.

Form the Guiding Team. Ensure that you have formed a powerful team to guide the change, one with leadership skills, credibility, communications ability, adequate authority, analytical skills, and a sense of urgency. Next, develop the Insider Threat Prevention Cyber Security Unification Change Vision and Strategy. Clarify how the future will differ from the past and how the Unification Program can make that future a reality.

Communicate for Understanding and Buy-in. Ensure that everyone understand and accept the vision and the strategy. Then empower teams to act. Remove as many barriers as possible to ensure that those who want to make the vision a reality can do so. Work to produce short-term wins. Create visible, unambiguous successes as soon as possible. Never ever let up. Press harder and faster after the first successes. Be relentless with instituting change after change until the vision becomes a reality. Create a new culture of Insider Threat Prevention Cyber Security Unification. Hold onto new ways of behaving and ensue that they succeed until they become a part of the new united Insider Threat Prevention Cyber Security culture.

Soft Systems Thinking

When we speak about changes in culture and the transformation of organizations and enterprises, we have entered the world of Soft Systems Thinking. This is the world of description rather than prediction. This is the world of Human Activity Systems (HAS), Social Technical Systems (STS), and Appreciative Systems and many other "soft" systems. Fundamentally, these systems have human beings as their primary components.

The "Systems Perspective" is the dominant perspective in this reality of organization transformation, evolutionary unfolding and self-guided evolution. How we approach soft systems challenges is far different from how we approach hard systems challenges. Using a Soft Systems perspective, we navigate the territory where we unify Continuous Performance Management and Insider Threat Prevention Cyber Security as a single environment.

We do this first by describing the problem situation unstructured existing in the real-world environment and then finalizing the problem situation expressed in the real-world environment. We next finalize the root definitions of relevant systems using systems thinking. Next, we build the conceptual models using systems thinking consisting of the Formal System Conceptual Models and models of other systems thinking. We then compare the Conceptual Models from above with the problem situation expressed earlier in the Real-World Environment. We further define the feasible, desirable changes in the real-world environment. Finally, we take action to improve the problem situation in the real-world environment.

Cultural Systems Methodology

Central to the challenge of designing new Human Activity Systems is the challenge of shaping the cultures that emerge during this process. As we move from a fragmented ITP Cyber Security environment to a Unified ITP Cyber Security enterprise, management actively directs, develops, and evolves organization cultures. Teams rapidly respond to the ever-changing opportunities and challenges that impact them as they unify CPM and ITP Cyber Security.

These teams respond by engaging continuous streams of cultural and logic-based analysis. In this respect, these teams begin to more clearly understand the history of the real-world problem situation. This enables them to more appropriately define the tasks and issues, identify relevant systems, build models and then compare the models against each situation under analysis. Moreover, project managers become better prepared to appoint the skilled "improvers" of the situation as they now analyze the situation as an aspect of the culture. Here, they analyze the intervention program, as well as the social and political systems the form the existing and now emerging cultures.

As the project managers engage the stream of logic-based analysis, they remind their teams to consistently determine the difference between the models and the real-world environment so that the organization will only institute the systematically desirable and culturally feasible changes.

Matter, Energy, and Information Subsystems

Miller (1978) wrote that all living systems transform matter, energy and/or information. Living systems consist of at least nineteen subsystems to transform these three classes of inputs into outputs. Collen (1988) referred to the evolutionary nature of Living Systems Theory when he mentioned Miller's later inclusion of a Timer Subsystem as a required subsystem that assists living systems with surviving in harshly variable environmental conditions. While specialized subsystems transform matter, energy and information, other subsystems transform only matter and energy, and still other systems transform only information. Subsystems that transform matter, energy and information include the Reproducer and Boundary subsystems.

Reproducer Subsystem

The Reproducer Subsystem produces the Human Activity System that engages in performance evaluation. It, then, reproduces the performance evaluation Human Activity System in other organizations and environments. Classically, the Reproducer Subsystem is the cause of the Human Activity System coming to be or coming into being. Ontologically, the Reproducer Subsystem is the First Cause, Causa-in-Esse, of the existence the Human Activity Systems as a living system in time and space.

Boundary Subsystem

As the Human Activity System emerges within an organization, it must ensure that it manages its boundaries. However, in the Human Activity System, boundary management challenges team management due to the fluid structure of the Human Activity System in organizations. Katz and Kahn (1966) wrote that:

Human organizations enjoy unique properties, however, which distinguish them from other categories of open systems. Perhaps the most basic of these unique properties is the absence of structure in the usual sense of the term - an identifiable, enduring, physical anatomy which is observable at rest as in motion and which in motion generates and performs those activities which comprise the systemic function. (p. 14)

Since the Human Activity System is an open system, it requires boundaries that are open to the environment. Katz and Kahn (1966) distinguish open systems through a recurrent pattern of events, differentiated from but dependent on the larger stream of life in which it occurs and recurs.

When discussing openness, boundaries and coding, they reason that openness is the most general systems concept. System openness is the most general of these concepts and refers to the degree to which the system is receptive to all types of input. Systems vary with respect to the general range of inputs they absorb and their openness to inputs.

For an ITP Cyber Security Human Activity System to remain viable, its boundaries must permit the flow of inputs and outputs between the Human Activity System and its suprasystem, the enterprise. The Boundary Subsystem maintains the dynamic equilibrium of the Human Activity System and manages the Human Activity System's negentropic functions. For the Human Activity System, the Boundary Subsystem is that system's mechanism that keeps the Human Activity System separate from the corporate environment of other organization systems and determines to what extent the boundaries remain secure.

Using the Formal Systems Model (Checkland, 1981), we see that boundaries define the limits of the Insider Threat Prevention Cyber Security Human Activity System in respect to its environment and the wider systems constraints and actors. The boundaries of the Human Activity System inform the enterprise that the Human Activity System is a system chartered by a corporation and consists of the appropriate human components of the Human Activity System and its facilities, hardware, software, physical space and other resources.

Matter and Energy Subsystems

The ITP Cyber Security Human Activity System depends on matter and energy to sustain its existence. It delivers the resources that permit it to achieve its goals and satisfy the enterprise's requirements. The following subsystems process matter and energy: Ingestor, Distributor, Converter, Producer, Matter-Energy Storage, Extruder, Motor, and Supporter.

Ingestor Subsystem

This subsystem consists of the components that bring people, material, hardware, power, supplies, and all other physical inputs into the Human Activity System. The Ingestor subsystem consists of the executive level program manager and those who support him or her in delivering resources.

Distributor Subsystem

After the Ingestor Subsystem brings matter-energy into the Human Activity System, the Distributor Subsystem defines the process that receives and transfers these resources by distributing them to each Human Activity System component. The Distributor Subsystem is a flow-oriented subsystem.

Converter Subsystem

Whenever the Human Activity System receives matter-energy in the form of physical resources from the Ingestor Subsystem via the Distributor Subsystem, the Converter Subsystem ensures that the resources are in a form that is usable by the Human Activity System.

Producer Subsystem

In the Human Activity System (HAS), the Producer Subsystem both manufactures the products that are returned to the environment and maintains the dynamic equilibrium of the Human Activity System. Katz and Kahn (1966) wrote that an open system transforms two classes of inputs: production and maintenance inputs.

The reason (1966) that production inputs involve the powerful flow which goes into procuring, transforming, and exporting the organization product. Maintenance inputs involve that powerful flow which enables the system to overcome the centrifugal and permeable qualities inherent in the unique function-structure of the human organization.

The Producer Subsystem is the only subsystem that processes both kinds of inputs. In the Producer Subsystem Human Activity System, production inputs are directly related to the work of the Human Activity System in unifying the ITP Cyber Security component. However, maintenance inputs are necessary to constrain the people in the Human Activity System and persuade them to execute their activities as members of the system (Katz and Kahn, 1966).

Matter-Energy Storage Subsystem

This subsystem consists of all matter-energy stored in the Human Activity System and the staff responsible for storing and retrieving that matter-energy.

Extruder Subsystem

This subsystem works with the Producer Subsystem to send products, and the associated waste, out of the Human Activity System into the environment. In the ITP Cyber Security Human Activity System, this subsystem consists of the project leaders and the external auditors.

Motor Subsystem

Through this subsystem, the Human Activity System moves through its environment and moves itself. The Motor Subsystem associated with the immanent and transitive capacities of the Human Activity System as the Human Activity System either moves itself by self-actualization or is moved by its environment in response to external motivation.

Supporter Subsystem

This subsystem delivers a sense of physical reality to the Human Activity System as a living system by incorporating the visible artifacts of physical structure such as walls, floors, desks, and partitions. This subsystem delivers a sense of space, separateness, and rigidity and sets the Human Activity System apart from other organization subsystems or work groups.

Information Subsystems

In addition to matter and energy, the Human Activity System requires information to remain viable. In the ITP Cyber Security HAS, information subsystems enable the Human Activity System to perform many activities. For example, this subsystem assists product developers with settling on product requirements and performing the activities of software development. It also enables teams to manage data flows and technical constraints and also train technical leads and their technical staff. The Information Subsystem also enables teams to track project progress and determine project success.

In supporting these activities during the execution of the ITP Cyber Security Unification Program, the HAS consists of the nine subsystems that manage all information transformation processes including the Input Transducer, Internal Transducer, Decoder, Channel and Net, Associator, Memory, Decider, Encoder, and Output Transducer Subsystems.

Input Transducer Subsystem

Operating like the Ingestor Subsystem, the Input Transducer Subsystem brings information into the Human Activity System.

Internal Transducer Subsystem

This subsystem carries information generated within the Human Activity System through the Human Activity System to the other subsystems. The behavior of this subsystem assists the Human Activity System with coordinating the activities of all subsystems. In CPM-ITP Cyber Security Unification software development and work flow groups, this system exists as a subsystem of the project management structure.

Decoder Subsystem

As information enters the Human Activity System from the environment via the Input Transducer Subsystem, the Decoder Subsystem transforms it into a form of information that has meaning and/or technical content. For example, the high-level design information obtained via the Input Transducer Subsystem from the environment conveys little meaning to the programming team. For understanding at the programming level, the Decoder Subsystem transforms this information into the detailed design models containing the mini-specs suitable for programming or coding.

Channel and Net System

As information enters the Human Activity System from the environment or is transferred from other subsystems of the Human Activity System, the Channel and Net Subsystems form the delivery process to act as a relay network.

Associator Subsystem

This subsystem is derived from learning theory and is the most conceptual subsystem of the Human Activity System. It exists in the training and development activities of the HAS and in the field of knowledge contained in the various knowledge bases of the HAS. The training and development activities link with any newly received information and associate this with other already attained knowledge. For example, the Associator Subsystem associates the knowledge of an organization's requirements with the knowledge of how to convert this information into appropriately detailed systems models.

Ultimately, the entire ITP Cyber Security Unification process becomes an association of one level and class of information with another. Moreover, this hybrid class of associated information becomes further associated with the tools, techniques, processes, hardware and software of development to produce a final product, which is just another kind of associated information, information termed knowledge.

Memory Subsystem

This subsystem consists of all the information storage components of the HAS. The Memory Subsystems reserves all the information flowing throughout the entire HAS for future use, backup and/or in compliance with management policy or formal regulation.

Decider Subsystem

The subsystem serves the dual functions of regulation and control. The Decider Subsystem focuses on feedback and adjustment. The Decider Subsystem delivers, communicates and maintains the organizing principles of the Human Activity System. It ensures that ab organization performs all information processing activity for the collective good of the Human Activity System in compliance with the charter of the Human Activity System which is its standard. Without the Decider Subsystem, the Human Activity System loses its purposeful characteristics (Banathy, 1984) that direct the course of its own evolution to meet project requirements.

Encoder Subsystem

This subsystem changes the internal information generated within the Human Activity System into meaningful information for the environment. The Insider Threat Prevention Cyber Security Unification Human Activity System is a technical/nontechnical group chartered to perform a large number of specialized activities.

Hence, it employs its own technical language to maintain the clarity and exactness of its mission to deliver software/hardware/business process products or problem solutions to a broad-based enterprise community within both a narrow-environment-of-interest and a wider-environment-of-interest.

As in other specialized groups, this Human Activity System employs a rigorous, technical language to achieve the required level of exactness in its products. However, after assuring the level of exactness, the Human Activity System must output its deliverables to the environmental subsystems in an understandable form.

The Encoder Subsystem encodes the technical language into the environmental language. In many cases, however, teams ignore the encoding process. Moreover, management anguishes over the deliverables for considerable time until it walks away and attempts a different solution often delivered by some other group. Human Activity Systems must respond to the needs of their environments or the environments will close themselves off to the Human Activity System. Closed HAS entropy and decay until they cease to exist.

Output Transducer Subsystem

This subsystem is the opposite of the Input Transducer Subsystem. After the Encoder Subsystem prepares information for release to the environment, the Output Transducer Subsystem releases the products, deliverables, or problem solutions to the environment. The Human Activity System employs various media to facilitate output including computer data base information, hard copy reports and summaries, electronic mail in its various forms, published directives, web pages, Platforms, and formally distributed documented systems models.

Summary of Living Systems Components

The preceding section introduced the fundamental subsystems involved in Insider Threat Prevention Cyber Security Unification. While the principal points of this section focused on the matter, energy and information subsystems defined in Living Systems Theory, it shaped the foundation for employing these subsystems in the design of the Continuous Performance Management-Insider Threat Prevention Unification Human Activity System, the CPM-ITPCS HAS.

Living Systems Theory is a high value component. It assists in the examination and redesign of the Continuous Performance Management Human Activity System. It is especially helpful in the analysis and design of the ITP Subsystem in regard to the past and current practices of delivering technical products to the Continuous Performance Management environments.

The use of Living Systems Theory as a systems thinker introduces a paradox of method in which the designer can only expand by reducing. We use a microscope to examine reality by reducing the object of investigation down to finer and finer levels of detail, including down to the quark level moving from the cosmos, planets, bodies, organs, cells, atoms, and loves while simultaneously using a telescope to examine the other side of reality to finer and finer levels of detail including superstrings, planets, stars, galaxies, and the cosmos. While in the former, we reduce boundaries inward, in the latter, we expand by identifying more and more detail outward. Learning about the expanded universe of astronomy requires the reduction of objects for examination.

In ITP Cyber Security Unification, the designer expands his or her field of inquiry by reducing Human Activity Systems to subsystems to expand his or her knowledge. The systems approach examines the relationships between the ever-reduced components of the Continuous Performance Management environment, regardless of the direction of such reduction.

In contemporary Organization Inquiry, we employ the same approach to redesign organizations to function as clusters of learning teams. Armed with an appropriate systems model, organization specialists are better equipped to guide organizations through the ITP Cyber Security Unification Program, from the transformation of competitive factions to the potency of cooperative teams.

3: Relevant System Descriptions

This chapter clarifies the concepts, expressions, and other terminologies that describe the environments and activities indicative of a program designed to unify Continuous Performance Management and Insider Threat Prevention Cyber Security. While a few of the concepts are unique to the design of the unification architecture, many others represent Systems Thinking, Behavioral Science, Enterprise Design, Cyber Security, Information Systems, and Project Management. Although the concepts are generally familiar to technical managers and executives, I am using them in novel ways in this series.

Appreciative System

Checkland (1986) described Appreciative Systems as interacting processes of continuous ideas and events which continually unfold. Appreciative Systems transcend themselves by critically reflecting on their past. An Appreciative System is a Human Activity System in which the guiding principle acknowledges the intrinsic value of human beings as the most valuable components of a goal directed and dynamic system. A potent Insider Threat Prevention Cyber Security environment leverages the experience and wisdom of employees.

People are more important than ideas. Sir Geoffrey Vickers (1983) described the Appreciative System as a dynamic, personal and social work-of-art sharing three defining attributes. They correspond with reality enough to guide action. Other people share them enough to mediate communications. They become acceptable enough to ourselves to make life bearable.

Design

Design in the generic sense includes planning, operations research, engineering design, architectural design, programming, and budgeting. Design also includes the activities we execute as we consciously attempt to change ourselves and our environments as we work to improve the quality of our lives," (Churchman, 1971).

Banathy (1984) wrote that design is creative and disciplined. It is a decision-oriented approach to inquiry that we execute in iterative cycles. During these cycles, we engage our skills to develop design solutions by exploring three spaces of design that surround the design solution space. These are the design knowledge space; design problem space; and design exploration space.

Design systems and designers work within the spaces of design to build a desired system. The evolutionary nature of design flows from the dynamics occurring within the design experience. Banathy (1984) identified divergence and convergence as two significant dynamics of design. Design commences with an image of the future system. Designers work to achieve the design through iterations of divergence and convergence.

The design experience delivers a description of a new system to be implemented. Design occurs through teleological or goal seeking behavior. Design enables Human Activity Systems to guide their own evolutionary unfolding (Banathy, 1984). Churchman (1971) argued that design consists of five core characteristics. He wrote that through design designers attempt to distinguish in thought between different sets of goals.

For example, designers try to estimate in thought how well each alternative set of behavior patterns will serve a specific set of goals. In this sense, designers aim to communicate their thoughts to other minds in such a manner that they can convert the thoughts into corresponding actions which in fact serve the goals in the same manner as the design indicated they would. Hence, designers initiate behavior that satisfies the goal of generality or methodology for similar goal-attainment problems, and enable the perceiver to describe the system such that the design alternatives are defined in terms of the design of the components and their interrelationships.

Design Inquiry

Design Inquiry investigates the design of methodologies by exploring the characteristics of the design problem situation; competence of the designers, and capacity of the Human Activity System that initiates design such as the resources available to support design (Banathy, 1986).

Evolutionary Competence

We attain evolutionary competence through evolutionary learning. This requires systems designers to nurture evolutionary values and attain competence in cooperative group interaction. Moreover, Evolutionary Competence systems designers learn to master systems thinking and action, anticipatory thinking, problem management, and system design (Banathy, 1987).

Evolutionary Guidance System

An Evolutionary Guidance System is a Human Activity System in which the components continually evolve toward evolutionary consciousness. Evolutionary Guidance should be moved to the very center of our societal systems. As a viable force of change, evolutionary guidance ought to be mapped into all systems, from the family to the global human community. It ought to be integrated into each and every dimension of human life. Evolutionary Guidance Systems are idealized or value systems.

Collen (1990) wrote: When a Human Activity System sets the direction of its own activities, activities which guide it in the pursuit of its specific mission, the Human Activity System becomes an Evolutionary Guidance System. The Metasystem, Hypersystem and Evolutionary Guidance System, as idealized Human Activity Systems, establish goals to form the organizing perspectives of the design inquiry. They provide a baseline for the design of the ideal system, a guiding notion of the unified CPM-ITP Cyber Security Human Activity System.

The ideal system describes the output model which becomes the quality assurance standard for evaluating all work engaged in by the unification human activity system. Through loops of feedback and adjustment, the output model guides the unification Human Activity System to the completion of its requirements for the environment and the attainments of its own goals. All Evolutionary Guidance Systems share four central traits. They present a holistic view of organizations as they co-evolve with the environment. They value and appreciate individuals and local communities as an ethical foundation. They form a social network of co-operative learning. They enable ecological axioms of strategic, tactical, and operational significance.

In the personal domain, the Appreciative Evolutionary Guidance System advocates self-awareness and self-management. They encourage respect for elected relationships and the associative level of work and career relationships. They promote the obligation of involvement people share in common as world citizens.

As an idealized Human Activity System, the highest level Evolutionary Guidance System performs three defining functions. First, they establish an organizing perspective to inspire executive leadership. They define idealized goals for core business processes. They also deliver a framework for designing the ideal business processes as a guiding notion for the new work environment vomited to Insider Threat Prevention Cyber Security.

Peter Checkland (1986) viewed Appreciative Systems as interacting processes of continuous ideas and events which continually unfold. They transcend themselves by critically reflecting on their past. Ideal business processes derived from a particular Evolutionary Guidance System describe an idealized enterprise model that becomes the new benchmark for evaluating all work performed by the core business processes.

Through loops of feedback and adjustment, the idealized model guides the business processes to meet the business requirements of the company, and attain their own goals. Evolutionary Guidance Systems share many of the attributes of Appreciative Systems. Sir Geoffrey Vickers (1983) described an Appreciative System as a dynamic, personal and social work of art. sharing three defining attributes. First, they correspond with reality enough to guide action. They are shared enough by others to mediate communication. They become acceptable enough to us to make life bearable

Leaders employ the Appreciative Evolutionary Guidance System model to inspire a HAS to meet environmental challenges and shape the internal values of the corporate culture. Guided by the Evolutionary Guidance System model, executives succeed in the future by capitalizing on realistic opportunities as the Evolutionary Guidance System (EGS) provides guiding principles of effective management practice such as diversity, optimization, cooperation, self-regulation, transformative change, connectedness, equivalence, and learning from experience.

The appreciative EGS model describes the new role of the postmodern leader as evolutionary guidance. This model provides an effective approach for succeeding by formalizing the role of appreciation, the appreciation of individuals, groups, society, and the environment. The EGS Model actually refines and enhances Continuous Performance Management to leverage the strengths of Insider Threat Prevention Cyber Security.

Hard System

A Hard System is a well-defined and structured system governed by laws that support measurable predictability. Hard systems are quantitative. While we most often associate CPM with Soft Systems, we introduce Hard Systems constraints through the introduction of Insider Threat Prevention Cyber Security.

Human Activity System (HAS)

A Human Activity System is a system in which the components are human beings. An HAS is a goal-directed or purposiveful system in which human beings share a common purpose. Checkland (1981) argued that HAS are notional purposive systems that engage the purposeful human activity that exists in the real world. Banathy (1986a) wrote that Human Activity Systems employ design to direct their self-guided evolution. Bogdanov (1984) argued that in conceptual design, Human Activity Systems evolve through the unity of experience rather than by discovery alone.

Hypersystem

Extending the work of Ivanov (1990) and Forsgren and Ivanov (1990) to support the design of unification Human Activity Systems, the Hypersystem becomes the locus of categories for all subsystems of the unification system and the relevant subsystems of the narrow-environment-of-interest such as the organization. During design inquiry, the Hypersystem clarifies the categories established during Metasystem Design as an examination and acceptance of the project values of the unification Human Activity System. Ivanov (1990) wrote:

> Systems structuring, with due consideration of ends-means hierarchies in both the physical artifact and the human-purposeful dimension is there attained in terms of not only morphological-structural (physical) categories that were implicit in most ideas of information about the physical world, but also in terms of functional classes and teleological classes which take into consideration more complex relations, including the human striving for goals and values.

The Hypersystem, as a learning social system, examines the values of the unification Human Activity System and its environment defined during Metasystem Design. It develops categories of consensus as a quality criteria baseline to support "Information Systems or OUGHT judgements".

It further achieves support for the goals, objectives and ideals of the unification system as expressed by the values identified or defined during Metasystem Design. These categories of consensus establish the systems management relationships of the unification Human Activity System between the subsystems of the unification system and their environments. Hypersystems and Metasystems emerge from the organizing perspective of the design inquiry.

The Hypersystem baseline is category dependent and category specific. Categories may range from primitives expressed as Client, Decision Maker, Planner, Systems Designer, System Philosopher to Soft Systems categories such Customers, Actors, Transformations, Weltanschauung, and Ownership (Ivanov, 1990 & Checkland, 1981).

Designers engage the Metasystem to determine the appropriate baseline categories for Hypersystem Design. The concurrent design of the Metasystem with the Hypersystem represents important cycles of design inquiry activation. The Metasystem and Hypersystem bring critical management values to the surface. These systems deliver a clarification method that places everyone on the same operational platform to share the same objectives, goals, and performance expectations.

Inquiry

This is an activity that produces knowledge where knowledge is understood as the ability to adjust behavior to changing circumstances in order to perform correctly. Inquiry enhances an individual's or organization's capability of adaptability.

Inquiring System

This is a system that produces the knowledge required to empower us to pursue goals consistently in a changing world. An Inquiring System does not produce knowledge in the hard or reductionist, scientific sense as a collection of information. An Inquiring System generates wide ranging knowledge that forms, corrects, and assures values, beliefs, and vision about the future individuals and teams.

Knowledge

When we speak of knowledge, we mean that we are at ease with a subject and deeply engrossed in it. Knowledge concerns knowing what one does. Knowledge is not about knowing and proceeding to become one with an entire area of living human activity. Intellectual understanding is about more than simply knowing. It is about mastering and applying knowledge to impact the narrow and wider range of experience.

Metamethodology (MetaM)

Metamethodology is a methodology for designing methodologies. It is a methodology that designers employ to design specialized methodologies. Human Activity Systems employ a Metamethodology to design a methodology appropriate to the type of systems problem encountered. A Metamethodology is "a generalization of all methodologies as a second level abstraction to provide a Metamethodology of all methodologies" (Newkirk, 1991a, p. 28).

Ontologically, as a second level abstraction, the Metamethodology exists in the province of mathematics. Thus, it retains intelligible matter and separates from common sensible matter. The Metamethodology has the imagination as its end point. Moreover, it exists as a contingent system in that it cannot exist without individual sensible matter. The Metamethodology defies understanding without intelligible matter (Hickey, 1976).

Metameethodology rests on the bedrock of philosophical inquiry and systems development. Designers require Metamethodologies to design methodologies appropriate to a given problem situation such as the unification of Continuous Performance Management and Insider Threat Prevention Cyber Security. Metamethodologies are based on theory and practice and enhance system's evolution. Metamethodologies organize methodologies and facilitate embedded systems building as they support multiple paradigms (Newkirk, 1991a).

Metasystem

A Metasystem is an organized value system consisting of a system of standard values used to make decisions. Concurrent Metasystem and Hypersystem design results in an understanding of the values implicit and explicit in the unification Human Activity System. These values relate to the design initiative. They further relate to the definition of the categories of the Systems Management relationships that we track and manage during unification Human Activity System design. Moreover, these relationships relate to the execution of the operational evaluation of the early unification system prototypes. Designers conceptualize the implicit and explicit values as dimensions of the Evolutionary Guidance System of the unification Human Activity System. Banathy (1987) identified these Evolutionary Guidance System dimensions as the Aesthetic, Economic, Education, Ethical, Political, Scientific, Social Action, Technological, and Methodology dimensions.

As we have seen, a methodology can be hard or soft. Banathy (1988) wrote that we define a methodology as a set of coherent, related, and internally consistent methods that we apply to pursuing a specific disciplined inquiry. Peter Checkland (1981) viewing methodology praxiologically, wrote that "a methodology will lack the precision of a technique but will be a firmer guide to action than a philosophy" (p. 162).

Flood and Carson (1988) discussed hard and soft systems methodologies by arguing that hard methodologies enable us to select an efficient means of achieving a known and defined end. Soft methodologies enable us to describe the efficient and effective known and defined ends. Focusing on systems, Collen (1985) argued that a systemic method delivers a formalized approach to studying a system.

Collen continues by writing that system methodology is the study of such methods, as well as the collective applications of these systemic methods to the study of a Human Activity System. Dillon (1983) seeing methodologies as imperfect argued that every methodology emerges from the human mind and every methodology is intended to bring some order out of the bewildering array of signals coming from the expanded sensory system. In systems science, a methodology forms a mental image or model of the thing or event perceived from a specific perspective.

Methodology building is a design challenge. It requires a design system to function as a Methodology Generating System, a Human Activity System that engages a Metamethodology to conduct Design Inquiry. Designers employ Metamethodologies to design methodologies. The design of a methodology requires a Metamethodology. Methodologies are valuable because they are prerequisite to advances in science (Misiak & Sexton, 1966; Branden, 1974). However, "advances in methodology are preceded by advances in philosophy" (Newkirk, 1991, p. 34).

4: Models and Model-Making

Overview of Models and Model Making

Some writers use systems, theories, and models interchangeably, as if they were synonymous. This is incorrect. Banathy (1983) wrote that a "model is a construct and/or description that represents or stands for something" (p. 36). Thus, we can model systems and theories. Trained observers can find models everywhere and in any medium. In this Digital Age, models have become commonplace.

Components of models include standards and benchmarks, diagrams, charts, verbal or textual narratives, various forms of design documentation, physical artifacts, illustrations, and explanations. Any medium may be useful in model building as the language of modeling permits. Moreover, models may consist of several different modeling languages simultaneously. In this case, skilled model makers employ languages appropriate to the type of model being built within a given context. For example, in the Information Technology domain, model makers, also referred to as designers, build prototypes as operational models of basic systems.

Types of Models

"Models are low-variety representations of systems" (Banathy, 1983, p. 37). We can model conceptual, theoretical, concrete and abstract systems, including systems of Continuous Performance Management-Insider Threat Prevention Cyber Security Unification. We can model existing systems and systems that do not yet exist. We can model existing systems to contrast conceptual, concrete or abstract systems (Banathy, 1983). We build solutions models to describe or represent something to be made. Process models become solution models when they describe or present an approach for designing and validating the design of a system, product or problem solution.

Depending on the conceptualized representations, models vary considerably by subject or system. Models may be deductive or inductive. We build deductive models to describe or model existing systems. We build inductive models to describe or model systems yet to exist. Solution models are inductive models but inductive models are not necessarily solution models. Since design focuses on systems yet to be built, designers usually build inductive models.

Model-makers build theoretical models to model causal explanations. These enable experimenters and systems designers to evaluate the consequences of the empirical assumptions guiding any design path or experiment. Model-making facilitates the design of systems. Systems design is a decision-oriented activity because it focuses on the utilization of knowledge during the evolutionary unfolding of systems, of what should be.

Model building is the paramount activity in technical and social systems design. Model-making, or modeling, is crucial to the design of Human Activity Systems and technical artifacts alike. Modeling provides decision-makers information about goals, values, what if scenarios, and even about the decision logic used in decision making.

Bakker (1979) categorizes such models as Preference, Consequence, and Decision Models. Banathy (1984) reminded us that Preference Models focus on a decision-makers goals and values and Consequence Models focus on the consequences of courses of actions. Decision Models deliver abstractions of the decision logic aimed at determining optimal solutions to a problem. Florian (1974) characterized models as Static or Dynamic, Descriptive or Normative, Aggregate or Desegregate, and Precise or Approximate.

Boar discussed Analytical Models by reminding us that such models deliver a potent framework for representing and understanding the whole problem, as well as the component parts and their relationships. Analytical Models improve comprehension since through them we can first agree on the validity of the abstraction (the model) and then carry that agreement forward to the immediate problem. Designers employ Analytical models to describe systems and theories.

Categories of Models

Models fall into three categories Specific, Generic, and General Models. The criterion for using models, however, is not how closely models mirror reality but how well teams can use them to attain good goals. Human systems models derived from Living Systems Theory form models of human systems that contribute to the design of the Continuous Performance Management-Insider Threat Prevention Cyber Security Unified environment.

Specific Models

The Disciplines employ specific models to attain goals. These models can be bottom-up or top-down, high-level or detailed representations. Occasionally, they reflect the activities of several disciplines concurrently working on the same applications problem. In design science, we refer to specific models as tools or instruments of design. Designers of the CPM-ITP Cyber Security Human Activity System employ specific models to facilitate implementation of unification tasks to meet program objectives.

ITP Cyber Security Human Activity Systems and their subsystems design business processes and unified organizations as specific models. Management employs these models to implement ministerial, educational and/or hierarchical objectives. In the ITP Cyber Security Human Activity System, specific models become test bed solutions to verify the feasibility of the required processes.

Generic Models

Some authorities find the concept of Generic Models argumentative. For others, however, Generic Models continually evolve as model-makers gain new insights and learn new approaches to model-making. Generic Models deliver a theoretical rationale for top-down design. While some designers argue that only one Generic Model can exist, others argue that different classes of Generic Models exist.

In the design of Human Activity Systems, designers adapt the Generic Model to each category of social and technical problem to which it is applied. Designers, then, add specifications to the meta-theoretical framework of attributes, phenomena, and conditions to maximize the goal-oriented problem situation under study. Adding these specifications result in a Specific Model. Lacking a Generic Model approach, designers commit the fallacy of under-conceptualization, a common fallacy in Information Systems design.

In Human Activity Systems design, the characteristics of Generic Models include the attributes, conditions, and characteristics that are common to all models used in the design of Human Activity Systems. Generic Models also include the properties that inform specific project-oriented technical models while not replacing them. The different versions of the Generic Model may be applied to different versions of Human Activity Systems. Beyond this, Generic Models also include the fundamental presuppositions of HAS Design Inquiry. These include such presuppositions as human existence and the ability to know things. Additional presuppositions include the capacity for forward and backward reasoning through logical structures and reasoning through referential relationships of inferred structures and archival representations.

General Models

The General Models Library serves as the repository for all design models. Designers build this Library as an integration activity during Human Activity Systems design. While designers of General Models integrate the Specific and Generic Models, the General Models Library stores the Specific, Generic and General Models. A final, executive level model produces, as a General Model consisting of the integrated Generic and Specific Models, the top-down with bottom-up view of the Insider Threat Prevention Cyber Security General Model.

General Models are comprehensive. They include all documentation about the Insider Threat Prevention Cyber Security Unification Program such as the environmental Human Activity Systems process design guidelines and system management designs.

The Modeling Environment

Making the models of Human Activity Systems remains a complex process. Since models must be appropriate to their context, designers build many types of models. Moreover, since the challenge of representativeness is a big one, model makers employ a language that is best suited to the model's own environment and the context of the situation. However, as powerful as any language or model may be, designers face limits. For example, a model is only a model; it is only a representation of the subject modelled.

This fact is significant. Obviously, modeling requires an adequate Modeling Support Environment to enable model-makers to execute the critical modeling tasks of specification, definition, alteration, execution, output display, and analysis. With the support of the Modeling Support Environment, model-making and models deliver advantages to social and technical systems designers seeking to design Insider Threat Prevention Cyber Security Unified Human Activity Systems. However, model-making remains an imperfect exercise having as many weaknesses as strengths.

Strengths and Weakness of Model Making

Models deliver advantages that make them important to designers. Models save time, reduce cost, clarify problem situations, and even minimize concept confusion by reducing errors. Models bring order, clarity, and structure to the problem solution. Models allow designers to do things they would not normally be able to do because of the risk, danger, and cost associated with special circumstances endemic in dynamic high technology areas. Lippitt (1973) wrote that models provide frames of reference, are easy to develop, and help put complex situations into perspective. Hanneman (1975) saws models as useful because they provide coherence in problem situations. Without models, progress in human development would not have occurred as widely and as rapidly as it has.

Model-making has disadvantages also. For one thing, models often fail to deliver what is expected. One reason for this is that inexperienced designers frequently submit to the fallacy of domain confusion. Banathy (1983) wrote:

The model-maker crafting a design makes images and seeks differences and news by defining criteria to evaluate interference and fit between two fundamental and similar systems: World of physical objects and events, and the World of human and social systems. Great difficulties occur when designers mistakenly apply processes and methodologies appropriate to one domain to the wrong domain.

Model-makers employ modeling languages to build models appropriate to a given domain and problem context. Thus, model-making requires an appropriate model making methodology. Lippitt (1973) wrote that a weakness of models is that they may encourage a model-maker to "over-generalize a situation". Domain confusion can occur whenever a model-maker over-generalizes a situation.

Additionally, master model-makers are well-suited to model making as a design activity. The less suited the model-maker is to model-making, the more the model-maker risks making many different types of errors including oversimplification, unrealistic mapping, pictorial realism, and overemphasis on form, symbols and rigor (Hanneman, 1975).

Human beings make many types of errors. Managers often reduce these errors by assigning the right person to the right job. For example, a serious weakness in model making is that model makers are so involved in model making that they become blindly dedicated to a particular model. In these instances, model makers respond to an inherent bias by attempting to make the situation fit the model.

In model-making, a goodness-of-fit is a necessity between the model-maker and the modeling task (Prigogine, 1976; Bateson, 1979; Banathy, 1984; Kremer, 1986). Banathy (1984) reasoned that goodness-of-fit is a function of specific internal criteria for selecting design methods including methodological power, systemic match, participation, and organization enhancement. When coupled with other external criteria, the goodness-of-fit between system and methodology ensures the adequate selection of design methods and the formulation of the design model.

The importance of goodness-of-fit raises questions about the characteristics of the model-maker. Model-making is not easy. It requires several personal strengths including discipline, abundant skill, and deep knowledge. It also requires the abilities to abstract, see entities from different perspectives and problems from different perspectives. It also demands an abundance of practice.

While some model-makers are adept at model-making from the very first day, others are less fortunate. This group must keep trying. The majority of model-makers require considerable training and development over an extended period of time to build their skills and techniques. Some can never make it, no matter how hard they try. Model-making is not for everyone.

Problems in the Transition of Models

Developers and end-users employ models differently. Developers use models to define design parameters, while end-users want models to serve the business either as operational prototypes or end products (McMillan et al., 1989). In the domain of Cyber Security systems, for example, senior executives are interested in the development of these systems as a strategic business product designed to enhance the performance of customer-centered Cyber Security product development. In commercial organizations, Cyber Security systems are envisioned as products that produce products. However, executives in research organizations which employ model-based analysis use Cyber Security systems to satisfy specific research aims.

In government, the concerns include all of the above. The design of Cyber Security systems evolves as the goals of each segment of human society evolves. Accordingly, Cyber Security systems design will become more successful as program management provides better information about the limits of the Cyber Security system designed for a particular environment and organization type. Thus, end-users can contribute to any discussion about resolving problems during the entire Cyber Security systems design process.

Lack of Representation

Interactive computer systems perform poorly whenever designers fail to consider how things really work in the real world. For example, while many functions in the field are knowledge-based, many computer applications are rule-based. This discrepancy leads to inefficiency, waste, and poor business performance.

Most performance studies, including studies of human performance, ignore organization and social psychology issues (McMillan et al., 1989). The design of CPM-ITP Cyber Security Human Activity Systems models will fail whenever designers focus on technical performance issues alone. An expanded design that considered the Human Activity System involved in the CPM-ITP Cyber Security Unification Program would more appropriately link the design to social, business, and security issues.

Characteristics of the Model Maker

Some designers find model-making a challenge because it is an abstract enterprise requiring appropriate languages, skills, tools and techniques. As mentioned earlier, the model-maker must enjoy a mind for abstraction. It is my experience that those lacking imagination have a difficult time as model-makers. Commentators have presented considerable material on the characteristics of the model-maker. For example, Lippitt (1973) suggested that model-makers require a tolerance for ambiguity, independence of judgment, situational sensitivity, and the ability to analyze and synthesize. They must be able to work comfortably in the gray areas of problem solving.

Banathy (1973) wrote that, first and foremost, model-makers should enjoy systems thinking. Secondly, it helps if they are evolutionary visionaries. I believe that model-makers require intellectual quickness, that is, quick on their intellectual feet. Successful designers are resilient and adaptable. They are endowed with a kind of mental flexibility that permits them to change course quickly while maintaining rigor in their ability to simplify large amounts of information in a meaningful way. The problem here, of course, is the risk that under certain conditions, adaptability might reduce resilience.

Defining a new role for management, Cavallo (1979) saw model-makers as managers who function as catalysts "in the flow of all the processes constituting a socio-technical system" (p. 86). Personal experience seems to bear out that different model-makers excel at building different models.

CPM-ITP Unification HAS Design Models

Human Activity Systems exist within an administrative/technical conceptual space termed the cooperative or participative management domain. We refer to the sociotechnical extension of cooperative management as cooperative processes. These empower individuals to participate concurrently on the same process or goal. In the domain of the ITP Cyber Security Unification Program, design inquiry delivers the approach which made the enterprise modeling environment possible. Thus, another revolution in Theory is currently shaking CPM.

Modeling of a Human Activity System, and its architecture, provides an innovative method of describing the cooperative nature of the transformation driven CPM-ITP Cyber Security Unification environment. Current reasoning suggests that Continuous Systems Thinking enhances HAS design practice.

Although plenty of wisdom certainly exists in this rationale, HAS architectures designed to describe the CPM-ITP Cyber Security Unification Program can become extremely complex. At such times, designers, unfortunately, generate a great deal of confusion when their designs confuse development teams, become insufficient to satisfy the intended tasks, or too difficult to facilitate project management.

Employing the systems models approach in the design of the CPM-ITP Cyber Security HAS reinforces the need to build descriptive models and bypass the analytical models. The Five Forces or Competitive Model is among the most unsuitable models for the unification program. We can certainly eliminate it from the CPM-ITP Cyber Security Unification design project. Other unstable models include the Processing Architecture Models or Information Technology and Systems Architecture Models. Also, we may eliminate the

Data Architecture and Strategic Analysis Model in this group. Beyond these, we may avoid Data Models, the 7 "S" Model, the Engineering Model, Core Competency Model, Medical Model, and the Configuration Model.

The generic models presented in this paper enable managers and designer to describe the essence of the Insider Threat Prevention Cyber Security Unification Program. These models provide a methodology for creating and leading fundamental change in how the enterprise defines the unified Insider Threat Prevention Cyber Security environment. For designers guiding the evolution of the Insider Threat Prevention Cyber Security Unification Program, and managers establishing the Cyber Security of enterprise processes, this presents a complex challenge. Simon (1962) wrote that complexity exists "when the whole is more than the sum of its parts, not in the ultimate, metaphysical sense, but in the important pragmatic sense that, given the properties of the parts and the laws of their interaction, it is not a trivial matter to infer the properties of the whole" (p. 468).

The design of Human Activity Systems consists of several levels of embedded activities that make such design efforts nontrivial exercises in the sense intended by Simon. According to Simon, complexity has much in common with ontological determinism (Bogdanov, 1984; Katsenelinboigen, 1989). The process of designing Human Activity Systems delivers to design teams and their managers a potent strategy for confronting their lack of knowledge about a change in understanding. The complexity associated with this strategy stems from the characteristics of design non-separability, design non-feasibility, systems self-motivation and observer interests (Ulrich, 1983) placed in the embedded requirements of the Human Activity System.

Models

For the purpose of Insider Threat Prevention Cyber Security Unification Program, we define models as "low-variety representations of systems" (Banathy, 1983, p. 37). This definition derived from the systems paradigm.

5: The Systems Paradigm

Paradigm

A Paradigm directs, guides, focuses, and influences our perception of the world, how it works and what it contains in any given situation. We perceive the world within the one world view or another which establishes any paradigm we may advocate for problem solving. Carrico (1989) described a paradigm as a representation for the internal model that human beings employ to think about something.

Kuhn (1970) wrote that paradigms "define the legitimate problems and methods of a research field" (p. 10). For Kuhn there is the pre-paradigm period, the period of normal science consisting of anomaly, crisis, and revolution. Powers (1984), wrote that a paradigm "is a basic image which acts as an organizing and filtering agent, a socially accepted way of seeing, modeling, and communicating about reality" (p. 2). Powers sees a paradigm as a larger philosophical system consisting of three crucial subsystems the Ontological, the Methodological, and the Epistemological.

As a systemist, I see a paradigm as a suprasystem consisting of Ontological, Epistemological, and Psychological subsystems which together inform a meta-methodology for making sense out of the world through design. Our paradigms influence our efforts at designing our own futures through design inquiry. While I see paradigms as ways of encountering the universe, others see paradigms as metaphorical (Morgan, 1986).

Principles, Laws, Corollaries & Guidelines

The Systems Approach is operationalized through its various statements, assumptions, pre-suppositions, and guiding notions as expressed in the form of principles, laws, corollaries and guidelines (Yourdon, 1989a). This "legal" and "disciplined" foundation derived from General System Theory stresses the nature of the systems approach as an expanded encounter with the world being perceived in the form of dynamical systems in interaction and interdependence through the interconnectedness of subsystems rather than as a background of static, discrete and non-interrelated components in isolation (Yourdon, 1989a).

An important corollary of the system approach is that as systems thinkers, we appreciate the uniqueness of a situation or element as a member of any system. If it is correct that a system is changed whenever a component or subsystem enters the system or leaves it, the component must be unique

(Mayon-White and Morris, 1982). From the human science perspective studying both the expanded domain of Human Activity Systems and the discrete organization structures and functions of Organization Development, this corollary defends the uniqueness and indispensability of every person. Every human person brings something unique into their systems. This something unique makes the system other than what it previously was (Mayon-White & Morris, 1982).

We derived the axioms, propositions, principles, laws, corollaries, and guidelines of the system approach from the basic definition of the concept system. Bertalanffy (1950), Ashby (1956), Miller (1956), Checkland (1981), Myon-White and Morris (1983), Bogdanov (1984), Christakis (1985) and Warfield (1987) have all contributed to this definition. As the system movement evolves, the laws and principles developed within this perspective will increasingly become influential.

Although not ever dictate of the systems perspective enjoys empirical credibility, experience with them indicates that they present logical content. Moreover, history demonstrates Checkland (1981) was correct when he wrote that the continual use of systems concepts in problem-solving will generate a parallel emergence of laws derived from the logic made explicit by the use of systems ideas. Today we derive these systems ideas from the systems perspectives that are continually evolving as a new paradigm of disciplined inquiry. Systems principles are implicit in the many new theories of corporate rebirth.

Social-Technical-System

Sociotechnical systems designers argue that the social subsystem consists of the division of labor, i.e., the roles of the ITP Cyber Security Unification teams, and the methods of coordination such as the hierarchy, rules, and regulations used to control the variances in the design and implementation processes. Growth in Human Activity Systems is associated with the informal and unwritten code of conduct that enforces the problem-solving approach followed by the advocates of the ITP Cyber Security Unification Program within the transactional environment, i.e., that environment in which teams engage secure business practices.

Since the social subsystem is the component Human Activity System that engages designers of the ITP Cyber Security HAS, they search for new configurations of procedures or tasks in the social subsystem to reduce the confusion in the development processes and practices. However, without commitment to achieve peak performance and sustain it, the carelessness, inattention, and alienation characteristics of all social subsystems, constrain the development of even the most dedicated teams.

HAS designers therefore, design systems that encourage commitment and involvement in the process. These most often take the form of special projects. Additionally, growth in Human Activity Systems is related to the informal, and often, unwritten code of conduct that enforces the problem-solving approach followed by the teams within the ITP Cyber Security Unification-Transactional environment. Designers will fail with this if they overlook several formative characteristics of the design contract.

First of all, the maintenance of program performance requires autonomy and discretion as clear guidelines to action. Designers and team member must have the opportunity to learn and continue learning in respect to challenges and feedback. Designers require the correct mix of variety in the design journey to encourage teams to develop a satisfying pace and style of commitment. Team members require an opportunity to build self-esteem by exchanging assistance and fostering mutual respect as an element of growth through the public recognition of individual accomplishment and potential during the unification design program.

Also, designers must make a meaningful contribution to the unification program in the respect that a designer's contribution to the CPM-ITP Cyber Security Unification Program represents the successful accomplishment of a challenging task. Designers and their teams need to understand that their practices contribute to the good of the Unification Program. Moreover, designers expect to have a fair opportunity for a meaningful future in respect to their need for advancement, personal growth, and increased meaningfulness.

Sociotechnical Systems (STS) design methodologies do a better job balancing Human Activity Systems with their technologies than do other methodologies. An expanded Sociotechnical Systems design approach delivers an path to developing highly effective Human Activity Systems through the design of the social and technical interfaces existing within the Insider Threat Prevention Cyber Security Unification Human Activity System.

Soft System

These systems deliver descriptions. They are descriptive. They are not governed by laws that lead to the generation of predictions. In soft systems design, measurement occurs through qualification rather than quantification. Each soft system requires methodologies appropriate to its system's type.

System

Mayon-White and Morris (1982) wrote that a system is an assembly of components of particular interest to someone. The components are connected in an organized way for doing something of interest to someone. Systems are structures consisting of organized components with the basic components being those which do not contain subcomponents (Churchman, 1971). The components are affected by being in the system in such a way that the system is changed if any component leaves it, or is added to the system.

System thinkers classify systems as natural systems, designed systems, Human Activity Systems, and social systems. Systems can be hard or soft, designed physical systems or designed abstract systems. Some authorities claim that systems exist which are beyond human knowledge; these are the transcendental systems (Checkland, 1981). In Living Systems Theory (Miller, 1988), systems consist of 19 subsystems. Today, we can add several more subsystems.

Systems Design and Relevant Dynamics

Systems Design occurs as a disciplined inquiry consisting of specialized techniques, general rules and universal principles. For Human Activity Systems to evolve, systems design must be continuous. This requires full stakeholder participation. Collen refers to the systems design methodology as the "Systems Design Journey" to reflect the continuous or evolutionary nature of design as distinct from planning.

Systems Perspectives

The systems approach is engaged in continuous debate. Debate rages over the efficacy of the movement itself. Some fear that it may be just a new way of expressing old ideas. Others wonder if the systems approach is so general as to be vague, vacuous, and meaningless (McCraken & Jackson, 1981; Freeman, 1983). Some even argue about the best approach to systems thinking.

Just as the systems perspective is a way of perceiving the world, there exist several ways of perceiving systems. Churchman (1979) wrote that the systems approach consists of a continuing debate between various attitudes about society. The advocates of science who build objective models have become the most influential debaters of the current period of systems thinking (Churchman, 1979). Churchman reasoned that many systems debaters exist who fall into one of four classes of systems thinkers. They are efficiency thinkers who study trouble spots. Or they are science advocates who build objective models. Other may be humanists who consider values while encouraging noninterference. A fourth kind of systems thinkers are the anti-planners who encourage experience at the expense of other rational approaches.

Systems Philosophy

Systems Philosophy provides internal consistency to system theory and systems methodology. It delivers a general world view or way of thinking about reality. Systems Philosophy informs all of philosophy with the systems view and brings forth an expansionist, dynamic (non-linear), synthetic, and holistic mode of thinking.

Systems Thinking

Checkland (1981) wrote that "Systems thinking in the tradition stemming from organismic biology regards its holism as manifest thinking in terms of 'whole' rather than 'the whole'" (p. 258).

Workflow Human Activity System

This refers to a Human Activity System that employs tools, techniques, software, hardware, and networked architectures in a transparently qualified manner on secure platforms. This system produces business products or problem solutions for a client environment within an enterprise, organizations, or team. (Newkirk, 1993)

Insider Threat Prevention Cyber Security (ITPCS)

Insider Threat Prevention Cyber Security is challenging because it is all about "Prevention". ITPCS is all about stopping an action before the action can occur. Detection is in the domain of prevention, but it occurs after a malicious intrusion has occurred. In ITP Cyber Security, Prevention means Prevention. Interestingly, the Prevention Paradox reminds us that prevention is so challenging because many conditions occur that prevent Prevention from succeeding. So, prevention is possible, but the wrong kind of prevention.

When I refer to ITP Cyber Security, I have two concerns in mind. First, ITP means "Prevention" before a malicious act has occurred. Second, ITP Cyber Security means "Prevention before a malicious act has occurred against any Information System, network, data base, repository, data file, electronic record, electronic product, power grid, standard, guideline, process, and/or procedure". I am sure, you get the idea.

Moreover, ITPCS also refers to the Prevention of any malicious act against any individual, group, or organization affiliated or associated with the information Technologies of the enterprise wherever these people are located. These individuals may be employees, contractors, or third-party vendors.

Technically, any person who has access to any information Technology element or system component can become an Insider Threat, or target of any malicious Insider Threat. Like I say, ITP Cyber Security is challenging. Perhaps this is why people commonly focus on the "low-hanging fruit" such as the external attacks which can be terrible, but not catastrophic. However, about 35 percent of the ITP CS attacks destroy their targets.

Continuous Performance Management

Continuous Performance Management is a big deal. Organizations have bet the farm on the potential of this management strategy to enhance workplace life and invigorate business operations. CPM is such a powerful movement that several institutes around the globe dedicate themselves to it as a cause of the day.

We can recognize CPM through about a dozen strategies referred to by CPM insiders as the Hallmarks of CPM. Generally, these include the migration to self-directed teams, transition of mangers to coaching roles, nurturing an atmosphere of openness and trust that grants employees access to corporate Information Systems, transformation of annual reviews into self-directed learning exercises, and many other Hallmarks that actually conflict with the strategies of Insider Threat Prevention Cyber Security that encourage the initiation of Zero Trust guidelines.

CPM-ITP Cyber Security Unification Program

Historically, organizations integrate their information systems, business processes, and enterprise architectures to develop a tight-coupling of the data flow and to simplify access to multiple systems. In the Age of Cyber Terror, Technical Integrations such as these generate a number of down-stream threats in which a single access point grants multiple entre points through multiple and integrated applications. Insider Threat Prevention Cyber Security changes these dynamics whenever it proposes a Zero Trust design strategy.

In the practical sense of business survival and expanded competitive opportunity, nearly every company will eventually become an ITP Cyber Security company if they wish to survive. Manufacturing companies will become ITP Cyber Security companies that do manufacturing. Research companies will become ITP Cyber Security companies that do research. I am sure you get the idea. Insider Threat Prevention Cyber Security will become the great challenge of the 2020's. Eventually, executives as well as managers will figure it out. When they do, they will see the need for new enterprise architectures that unify these with the architectures of Insider Threat Prevention Cyber Security. Integration will never be good enough, too many gaps that invite malicious access.

Although this series discussed the unification of Continuous Performance Management and Insider Threat Prevention Cyber Security, it did so as an illustration of the challenges faced by every enterprise. Whether you favor the Continuous Performance Management architecture or something else, you will eventually face the problem of Insider Threat Prevention Cyber Security. What will you do then? If you wish to remain competitive, your will perhaps realize that architecture integration really is insufficient to carry the day. Perhaps you will once again redesign your enterprise as a single enterprise unified with ITP Cyber Security. Your company will become a security company that has unified Cyber Security with your enterprise, business or industry model.

Unifying Continuous Performance Management and Insider Threat Prevention Cyber Security creates a substantial strategic and operational challenge for even the most accomplished manager and technical specialist.

6: Designing Unified Systems for ITPCS

Even in the Age of Digital Transformation, the unification of Insider Threat Prevention Cyber Security with business architectures remains a non-trivial project. At the least, success requires managers to master Soft Systems Thinking, Design Inquiry, Cultural Systems Methodology, Systems Modelling, Visioning, and Human Activity Systems Design. Through the mastery of systems thinking, an enterprise enhances its probability of succeeding with the unification of Insider Threat Prevention and the adopted business architecture it employs, such as Continuous Performance Management.

From Adaptability to Resilience and Beyond

It is through the implementation of unified business and Cyber Security architectures that companies finally gain the capability to more rapidly adapt to the attack strategies of the malicious inside actors that will come their way. Above and beyond mere adaptability, however, success through ITP Cyber Security occurs as organizations and teams achieve a high level of resilience, authentic resilience.

This will deepen the capacity of organizations to absorb the Cyber Attacks that come along and reorganize the business environments that may need to adjust. The key here is that as the enterprise reacts to the need to make appropriate changes to its environment in response to the Insider Cyber Attacks, they may be required to support the same functions, rely on the same structures and identities, and the same feedback and adjustment loops.

While organizations have historically valued the functional advantages derived from adaptability, the same cannot be said about resilience. This is more of a new concern thanks mostly to the cyber-terrorist. Common thinking has it that organizations, like people, are either resilient or they are not. Resilience cannot be developed; it is simply a natural trait. Some organizations have it, and some organizations do not. Of course, this kind of thinking is incorrect. Although it is quite true that organizations enjoy different levels of resilience, just like people, organizations can continue to develop resilience throughout their existence, just like people, if management chooses to do so.

Adaptability and resilience are connected. They are defined by their constraints. For example, when we speak of adaptability, we are really saying that the people in an organization can influence resilience. A relationship exists between adaptability and resilience in that adaptability is the capacity of employees to influence resilience. In Social Ecological Systems, for example, human beings possess the capacity to manage resilience. This capacity is a function Latitude, Resistance, Precariousness, and Panarchy.

Latitude reminds us that an organization can be adaptable, but not infinitely. Every organization has limits to it capacity to adapt or recover from a Cyber-attack. How much change can your organization take before it loses its ability to recover? Every organization has a built-in limit to recover from the change that a Cyber-attack introduces to the organization. When you cross that limit, the organization cannot recover. Every organization has to contend with a Cyber–attack threshold.

Latitude, of course, is associated with Precariousness. If an organization is close to its attack threshold, that point where Cyber Security fails, we can think of it as being in a precarious situation. This is not where one should hope to be unless, of course, one is a malicious insider seeking the destruction of a target.

Naturally, the question comes up: How much resistance remains in the organization if Cyber Security has become so precarious? Will the malicious insider find the target highly resistant to the attack or not resistant at all? Will the malicious insider encounter little resistance to the attack or find every effort to penetrate the system extremely difficult? Moreover, if the attacker succeeds and brings down the system, will the people in the organization be resilient enough to rebuild the organization, or the system at the least?

Adaptability & Resilience Framework

From the foregoing, we can see that any discussion of adaptability leads us into a consideration of resilience. Can an organization, or any person for that matter, be adaptable if the person lacks resilience? Indeed, can any organization be resilient if it is unable to adapt to even a minor situation? Although resilience and adaptability are not synonyms, they share some attributes. It is the attributes of adaptability and resilience that make them good and bad partners in Cyber Security. Just consider the "Paradox of Efficiency" for a moment and you will understand what I am getting at.

For example, efficiency is ordinarily a highly respected and sought after organization characteristic. Many managers dedicate their entire careers to optimizing efficiencies of scale. Of course, efficiency is one of those characteristics of human enterprise that if you have too much of, you will destroy your organization.

Aristotle is correct, after all. Too much of a good thing is a bad thing. Or let me put it in terms modern people understand: The Golden Mean means gold. So how can efficiency ever be a bad thing? You can actually ruin a market through efficiency. Moreover, an organization can become so efficient that it may reduce resilience and further complicate the range of adaptability. Also, high efficiency means low adaptability. Low adaptability can influence organization resilience. This is a complicate relationship with high potential complication. Although resilience and adaptability are not identical characteristics, one can affect the other. What we are talking about here is that adaptability and resilience are different aspects in a single framework that I refer to as the Insider Threat Prevention Cyber Security Panarchy.

ITP Cyber Security organizations increase their range of success when they are supported by teams, knowledge platforms, and networks that learn and store knowledge and experience virtually. They enhance their adaptive capacity whenever they leverage their knowledge and problem-solving resources to deliver flexible Cyber-Security solutions. The goal in this case would be to expand the adaptability of management and security teams in conformance with the Law of Requisite Variety.

ITP Cyber Security organizations that conform to the Law of Requisite Variety enhance their adaptive capacity to re-configure their organization without the burden of making notable changes in the core functions or suffer a decrease in ITP Cyber Security performance. Without gaining the advantages delivered by the Law of Requisite Variety, the ITP Cyber Security organization weakens its adaptive capacity to design new solutions for ITP Cyber Security. Such a failure further reduces the available options that support the inevitable enterprise-wide CP-ITP Cyber Security redesign and renewal projects.

Enhancing ITP Cyber Security Adaptive Capacity

The quest for resilience remains a powerful concern for the success of ITP Cyber Security. Like the rest of the technical world, the dark universe of Cyber Terror is continually changing and evolving. Thus, ITP Cyber Security requires insights and solutions that enable ITP Cyber Security specialists to strengthen the adaptive capacity of ITP Cyber Security as it continually seeks new way to assist the enterprise.

Remaining on the reliability path forward, ITP Cyber Security management tracks how organizations and their people behave during periods of malicious insider generated duress. Consistent ITP Cyber Security success requires that ITP Cyber Security leaders note how organizations respond following a successful cyber-attack. Unfortunately, this kind of attitude tracking is for the most part neglected. Perhaps this is the reason why the attitude of organizations about Insider Threat Prevention Cyber Security is the least understood aspect in Resource Management and science (Gunderson and Holling 2002).

Back in 2002, Folke et al. clarified the four critical factors that interact across the Panarchy of the temporal and spatial scales that address the dynamics during periods of change and reorganization. We can argue that these dynamics include how people learn to live with Cyber Security change and uncertainty and how Cyber Security organizations nurture the diversity of solutions to better enhance resilience. Additionally, these dynamics concern the ways people combine different forms of knowledge to learn how to create opportunities for enterprise-wide self-organization necessary to consistently master ITP Cyber Security.

Role of Resilience in ITP Cyber Security

In the world of Insider Threat Prevention Cyber Security, resilience refers to the depth and breadth of positive coping capacity. Resilience means more than merely coping; it really is all about remaining positive during trying times. It is about stay confident and keeping focused on the challenge ahead. A positive attitude is important because we know that during a crisis positive people remain creative and are more energized to get things done. They recover quicker and stronger and design better solutions.

While people formerly believed that an individual's capacity of resilience was fixed, today we know that resilience is flexible, depending on the nature and environment of the challenge encountered. Regardless of the kind of resilience an individual may have developed, it requires the continual nurturing and strengthening that can occur through workplace experiences and the events of personal life.

Since everyone is different, everyone copes differently. Individuals who enjoy high-capacity resilience consistently spring back more rapidly from malicious insider attacks. As organizations continually work to enhance their reservoir of resilience, they address the entire spectrum including psychological, individual, group, team, organization, cultural, and enterprise resilience.

Resilience is not about being a ITP Cyber Security super hero. It is not about becoming a super stoic with every emotion under control every day all the time. It is not something that people turn on and off like a water faucet. Resilience is a behavioral response to an unpleasant event. It does not turn a person off but focuses a person to more rapidly access knowledge and skills that have been learned and mastered throughout life.

Resilience is the behavioral skill that enables people to manage anxiousness, disappointment, sadness, impatience, pain, or many other challenging emotions that paralyze the less resilient individual. If one is resilient, one can still cope and take right action while being energized by a positive attitude still attached to reality. Through resilience, people can still focus their emotions and impulses in a way unavailable to the less resilient.

The Resilience Architecture

We can clarify the value of resilience to Insider Threat Prevention Cyber Security by describing its Panarchy, its organizing architecture. Although fundamentally the same in its core characteristics, we can describe resilience from psychological, individual, group, team, organization, cultural, and enterprise perspectives. Since we have discussed the psychological above, we will begin here discussing Individual Residence.

Individual Resilience

Individual Resilience enables a person to cope well during high levels of stress and adversity and to function effectively despite the challenges and setbacks they face. Highly resilient individuals believe in their ability to succeed. These people remain optimistic and enjoy mature self-esteem.

Many factors come together to energize Individual Resilience. These factors include cultural background and ethnicity; personality and socioeconomic; status and family history; physical and mental health, and history of past traumatic events and social experiences. A person's social support networks consisting of family and friends; colleagues and co-workers, and even the community play a formative role in building resilience. They deliver emotional security and establish connections with a range of people who can offer other supportive resources.

Group Resilience

While the direct impact of traumatic events are obvious because they are up close and personal, the indirect effects can spread out everywhere in the wider environment. For example, a malicious insider attack that targets a single person may impact a larger number of people including witnesses to the event, co-workers, and even family and friends and the larger community outside the workplace.

Team Resilience

The risks associated with Insider Threats can reduce the performance of an organization. Moreover, they often create conflicts among business teams, their managers, and technical partners over strategies and tactics designed to prevent insider attacks. Team Resilience refers to the coping process shared by an entire team. Management employs directed relationship processes to reduce the severity of stress suffered by team members and their managers. It reduces the impact of stress and facilitates the adaptation of ITP Cyber Security strategies.

Resilient teams impart acceptance and belonging that enable team members to overcome the Cyber Security challenges they face as the meet the needs of teammates. Such teams enable teams to cooperate better as they work to find ITP Cyber Security solutions that can rapidly neutralize the insider threat. These teams resolve their ITP Cyber Security problems through innovative practices, deep cooperation, and a spirit of openness. They emphasize social support as they value the necessity for connectedness. Moreover, overt resilience occurs when team members freely demonstrate confidence, hard work, cooperation, and innovation.

Organization Resilience

Organization Resilience refers to the collective capacity to respond to adversity and bounce back as a community of colleagues and workers. Organization Resilience is increasing critical in the age of Cyber Terror. However, Insider Threat Prevention Cyber Security is still the weak child in the Cyber Security family.

Implementing appropriately designed unified architectures will enable organizations to respond effectively against the malicious insiders among them. Indeed, the business architecture- ITP Cyber Security Unification Program will involve the enterprise in developing new approaches of critical analysis,

ITP Cyber Security skill building, and Governance Risk Management and Compliance. When properly managed, the Unification Program will foster deeper attitudes of cooperation and support in the drive to secure each organization and team against the malicious insiders among them.

Cultural Resilience

Cultural resilience refers to the ability of an organization and its teams to develop and deepen a, ITP Cyber Security sensitive cultural identity. This special identity emerges from the critical cultural knowledge and practices of ITP Cyber Security in a business environment. At the personal level, the newly unified culture will impact at the least the intensity and frequency of interpersonal communication. It may also influence the emotional life of teams. Beyond this, such a program will align the values of the organization with ITP Cyber Security and assist everyone with the development of individuals and team coping skills. Cultural expectations will change as employees begin to understand the hidden dangers of malicious insider attacks. Since beliefs and values are deeply personal, success with ITP Cyber Security requires everyone to be on the same page. If it is indeed the case that an individual's cultural formation deeply influences the way that person reacts to stressful events, management has to ensure that the effort to establish a security conscious includes everyone.

No one is the Borg here. We are talking about new levels and programs of ITP Cyber Security, not radical assimilation. Cultural Resilience is a positive attitude that enables employees to bounce back after an unforeseen malicious event. Any acceptable culturally derived coping strategy would have to bring the teams together, not fragment them. Fragmentation is always the undercurrent when management attempts to introduce programs intended to build Cultural Resilience.

Enterprise Resilience

This brings us to our last category of resilience, Enterprise Resilience. While individuals, teams and organizations have developed their singular and collective resilience, an entire enterprise may need to rapidly recover from an insider generated cyber-attack. Enterprise Resilience refers to the capability of an enterprise to bounce back from malicious cyber-attacks that do major harm to the economics of business operations, and damage to systems and data, or disrupt special programs of strategic importance.

In the Age of Cyber Terror, Enterprise Resilience is a necessity if organizations are to adequately recover from the malicious insider attacks that span enterprise systems. At the very least, executives and their managers are obligated to identify the factors that enable an enterprise to rebound and then sanction the projects that implement these factors. Obviously, every level of resilience, from the psychological to the enterprise, requires resilience building systems, procedures, and contingency plans that increase resilience while decreasing Cyber Security risks.

Building confidence, these interventions include training on the processes required to reduce the impacts of a malicious attack. Ultimately, an effective resilience building process enhances the primary activities of Cyber Security: Observe the problem situation; Approach involved teams cautiously to offer assistance; Stabilize the emotional environment; Interact with offended teams and organizations to defuse the situ ation, and Support everyone impacted by the Cyber-Attack.

Potential Resilience

Potential Resilience refers to the deepening of the capacity for attaining resilience. The previous examples of resilience concerned Actual Resilience. Potential Resilience is about build resilience across a wide range of situations. Every day is a new day and as such really is unknown. Anything can happen.

Potential Resilience is about developing the emotional and intellectual strengths required to overcome the most unexpected, difficult, unimaginable, unique, and extreme attacks (Carpenter et al. 2009b). In the universe of ITP Cyber Security, management also faces the risks that accompany openness, short term contracts, multi-culturalism, compartmentalization, continuous monitoring, indifference, and unearned trust (Carpenter et al. 2012a). Potential Resilience is expansive in that it can increase an individual's capacity to bounce back from all of these either gradual or sudden shocks within the enterprise at-large.

Since uncertainly never ends, the expansion of Potential Resilience forms a potent foundation for engaging Actual Resilience. One might say that Actual Resilience is Potential Resilience actualized. Potential Resilience is the reservoir of resilience that enables individuals to go beyond the ordinary in proactivity responding to ITP Cyber Security threats. Unfortunately this response comes with a cost.

The need for Potential Resilience never diminishes and thus requires continual development. This can become quite expensive depending on the critical nature of the specific organization, number of people involved and their current state of resilience, level of Cyber Security maturity, complexity of work practices, and range of ITP Cyber Security unification with the enterprise. The progression of Potential Resilience into Actual Resilience is actually an individual adaptation that also depends on an individual's capacity for adaptation.

As we have seen above, Folke et al. (2003) proposed four key features for building the kind of resilience necessary to enhance adaptive capacity. These are features that interact across temporal and spatial scales and influence the dynamics in Insider Threat Prevention Cyber Security organizations. The first key feature refers to the potential to respond effectively during periods of uncertainty, unplanned changed, a sudden crisis. Resilient people respond creativity by leveraging the disaster for downstream success. Secondly, resilient teams rapidly employ their diversity of insight to develop new paths of success using the collective innovation that resilience may deliver.

Third, resilient ITP Cyber Security teams leverage their experience, knowledge, and understanding about the dynamics of malicious insider threats to enhance management practice and ITP Cyber Security tools and techniques. Fourth, Insider Threat Prevention Cyber Security teams employ their Potential and Actual Resilience to guide their evolutionary unfolding, improve Governance, Risk Management, and Compliance (GRC). These teams also leverage internal drivers of insider threats to master the inter-systems dynamics between diversity and complexity (Folke et al. 2003) that often lead to malicious insider Cyber-Attacks.

Seven Principles of Actual Resilience

Biggs et al. (2015) identified seven principles that may deepen the Actual Resilience of ITP Cyber Security teams. These principles enable people to bounce back from unanticipated disruptions and sudden changes in the behavior of strategically placed employees who make the malicious Cyber-Attacks that test the effectiveness of ITP Cyber Security organizations and systems.

As we have seen in an earlier book in this series, effective ITP Cyber Security organizations continually monitor a wide range of threats from many sources. Since diversity is both good and bad, ITP Cyber Security teams monitor the special threats that emerge from the different kinds of diversity that characterize each enterprise and the imbalance generated by incompatible CPM and ITP Cyber Security architectures. Other areas of ITP Cyber Security concern that could invite malicious intruders include the challenge of redundancy, optimization of systems and software connectivity.

Beyond these interest areas, ITP Cyber Security organizations do best when they design and implement prevention controls designed to "Prevent" malicious intruders from delivering unwanted surprises. Such controls are especially important in organizations that function like complex adaptive systems. In these systems, team members may inadvertently introduce variables under the radar that may encourage the risk-taking behavior of a malicious insider who is operating under the radar.

Additional areas that directly impact ITP Cyber Security quality and effectiveness are Training and Development or T&D. Here, Cyber Security and business organizations have a chance to look back and look forward, that is, to connect the past with the present. Organizations look back by teaching their people about what has occurred in the past and they look forward to try to understand what methods the malicious insiders might employ in the future. The point here is that teams ought to learn from the past and then try to understand what malicious insiders might to in the future. They do not try to predict the future. Through T&D, employees gain a chance to learn about "what they did in the past" and "what they might do in the future".

Beyond Training & Development, management has to learn to address the challenges associated with the expanded participation of employees in organization-wide ITP Cyber Security and the adoption of more responsive polycentric governance systems. Quinlan et al. (2015) reminds us that the unified CPM-ITP Cyber Security architecture can focus on the resilience of the unified enterprise as a social-technical system or on the resilience of the architecture structure as a dynamical system. Management can unify these strategies in the newly unified architecture.

Summary of Resilience

Resilience does not come easy. It actually begins to develop in childhood and continues throughout one's lifetime. Resilience is not fixed in stone as are the color of one's eyes. Resilience has an ebb and flow about it that can be mastered and improved upon as a person works to deepen and strengthen it. Resilience is not about bravery; it does not make a person brave or cowardly. Resilience is about coming back again and again to get the job down. Resilience follows the law of my old friend Jerry Cooper. I call it "Cooper's Law":

> "I'll be back. You can beat me up and you can kill me, but you can't eat me
> because that's against the law. I'll be back". —Jerry Cooper

Now that is resilience. Jerry was a hardworking and positive guy who overcame many setbacks during his life, and he always came back. He exuded resilience. He never ever gave up, and he did it all with a smile on his face and a chuckle in his heart. So how much resilience does anyone have? I do not know that answer to that question. However, I do know that whatever you have, you can still develop more. Resilience describes the degree to which the ITP Cyber Security organization remains capable of self-organization, learning and adaptation (Holling 1973, Gunderson & Holling 2002, Walker et al. 2004).

ITP Cyber Security teams must be resilient to do their job. When resilience is enhanced, an ITP Cyber Security team is likely to withstand a malicious attack without falling apart or being forced to adopt a new set of ITP CS processes to remain effective. Authentic resilience in ITP Cyber Security enhances the capacity of teams to anticipate change and, therefore, influence future pathways to ITP CS.

Reduced resilience increases the vulnerability of ITP Cyber Security teams to even smaller disturbances than usual. Even a gradual decline in resilience among team members can generate a dangerous ITP Cyber Security reaction in which the viability of Cyber Security processes becomes less effective. Even a small decrease of resilience may make attack recovery impossible. Research suggests that recovery of ITP Cyber Security teams to previous levels of capability may require a return to the readiness posture that existed well before the occurrence of last malicious insider cyber-attack (Scheffer et al. 2001). While a number of theoretical advances for Cyber Security have emerged over the last several business quarters, they have mostly neglected Insider Threat Prevention Cyber Security. Psychology is a global concept and the Psychology of Insider Threat Prevention Cyber Security impacts both the threat domain of Cyber Security and the ITP Cyber Security domain.

Insight into Insider Threat Prevention Cyber Security Resilience, Potential and Actual, stresses the importance of balancing diversity and redundancy to enhance the resilience of Cyber Security teams during periods of sudden change. Achieving balance further requires management to govern and adapt connectivity and modularity between organizations and their systems as internal data, systems, and networks become compromised.

Moreover, since organization variables become friction points for GRC teams, due to the irregular pace of feedback about risks and threats, ITP Cyber Security organizations can ensure that focused communications systems deliver real-time reporting and feedback capabilities. Also, because of the significant uncertainty associated with the feedback, however, the complex adaptive-systems thinking characteristic of ITP Cyber Security can improve team results by tracking the potential nonlinearities and thresholds of employee behaviors while still allowing for diverse types of knowledge to emerge by experimenting with new methods and monitoring the results they deliver.

Beyond this kind of learning approaches, ITP Cyber Security teams can develop expertise by participating in Innovative Problem Solving to build social capital and join in collective ITP Cyber Security action with nontechnical organizations. Establishing an enterprise-wide polycentric-enabled overarching set of standards and regulations, the ITP Cyber Security organization can leverage two or more decision centers with their own limited and autonomous prerogatives to enable teams through the enterprise to master a range of resilience building principles.

In this way, ITP Cyber Security teams become better prepared to clarify specific short-range and long-range ITP Cyber Security goals and define and track related metrics for each resilient building principle. Employing the polycentric-governed unification approach, the ITP Cyber Security organization becomes better prepared to employ multiple knowledge streams to refocus efforts from efficiency to effectiveness as well as planning for uncertainty and surprise. Moreover, using a polycentric approach, ITP Cyber

Security teams can potentially become more flexible as they create spaces for spontaneous exploration and more effectively learn to build informed trust while expanding social capital (Biggs et al. 2015).

The principles of ITP Cyber Security are never end-goals, including those that (1) build team resilience, (2) guide collective action (e.g., Ostrom 1990) through difficult times, or (3) govern the adaptation of organizations (e.g., Folke et al. 2005) in response to insider threats. Rather, they are means-goals. They assist in generating the conditions that resolve the challenges found in the collective actions associated with the trade-offs made by ITP Cyber Security organizations, especially when they function as complex social-technical systems.

ITP Cyber Security lacks even the most basic predictive models. No universal solutions or magic potions or any concrete principles exist that enable ITP Cyber Security teams to do their job effectively in every case (Holling et al. 1998, Ostrom 2007, Pahl-Wostl et al. 2012, Biggs et al. 2015, Clarvis et al. 2015). More than rules and regulations, ITP Cyber Security requires inspired creativity, deep reflection, continuous learning, and rapid adaptation to respond to the rapidly changing threat state created by 21st Century Cyber Terror.

Successful ITP Cyber Security teams continually seek a deeper understanding of complex, multi-variable, nonlinear, cross-scale, and continually changing attack scenarios that threat actors employ during their well-planned, and not so random, malicious attacks. Such understanding is essential if ITP Cyber Security teams are to have any chance of gaining the upper hand against their malicious Cyber Terrorists. This is especially the case if ITP Cyber Security teams hope to maintain the integrity of the enterprise-wide environment.

A few ITP Cyber Security organizations attempt to implement frameworks that not only enable them to better understand what goes on in the Cyber Terrorist's mind but to predict it as well. These organizations would probably achieve better results by seeking understanding and leaving prediction to Las Vegas. While understanding is, no doubt, a noteworthy goal, prediction is a roll of the dice.

Rather than attempt prediction, successful ITP Cyber Security organizations adopt an adaptive management approach for combating the threat. They hope that this approach will enable them to better identify the uncertainties of ITP Cyber Security and then implement methodologies to test hypotheses about these uncertainties. For these organizations, adaptive management becomes a tool for not only learning about the ITP Cyber Security system but also to change the ITP Cyber Security system.

The ITP Cyber Security management approach differs from the usual management 'trial-and-error' decision-making that uses the available knowledge to generate the 'best guess' management strategies that proliferate in many organizations where "the guess is the solution". The achievement of the ITP Cyber Security objectives requires access to data and information about the past, present and future ITP Cyber Security operations within the enterprise specifically and then access to data and information about the industry generally.

Adaptive management requires political openness. As an adaptive process, ITP Cyber Security has to function as a social as well as a technical process. ITP Cyber Security focuses on the development of new Cyber Security methods, techniques and strategies just as much as it focuses on the possible threats of malicious insiders.

The adaptive management approach of ITP Cyber Security employs systems science to deepen understanding and otherwise enhance ITP Cyber Security flexibility. Hopefully, the insights gained from systems thinking may generate new methods and approaches to ITP Cyber Security that anticipate the trends and techniques of malicious actors in rapid real-time. Armed with this knowledge, teams then can design an appropriate response that consistently prevents insider threats enterprise-wide.

In system thinking, we learn that management cannot understand or manage any organization by focusing on a single component of the system. All systems, and Insider Threat Prevention Cyber Security Systems, especially, function across multiple scales of time, environment, social organization, and interactions. ITP Cyber Security teams employ the interactions across hierarchically structured scales, the Panarchy (Gunderson & Holling, 2003), to estimate the dynamics of an attack threat at a specific focal scale.

In sum, Panarchy is a framework of ITP Cyber Security rules that enable ITP Cyber Security teams to clarify the interactions between a malicious attack and the persistence required to sustain the attack. In this sense, then, Panarchy describes evolving systems with multiple interrelated elements such as threat systems and Cyber Security systems. Holling et al. (2002) discuss the concept of "hierarchies of influences between embedded scales, i.e., pan-archies, to represent structures" that confront sustained attacks, validate the outcome of the attacks and enable the adaptive evolution of the ITP Cyber Security Framework. In this way, the slower and larger attack mitigation strategies set the conditions within which the faster and smaller attack mitigation strategies behave.

Throughout this process, management rules moderate the state within the existing ITP Cyber Security rules to control the range of security options that the teams can access for any specific threat scenario. This moderation process periodically generates the variability and novelty of the solutions employed upon which Insider Threat Prevention Cyber Security depends. As a result of the periodic and transient cycles of malicious cyber-attacks and mitigation attempts, the ITP Cyber Security organization's components, processes, and relationships may require redesign.

This effort results in a new design that offers novel opportunities for updating and improving the capabilities of the ITP Cyber Security organization. This adaptive process explicitly transforms the ITP Cyber Security organization as the outcome of a planned process that impacts each level of networked relationship. Moreover, this adaptive process does not risk the integrity of the enterprise or the ITP Cyber Security organization. Moreover, as the characteristics of an organization continue to change at a variable rate over a variable span of time, the capacity to generate fundamentally new systems become more urgent as ecological, economic, social, or political conditions make existing ITP Cyber Security teams ineffective. Transformation occurs as the speed and force of the change increases and passes that point where the structure adopts a new design.

7: Design of ITP Cyber Security Systems

Systems Thinking is paramount when describing complex dynamical problems. The systems approach to inquiry delivers a deeper perspective about the components, processes, and interrelationships of problems as systems and the environments that "ignite" them. Contributors to the development of the systems perspective are many. Their names are well-known: Ackoff, Warfield, Checkland, Cristakis, Rahmatian, Miller, Bertalanffy, Banathy, Collen, and many others. These contributors to the continually emerging systems perspective either reinforce previously understood aspects of systems Design Inquiry or introduce additional insights which become assimilated into the presently existing knowledge space of this five books series. Naturally, this means that I approach these five book series with a level of competence consistent with the requirements of conducting a Design Inquiry into The Psychology of Insider Threat Prevention Cyber Security. Banathy (1987) defined these requirements (1987).

Understanding of the Systems of Design Inquiry

Insider Threat Prevention Cyber Security involves a significant number of systems that come together to achieve conflicting goals. I used names for these systems that make their goals obvious. They include the Target Systems, the Prevention Systems, the Malicious Insider Systems, the Management Systems, the Knowledge-Base Systems, the Configuration Management Systems and Change Management & Version Control Systems.

Each of these systems consists of human and technical components. Also, these systems are driven by an organizing perspective based on the charter of the ITP Cyber Security function. They are Human Activity Systems that are socio-technical.

Target System

Target Systems are the systems under threat, the ones at risk. These systems reveal the motives of the malicious insider. They tell us about the scope of the risk and reveal something about the possible enemy associated with the malicious insider. The Target System will even tell us if the malicious insider attack is a lone wolf attack. Determination of the Target System may even reveal something about the history of the malicious insider within the organizations, including insights about workplace relationships, position in the organization, and motive for the crime.

Prevention Systems

Prevention Systems are the systems that respond to prevent the malicious insider from acting on his or her plan to launch an insider generated cyber-attack. These systems exist as a family of interconnected systems. Collectively, they form a single, enterprise-wide, anticipatory system. These systems monitor, assess, evaluate, track, record, estimate, rationalize, and direct responses to perceived threats. Prevention Systems engage in Command, Communications, Control, and Coordination functions. They note changes in the behavioral patterns of individual employees and teams and record personal histories within the organizations. Prevention Systems work together to prevent an Insider Threat from succeeding at any time.

Malicious Insider Systems

We access Malicious Insider Systems to develop and test profiles of malicious insiders. These systems contain historical information and data points about everything to do with insider attacks including strategies, technologies, methods, approaches, attack styles, motives, innovations, duration, damages, attack multiples, schedules, languages, depth of attacks, range of attacks, attack ratios, triggers, accomplices, damage outcomes, prevention keys, psychological techniques, degree of attack difficulty, penetration plans, special algorithms, special hardware tools, special software routines, internal attack leverage aids, preparation scenarios, preparation schedules, attack plans, attack resources used, attack budgets, overriding attack success factors, attack failure factors, attack prevention factors, attack ratings in degree of difficulty, attack openness or subterfuge, and many more.

Management Systems

We access Management Systems to review chain-of-command report expectations, standards, guidelines, procedures controls, decision rules, ITP Cyber Security Prevention protocols, intra-departmental participation guidelines, management sign-off rules, confidentiality requirements, special project authorizations, limits to Insider Threat Prevention Cyber Security team recruitment guidelines, ITP Cyber Security organization charters, ITP Cyber Security confidentiality rules, special project Command, Communications and Control guidelines, information sharing guidelines and authorizations, systems access guidelines, publishing rules and regulations, content storage and retrieval, ITP Cyber Security technology acquisition guidelines, Non-disclosure Agreements, content storage and access control, and management security infraction reporting guidelines.

Management Systems govern the management and control of the Insider Threat Prevention Cyber Security process from mission concept, training and development to Insider Threat Prevention Cyber Security Governance, Risk Management, Compliance, threat mitigation and risk reduction.

Knowledge-Base Systems

Knowledge-Base Systems describe and characterize the Systems of Design Inquiry. They store and deliver expert knowledge and intelligence about the relationships of the systems of Design Inquiry. Lacking a disciplined approach to Design Inquiry, the systems approach falters and loses its appeal as a descriptive science. Knowledge-Base Systems store whatever information ITP Cyber Security organizations, and their managers, decide they should store. This decision, of course, depends on the information ITP Cyber Security teams and managers regard as pertinent to their vision and mission in closing the gap between threat identification and threat prevention.

Configuration Management (CM)

Configuration Management (CM) refers to the tracking, recording, and updating of every modification made to every system component of the ITP Cyber Security System. It also refers to the maintenance of the historical record regarding the modification to any component of the Insider Threat Prevention Cyber Security System.

Change Management & Version Control System (CMVCS)

Change Management & Version Control Systems are highly valuable systems that reduce unnecessary redundancy in the expansion of the Information System's footprint. This system assists Insider Threat Prevention Cyber Security teams and enterprise managers with recording and tracking every change to each ITP CS system component in response to changes in the attack profiles of every malicious insider Cyber-Attack.

CM & VCS deliver and maintain historical libraries that detail the complete life-cycle of each module and component of the ITP Cyber Security hardware, network, and software systems. The Version Control component of the system identifies, maintains, and delivers the currently approved and promoted operational Insider Threat Prevention Cyber Security System of record.

Interaction Dynamics of the Systems of Design

High levels of operational competence in using the systems of Design Inquiry provide designers with an essential framework for conducting any project which culminates in the design of a new system or the redesign of an existing system. When the designer has obtained the required level of competence in the areas suggested by Banathy, that designer will be equipped to realize the admonishment of Rapoport:

The most promising course is the complete rejection of isolated consideration of individual aspects of the management relationships and transition to a new subject-matter of analysis and improvement-complex (general) relationships. This orientation of effort will allow designers to realize the advantages of the systems and contingency approaches to the design of management organization structures (Vladimar S. Rapoport, 1987, pg. 72).

The application of Banathy's Design Inquiry Model (1987) provides that "promising course" encouraged by Rapoport. Banathy views the design experience, meaning the process of design, as the spiral-like movement of the designer from the contextual space through the design solution space to the space of the future system. As the designer works toward the design of the future system in the future system space, the designer encounters all the spaces of design enclosing the design solution space, i.e., the contextual space, the knowledge space, the experience space.

"Systems Dynamics of Design" (Banathy, 1987) formally refers to the pattern of activities that moves designers through the spaces of design. The Systems Dynamics of Design include: The Dynamics of Iterative and Spiralic Design, Dynamics of Feedback and Feedforward, Dynamics of Divergence-Convergence, Dynamics of Multi-Systemic Thrust in Design, and Dynamics of Participative Design.

The Dynamics of Design only succeeds when the designer possesses a "clear understanding of the systems that are involved in design inquiry". These systems are summarized by Banathy (1987) as: Design Inquiry System, Decision Support System, Design System, Design Genesis System, Systems of Design Testing, Knowledge Base System, and the System to be Designed. Moreover, Banathy describes the environmental systems which surround the various design systems and collectively form the design suprasystem. He identifies these as: Systemic Environment of the Design System, Systemic Environment of the Design Genesis System, Systemic Environment of the Future System, and Knowledge Environment or "Knowledge Stock" System from which designers derive Design Relevant Knowledge.

Insider Threat Prevention Cyber Security begins and ends with design. Design is the discipline that adequately orders all the parts of the ITP Human Activity System (HAS) to function as intended. Design Inquiry is the discipline that describes the components of the HAS, their relationships to each other, and describes how they work together to form a coherent whole. In a significant way, Design Inquiry is a systems design discipline, especially so when organizations unify the business environment of Continuous Performance Management with the technical environment of Insider Threat Prevention Cyber Security.

The application of Banathy's Design Inquiry Model (1987) to the development of a unified Continuous Performance Management and Insider Threat Prevention Cyber Security architecture delivers that "promising course" encouraged by Rapoport. In this case, designers engage in the spiral-like movement from the contextual space of two separate systems through the design solution space of a unified architecture to the space of the fully realized unified CPM-ITP Cyber Security HAS as the future system. As designers design the future CPM-ITP Cyber Security unified HAS in the future system space, designers elaborate all the spaces of the unified architecture that enclose the final unified HAS architecture as the design solution space. This includes the contextual space, knowledge space, and the experience space of the final unified architecture, the unified CPM-ITP Cyber Security Human Activity System.

The "HAS Dynamics of Design" (Banathy, 1987) formally refers to the pattern of design description and examination activities that move the teams of designers through the spaces of unified architectural design. Here, design teams engage the Dynamics of Design for the unified CPM-ITP Cyber Security design program by iteratively progressing through Iterative and Spiralic Design; (2) Feedback and Feedforward; (3) Divergence-Convergence; (4) Multi-Systemic Thrust in Design, and (5) Dynamics of Participative Design.

Design occurs through iterations of design activity that occur through spirals of progress governed by occurrences that deliver results impacting management through feedback or not impacting management through feedforward. Additionally, as the CPM-ITP Cyber Security unification program moves forward, elements of the design process come together through convergence to generate design iteration or move apart through divergence to change the design iteration.

Throughout the design process, designers concern themselves with the impact that the unified system will make on the environment and the impact the environment will make on the CPM-ITP Cyber Security unified system. To be sure, as the design iterations continue, designers eventually involve all the stakeholders of the embedding systems and the relevant systems to build consensus about the purpose and operations of the unified system currently being designed. The emerging design project is dynamic and holistic, interactive and integrative, spiralic and interative, participatory, dialectical, and consensus seeking (Banathy, 2010).

The design of the unified system only succeeds when designers have developed a clear understanding of the CPM and ITP Cyber Security systems that are involved in design inquiry. Technically, in the case of this project, competent designers have experience with the following systems: Design Inquiry System, Decision Support System, Design System, Design Genesis System, Systems of Design Testing, Knowledge Base System, and the System to be Designed (Banathy, 1987).

Moreover, designers working on the unification project will be expected to describe the Environmental Systems. These systems surround the Design Systems and collectively form the Design Suprasystem. Banathy (1987) identifies these as the Systemic Environment of the Design System; Systemic Environment of the Design Genesis System; Systemic Environment of the

Future System, and Knowledge Environment or "Knowledge Stock" System from which designers derive design relevant knowledge. In ITP Cyber Security, these systems will be extensive and emerge from the Design Genesis System.

Systems Models of HAS Design

Following his explanation of the Spaces of Design and Design System, and his description of the Environments of Design, Banathy presents an approach for "Modeling the Systems of Design" (1987, pp. 105-107). Here, Banathy presents a three dimensional examination or characterization of the Human Activity Systems Environment, Structural, and Behavioral Models. Designers build these models to describe the new unified CPM-ITP Cyber Security architecture.

Systems Environment Model

The System-Environment Model describes and examines the relationships and interactions between the CPM and ITP Cyber Security specific systems and each system's environment. In this sense, then, the designers examine the boundaries of each system in view of their attributes, i.e. open system or closed system. Designers also evaluate the environment's requirements to permit an appropriate system's response. Designers work to insure that the System-Environment Model describes the environment's inputs and each system's outputs and further describes the dynamic processes of mutual cooperation, adaptation and co-creation.

Systems Structural Model

The Systems Structural Model describes and examines each system of the unification project within its own boundaries. Designers examine the "whatness" of each system and its organization. "This model displays the system, its contents, and the relational arrangements of its content (Banathy, 1987, pg. 105)." Also, designers describe the purposes/goals and functions of the Structural Model. Designers also describe the components and the data and information and everything else that integrates the components to form the model. This prepares the model for the deeper examination, definition, description and system building that follows in the next iteration of design.

Systems Behavioral Model

The Behavioral Model or Process Model examines the changes occurring in a specific system over time. Hence, it is a complement to the structural model. The conceptual area of interest in the Process Model concerns the system's operations. Here, designers employ the Behavioral Model to describe the input, transformation, output, and feedback and adjustment operations. The system received inputs from the environment, transform these inputs into substantially different elements, and then return them back to the environment in the transformed form. Cycles of feedback and adjustment govern this transformation process. These cycles enable the system to ensure that the transformation process accepts all relevant inputs and returns them to the environment as outputs in a form which conforms to the goals or requirements of the environmental suprasystem. Feedback and adjustment occur at two levels and ensures that the system adjust itself in response to:

(1) the environment;
(2) its own self-directed purpose, and
(3) in response to continuous cycles of output assessment.

Possibility Thinking in Design

Building upon the theme established by Banathy (1987), Curt McNamara (1987) moves from a discussion of the design of the future environment to an examination of the design of a future state. McNamara writes about "The Possibility-Space and the Information Environment. In his paper, McNamara notes several central implications for the CPM-ITP Cyber Security unification project. McNamara writes: "If a system does not take actions to consciously build the future, then the environment of the system builds the future for it as the Input and output operations link the system to its environment (1987, pg. 131)."

If this is indeed the case, perhaps we can better understand the necessity for designing a unified CPM-ITP Cyber Security Human Activity System that is a self-directed and purposeful system with goals. In some cases, I have observed an interesting phenomenon that appears to validate McNamara's assertion. In these situations, the ITP Cyber Security team indeed abdicated to its environment the responsibility of building the team's own future. In these cases, the environment dominated the ITP Cyber Security development project by permitting the CPM subsystem to unrealistically expand the CPM cyber security requirements.

Here, the CPM unification organization drifted "out of control" and management eventually canceled the project or the unification project fails in some other way. Whether McNamara is stating a law here is uncertain, but he certainly identified an important operating principle that can impact the performance of the ITP Cyber Security unification team. A consideration of McNamara's observation leads me to suggest the following CPM-ITP Cyber Security unification program design principle: Successful CPM-ITP Cyber Security unification design requires the design of a pro-active foundation for executing the activities of pro-active design. McNamara (1987, pg. 131) outlines these activities as:

- Identifying possible future states;
- Determining which possible future states are desirable, and
- Forging and implementing a plan to get from the present to a desired future state.

Moreover, McNamara writes about design possibilities. He identified and defines the Possibility-Space; Possibility Domain; Anticipation Space; Possibility Pathway; and Information Environment. Aside from additional clarification, Banathy had expressed most of these ideas previously. For example, when McNamara speaks of the Possibility-Domain and states that "an individual's 'mental images, values and realities' determine his/her possibility domain", he is simply presenting a variation on the theme of Banathy.

Writing that the Design Contextual Space "also includes images, purposes, and aspirations that are the genesis of design" (Banathy, 1987, pg. 101), Banathy was arguing that the Possibility-Space is the set of all future states expanded. By this I mean to say that the Contextual Space consists of the collection of all future states relevant to the genesis of design, and this is the Possibility Space. The Possibility Domain of the Contextual Space is the visible reality of the Contextual Space at any given point in time depending upon the level of activity completed by the ITP Cyber Security Design Human Activity System as it studies, defines, and characterizes "design relevant systems and systems of problems that are relevant to design inquiry" (Banathy, 1987, pg. 101).

What we are actually talking about here is the implied striving for simplification, an effort to make design understandable and somehow less complex. Both Banathy and McNamara illuminate operational principles that can make a successful design experience more realizable. For example, Christakis (1987) does the same in his paper, High Technology Participative Design: The Space-Based Laser.

In this respect, he discusses the "Laws of Design", presents the Principle of Reconciliation and argues that the Interactive Management approach "is capable of satisfying the Principle of Reconciliation" (1987, pg. 143). Both the Laws of Design and the Principle of Reconciliation are important considerations of the effort to manage complexity as organizations build CPM-ITP Cyber Security unified architectures. One can say that Christakis appears to be implicitly arguing that any CPM-ITP Cyber Security unification project should occur as an in-depth redesign of both CPM and ITP Cyber Security architectures as a single redesigned architecture.

. As a way of affirming Christakis, Nadler (1987) borrows from Warfield to caution about the need to reconcile the Law of Requisite Variety and Requisite Parsimony without addressing either one:

Complexity has a way of feeding on itself. As the complexity of a problem causes many minds to be applied to it, a new complexity arises, that of sharing among these many minds the products of each other's thoughts and actions and this in turn leads to another complexity, that of interrelating and distilling group effort and bringing them into a format where they assume utility (Nadler, 1987, pg. 118).

The arguments presented by these systemists potentially impact Insider Threat Prevention Cyber Security. They are worthy of consideration as an ITP Cyber Security organization makes progress on the redesign of the unified CPM-ITP Cyber Security architecture. It is obvious that Systems Thinking is critical for the success of any CPM-ITP Cyber Security unification re-design effort. Moreover, unification design teams require an understanding of design as a decision oriented, creative activity requiring:

- purpose;
- self-direction, and
- openness with the suprasystem.

Moreover, organization do best when they base design activity on established principles of design methodology. This means that organizations must:

1. Become knowledgeable in the systems and spaces of design;
2. Reconcile the laws of Ashby and Miller;
3. Design a methodology appropriate to the subject of design, and
4. Become a systems thinker informed by the theory of Human Activity Systems Design.

Given this, it is obvious that the effort to redesign the ITP Cyber Security organization as a unified organization with the business environment is not a trivial exercise. Such an effort requires a level of expertise consistent with the requirements of conducting a formal Design Inquiry. Banathy (1987, pg. 102) defines these requirements as:

- Understanding of the systems of design inquiry;
- Knowledge about the description and characterization of the systems of design inquiry;
- Knowledge about the relationships of the systems of design inquiry, and
- Appreciation for the entity or entities emerging from the interaction of the systems of design.

Such levels of expertise in the Systems of Design Inquiry provide CPM-ITP Cyber Security Unification designers with an essential framework for conducting any project which culminates in the design of a new unified system or the redesign of an existing system. When designers have attained the required level of expertise in the areas identified by Banathy, they will be better equipped to realize the admonishment of Rapoport stated earlier.

8: Deepening the Paradigm

Design Inquiry Metamethodology

The preeminence of the engineering paradigm as the exclusive approach to the re-design of an organization is responsible for many of the problems associated with the art and delivery of ITP Cyber Security. The problems are numerous and include the:

1. Design of poor solutions;
2. Cost overruns;
3. Schedule slippage;
4. Poor Insider Threat Prevention Cyber Security;
5. Low staff morale;
6. Unhappy end-users, and
7. Inability to determine the feasibility of CPM-ITP Cyber Security unification using potent information systems and networks.

The engineering paradigm minimally addresses the issue that the design of the unification architecture begins with the design of the Human Activity System that designs the architecture rather than with the implementation of a standard design methodology used to evaluate the hardware and software to be shared by the CPM-ITP Cyber Security organization.

Designers adopt systems thinking to expand their view of the unified CPM-ITP Cyber Security organization. Such a descriptive view is central to the success of the entire design process. Prior to engaging a design methodology to design the unified system, designers initiate a Design Inquiry to prepare for the design of the ITP Cyber Security HAS that then designs the methodology to use during the design of the unified CPM-ITP CS system. Collen (1990) reminds us that Design Inquiry serves designers in several ways. First, Design Inquiry assists designers with preparing for the design project. Next, it enables designers to design the ideal system. Third, Design Inquiry assists designers with designing the enabling systems. Finally, Design Inquiry enables designers to plan all transformations and implementations in the most effective way. Banathy (1990) refers to these stages of Design Inquiry as a map of the design journey to create the future. Designers focus on describing the ITP Cyber Security HAS well before they commence an Operational Evaluation of the unified CPM-ITP Cyber Security environment.

Under this expanded approach, the ITP Cyber Security HAS is seen to exist in a narrow-environment-of-interest and a wide-environment-of-interest. The HAS receives matter, energy and information from its environments as inputs and transforms these before returning them to the environment as outputs. To perform the various systems operations including feedback and adjustment, the ITP Cyber Security HAS consists of at least 19 component systems as subsystems. Each subsystem performs functions to achieve the purpose (or goals, depending on the type of system) of the ITP Cyber Security HAS. Like all open HAS, the subsystems process matter, energy and information.

The subsystems of the ITP Cyber Security HAS perform their functions through the systems operations of input, transformation, output, and feedback and adjustment. Designers construct a process or behavioral model to illustrate the operations of the ITP Cyber Security system as a living system. As noted above, a complete systems model consists of environmental, structural and behavioral models. Living Systems Theory (J. G. Miller, 1985) provides constructs describing the generic subsystems of a HAS and their functions that are useful to designers when employing the Systems Models Approach (Banathy, 1973) or the Design Architecture described by Banathy (1984).

In this expanded systems approach to the design of the ITP Cyber Security HAS, Design Inquiry delivers an approach to designing the ITP Cyber Security HAS. This HAS then engage in Design Inquiry to design the methodology that will generate the ITP Cyber Security design. "Design into design" provides the foundation for investigating many methodological design issues that are "beyond" or "meta" any particular methodology. In this regard, I view Design Inquiry as a "metamethodological" approach to design.

The evolving ITP Cyber Security HAS design paradigm focuses on the wholeness of living systems. It views systems complexity as something which exceeds reductionism. Moreover, HAS design is the foundation of ITP Cyber Security systems design. In this way, subjectivity and purpose become crucial while problem identification and uniqueness gain new prominence (Ulrich, 1983). For strategic organization change programs such as the CPM-IOTP Cyber Security unification program, design is more than a hard scientific engineering discipline alone as customarily perceived; it is social systems science.

The design of an ITP Cyber Security organization is based upon the interpretation of only sometimes expressed human requirements, often in domains that are unfamiliar to CPM organizations and ITP Cyber Security designers alike. Problem description remains an overriding concern that design teams often ignore or replace by the "drive" to decompose a perceived problem into its most basic parts. While each end user's problem or requirement may be truly unique, ITP Cyber Security designers argue that "if you've seen one, you've seen them all" (Simon, 1991). Ignoring the uniqueness of the end-user's problems often leads to later difficulty.

When designing the ITP Cyber Security HAS and employing Living Systems Theory as the theoretical framework, Design Inquiry engages multiple iterations of divergence and convergence among the various systems, spaces and environments of design using Living Systems Process Analysis (LSPA) and Living Systems Process Design (LSPD) to form the Living Systems Methodology (LSM) (Collen, 1988). Collen (1988) writes that:

> "Systems design inquiry as disciplined inquiry is usually conducted as a process involving a design team. The inquiry provides focus, context, and synthesis of a system and its subsystems as envisioned at some future time" (p. 5).

Joining LSPA with LSPD forms an inquiry journey from divergence to convergence and provides a rationale for the use of "the underlying dynamic of analysis-synthesis" (Collen, 1988). Using Design Inquiry to integrate the Systems Models Approach (SMA) with Living Systems Theory (LST) as an approach for designing the Insider Threat Prevention Cyber Security HAS provides a "convergence that suggests a more generic methodology, that is a metamethodology, which may unite all the systems methodologies stressing analysis and design" (Collen, 1988, p. 11).

As a generic model, the approach is both conclusion and decision-oriented inquiry. It is conclusion- oriented in that the ITP Cyber Security HAS discovers new facts. It is decision-oriented in that the ITP Cyber Security HAS makes recommendations regarding the feasibility of a redesigned CPM-ITP Cyber Security architecture.

Metasystem

Every HAS is derived from its own unique value system. The ITP Cyber Security HAS is a value system. The metasystem is the system of values informing the ITP Cyber Security HAS. Such values are operationalized as embedded systems governing ITP Cyber Security HAS initiation, design, behavior, evaluation and vendor selection. Embedded value systems are metasystems in that they are the systems of objectives and criteria of other systems. In ITP Cyber Security HAS design, metasystems design is a management challenge in that it represents the value system design component of the HAS (Hall, 1989).

During value systems design, also called normative scenario production, designers model the set of objectives or goals that assist the search for alternatives and provide the multidimensional decision criterion for selecting the most appropriate or optimum third party design solution (Hall, 1989). Hall (1989) reasons that guided by metasystem design, decision making involves management evaluation of the design alternatives tested by the third parties "and incorporating these evaluations into the decision criterion so that management can compare all alternatives relative to the criterion, to the end that one or more of the alternatives can be selected for advancing to the next phase" (p. 31).

In ITP Cyber Security design, metasystem formulation incorporates several activities as a management subcycle nested in Request for Information (RFI) definition. These activities include: Problem definition, meta-metasystem design (design inquiry), metasystem synthesis, and feedback from physical system design (Hall, 1989). Metasystems are designed around clusters of values ranging from the improvement in human artifacts, and the attainment of a higher quality of life to self-fulfillment and the satisfaction of aesthetic needs. As defined in the RFI, management often associates the metasystem of the CPM-ITP Cyber Security unification program with the improvement of human behavior and artifacts involving the most basic of technical value systems.

The subjective value systems of the project staff becomes unified with the official metasystem to act as informal metasystems. These value systems covered the gauntlet of possibilities from improving the quality of Insider Threat Prevention to personal security-enhancement. Organizations can view metasystems design as the means to designing a unified CPM-ITP Cyber

Security HAS methodology. In organizations, metaystems influence both strategic and operational planning in that they set the implicit tone of what is acceptable in the work environment in respect to strategic ITP Cyber Security directions and corporate goals.

Hypersystem

Extending the work of Ivanov (1990) and Forsgren and Ivanov (1990) to support ITP Cyber Security HAS design, the hypersystem becomes the locus of categories for all subsystems of the ITP Cyber Security HAS and the relevant subsystems of the Narrow-Environment-of-Interest such as the end-user. During the Design Inquiry, the hypersystem clarifies the categories established during metasystem design as an examination and acceptance of CPM-ITP Cyber unification project values. Ivanov (1990) writes:

> Systems structuring, with due consideration of ends-means hierarchies in both the physical artifact and the human-purposeful dimension is there attained in terms of not only morphological-structural (physical) categories that were implicit in most ideas of information about the physical world, but also in terms of functional classes and teleological classes which take into consideration more complex relations, including the human striving for goals and values. (P. 2)

The hypersystem is a learning social system that examines the values of the ITP Cyber Security HAS and its environment defined during metasystem design. It develops categories of consensus as a quality criteria baseline to support "Information Systems or OUGHT judgements" and to achieve support for the goals, objectives and ideals of the ITP Cyber Security system as expressed by the values identified and defined during metasystem design. These categories of consensus establish the systems management relationships of the ITP Cyber Security HAS between the subsystems of the HAS and their environments. Both hypersystems and metasystems are aspects of the organizing perspective of the Design Inquiry.

The hypersystem baseline is category dependent and category specific. Categories may range from primitives expressed as End-User, Decision Maker, Planner, Systems Designer, Systems Philosopher to Soft Systems categories such as Customers, Actors, Transformations, Weltanschauung, and Ownership (Ivanov, 1990; Checkland, 1981). Designers engage the metasystem to determine the appropriate baseline categories for hypersystem design. The concurrent design of the metasystem with the hypersystem represents important cycles of Design Inquiry activation. The metasystem and hypersystem brings important management values to the surface and provides a method of clarification to get everyone of the same operational platform in respect to objectives, goals, and performance expectations of the ITP Cyber Security HAS.

Evolutionary Guidance System

Concurrent metasystem and hypersystem design assist in understanding the values implicit and explicit in the ITP Cyber Security HAS. This is in respect to the operational evaluation and the definition of the categories of system management relationships. Moreover, designers and managers track and manage these categories during the design of the ITP Cyber Security HAS and the execution of the Operational Evaluation.

The implicit and explicit values are conceptualized as dimensions of the Evolutionary Guidance System of the ITP Cyber Security HAS. Banathy (1987a) identifies these dimensions as the aesthetic, economic, educational, ethical, political, scientific, social action and technological dimednsions. Evolutionary Guidance Systems are idealized or value systems. Collen (1990) writes:

> "When a HAS commands the direction of its own activities, activities which serve to guide it in the pursuit of its mission, the HAS seeks to become an EGS" (p. 8).

The metasystem, hypersystem and evolutionary guidance system as idealized HAS form the organizing perspectives of the design inquiry and provide a baseline for the design of the ideal system, a guiding notion of the ITP Cyber Security HAS.

Matching Design Methods to System Type

As designers engage in Design Inquiry and understand the organizing perspective of the Design Inquiry through metasystem, hypersystem, and evolutionary system design, they also differentiate systems types (Banathy,

1987a). Banathy (1987b) has argued that general and specific implications for Design Inquiry, design education, and design research exist in matching Human Activity Systems to design methods. Banathy describes Human Activity Systems as a continuum consisting of Rigidly Controlled, Deterministic, Purposive, Heuristic and Purpose Seeking Systems. He argued that a relationship exists between design methodology and systems type. Such a relationship is explored through the Systems Models Approach using Living Systems Methodology. In the domain of Information Technology, Eason (1988) describes design systems as one of five types:

1. Traditional Data Processing Design
2. Structured Design Methods
3. Participative Design Methods
4. Local Technician Developed Systems
5. End-User Developed Systems

Territory of CPM-ITP Cyber Security HAS Unification

Thus far, we have discussed the concepts, methods and guidelines that form the territory of Continuous Performance Management-Insider Threat Prevention Cyber Security unification. Human Activity Systems design is a professional pursuit that consists of cycles and iterations of "designerly" activities and processes that create new Human Activity Systems in the future. As Banathy (1990) so eloquently stated it, we can see the design journey as a process to "create the future". Design is about recognizing where we are today and where we are going to do from now to shape the future through our own vision.

Design is very powerful. When done right, designers do "create the future". When done wrong, designers create would could become a disaster. Design is one of those human activities that if worth doing is worth doing right. Perhaps, this is why design is so rigorous and yet so creative, so simple and yet so complex, so exhilarating and yet so fatiguing. Design is perfect for the creative person who is disciplined and intelligent. Design is for the big picture person who understands that success is in the details. It is not for the weak-hearted, intellectually lazy person who resists change. Design, however, is for the person who appreciates a disciplined approach to change that creates a more hopeful future.

As an element of its agenda to consider the Psychology of Insider Threat Prevention Cyber Security, this five books series examined Systems Thinking and the design of human systems, methodologically. Moreover, it presented the architecture and rationale of the Insider Threat Prevention Cyber Security organization as a dynamical Human Activity System. The following chapter puts it all together as a new Enterprise-wide Framework for unifying Continuous Performance Management and Insider Threat Prevention Cyber Security. This section summarizes what we need to know about systems thinking to build this Framework.

9: Subsystems of Systems

Framework of CPM & ITP CS Unification

If we wish to master the Psychology of Insider Threat Prevention Cyber Security, we do well to master several disciplines and paradigms simultaneously. The disciplines include:

- Psychology,
- Sociology,
- Behavioral Science,
- Philosophy of Science,
- Management Science,
- Computer Science,
- Physics,
- Systems Design,
- Organization Design,
- Operations Research,
- Assessment and Evaluation,
- Methodology Design,
- Communications,
- Cyber Security,
- Quality Assurance and Control,
- Game Theory,
- Ethics and Morals

The paradigms include:

- Systems Science,
- Quantum Science, and
- Reductionism.

Perhaps we will not use all of them, but many for sure. Obviously, the disciplines and paradigms span a lot of territory. A few of these disciplines involve several specialties concurrently as when Psychology involves Social Psychology, Community Psychology, Clinical Psychology, Developmental Psychology, and Assessment and Measurement. Obviously, the Knowledge

Base of Insider Threat Prevention Cyber Security is also daunting. Perhaps this is the reason so many organizations all but ignore it. Such architecture unification projects are not for the faint of heart.

Mastering CPM and ITP Cyber Security and then unifying them to build an enterprise-wide hybrid architecture demands an incredible amount of intellectual horsepower. It is what this series has been working toward since Book One. Now we will summarize the components that form the Framework of the CPM-ITP Cyber Security Unification development program. There are about 16 components that comprise the Framework of the unification development program.

Spaces of Design

The Spaces of Design refers to the conceptual spaces where the designers do their work and crates their design deliverables. Four specific design spaces exist:

1. Design Solutions Space;
2. Knowledge Spaces;
3. Problem or Contextual Space, and
4. Experience Space.

Design Solution Space

The Design Solution Space refers to the conceptual space where the Insider Threat Prevention Cyber Security Unification design team establishes the purposes and goals of the CPM-ITP Cyber Security Unification Program.

The interactive dynamics of design occur in this space to assist management with initiating the design process by defining the purpose of the Insider Threat Prevention Cyber Security Unification Program and establishing the Program's ultimate goals, such as protecting the enterprise against malicious insider cyberattacks while maintaining a Continuous Performance Management environment consistent with Insider Threat Prevention Cyber Security. The Reproducer subsystem functions in this space.

> Reproducer Subsystem: Refers to the subsystem that functions as a self-design model for a system that produces other systems similar to itself in other organizations. The Reproducer Subsystem accepts appropriate inputs in the form of matter-energy and information to produce systems with components and functions similar to itself.

Knowledge Space

The Knowledge Space refers to that space that contains all the knowledge that designers use during the design process. This space is comprehensive and consists of specific, generic and general design knowledge. It includes additions to existing knowledge such as strategic rules; knowledge about the Unification Tools and Techniques; learning requirements; business process management; new scenarios specific to specific and general design knowledge. It includes knowledge from the disciplines identified above.

Problem, or Contextual Space

The Problem or Contextual Space refers to that space that contains all the sources for defining, studying, and characterizing all the problems, values, and subsystems relevant to the design project. This space contains the use cases, rapid solutions, cultural challenges, and the unresolved issues that impact Program Maintenance for systems, process and assessment occurring throughout the life-cycle of the development program.

Experience Space

The Experience Space refers to the conceptual space where designers test alternative Process, Structural, and Environment models of Continuous Performance Management and Insider Threat Prevention Cyber Security Unification against reality. This space consists of the environments and systems of design specific to the knowledge base systems, the existing Human Activity Systems, the support systems, and the design inquiry system. Value systems design occurs in the experience space. Designers also implement Continuous Monitoring System Implementation; Data Management/Metrics; Change Management, and Assessment.

Metasystems of Design

The Continuous Performance Management Insider Threat Prevention Cyber Security Unification Program unfolds as the product of the Metasystems of Design as designers and managers collaborate together to design tools and techniques that will be used to eventually produce the Insider Threat Prevention Cyber Security Unified environment. The Metasystems of Design assist designers with articulating the:

1. Enterprise-Wide Insider Threat Prevention Cyber Security Sociotechnical Systems;
2. Situation Mitigation Systems;
3. Mutual Support Systems, and
4. Coaching Systems.

Design Models

Insider Threat Prevention Cyber Security Unification Program generates a large number of models of the hard and soft systems kind that come together to form the unified CPM-ITP Cyber Security environment. Collectively, designers build process, structural, and environmental models of Human Activity Systems of the old and new enterprise to complement the technical hard systems models that describe the flows of information throughout the enterprise and its networks of systems.

Interaction Dynamics of Design

Through the Interaction Dynamics of Design, designers engage specialized interactions and dynamics that form the workflows of the design process. Design occurs as a non-linear process consisting of discrete stages of analysis-synthesis and evaluation. Fundamentally, design occurs as a process of interactive cycles consisting of the integration of the five principal classes of dynamics.

Dynamics of Interactive and Spiralic Design

Through the Dynamics of Interactive and Spiralic Design, designers visit and revisit the conceptual design spaces outlined above until the desired new design emerges to replace the former multiples enterprise designs of Continuous Performance Management and Insider Threat Prevention Cyber Security.

Dynamics of Feedback and Feedforward

Through the Dynamics of Feedback and Feedforward, designers discern the iterative requirements of design that ground the work at each level of development. These dynamics enables designers to keep the unification program on the reliability path forward as they make positive progress at each level of development.

Dynamics of Divergence and Convergence

Through the Dynamics of Divergence and Convergence, designers search for alternative systems designs while settling on the most appropriate design according to the goals and objectives of the design project. Bogdanov (1984) argued that systemic divergence moves toward evolution to forge complementary connections. Contra-differentiation through conjunction leads to quantitative equalization which reduces systemic contradictions so that the system evolves.

Thus, through Divergence notable differences in the system design emerge in such a way that a version of the design of the current system breaks away and produces a new system. This is emergence. Bogdanov (1984) reasoned that convergence results from a similarly directed selection within a similar environment. Here the aspects of the system design that breaks away from the current system come together to form a new system that either fulfills the requirements or approaches the requirements. If it fulfills the requirements, the process ends. If it merely approaches the requirements, the process continues.

Dynamics of Multi-Systemic Thrust in Design

Through the Dynamics of Multi-Systemic Thrust in Design, designers coordinate and refine the preliminary designs, at all levels of the design hierarchy, to ensure that they do not ignore any of the expediencies of design. The Dynamics of Multi-Systemic Thrust in Design occurs at multiple levels in the design hierarchy concurrently.

Dynamics of Participative Design

Through the Dynamics of Participative Design, designers navigate the exploratory and issues-resolution cycles of the design program. These Dynamics ensure that designers examine the relevant information and hear all voices. The underlying assumption here is that design occurs as an iterative human activity.

Systems of Design

The Systems of Design refers to the six specialized types of systems that participate in the unification of Continuous Performance Management and Insider Threat Prevention Cyber Security. This unification requires the:

1. Design and implementation of an appropriate business infrastructure;
2. Nurturing of the right attitudes and commitments, and
3. Introduction of the potent technologies and evolutionary approaches that enable transformative success.

The unification of Continuous Performance Management and Insider Threat Prevention Cyber Security, when carefully executed, enables organizations to leverage the best that Continuous Performance Management has to offer with the deep security of a resilient environment to accelerate Business Value Realization (BVR).

Through such a transformative program, the enterprise becomes an embedded Insider Threat Prevention Cyber Security Human Activity System. Anticipating the emerging conflict between Continuous Performance Management and Insider Threat Prevention Cyber Security, we have designed a model environment that facilitates CPM and Insider Threat Prevention Cyber Security Unification. This model consists of the Methodologies of Design, Systems of Design, and Environment of Design, and the Spaces of Design. The Systems of design consists of the following:

System of Problems, Ideas or Intention

The System of Problems, Ideas, or Intention focuses on the problem context, including the existing problems in the current Continuous Performance Management Human Activity System such as the failure to define normative categories for Insider Threat Prevention Cyber Security system development.

System to be Designed

The System to be Design focuses on the "Ideal System" that is to be designed by the cooperating business, technical, and security teams. It will become the future Unified CPM-Insider Threat Prevention Cyber Security Human Activity System.

Design System

The Design System produces the new Unified CPM- Insider Threat Prevention Cyber Security Human Activity System. In doing this, the Design System references the models of the "Ideal System" developed by the value system as a product of the metasystem. The Design System conducts the Design Inquiry.

System of Operations

The System of Operations consists of all operations required to initiate the systems methodology. It energizes the component systems in the Problem Solution Space.

Knowledge System

The Knowledge System comprehensively delivers the knowledge relevant to the entire design project. This System delivers inputs to the Design System to energize the System of Operations within the Problem Solution Space.

Design Support System

The Design Support System energizes the Design System through the initiation of management and maintenance functions. This System empowers the Design System to manage the design inquiry and maintain itself as it designs the "Ideal System".

Ideal System

The Ideal System is informed by the Value System and emerges as a product of the metasystem. This system establishes the model of the best of all possible designs and employs this model to maintain the Design Support System as the Design Support System designs the Ideal System.

Environments of Design

At a fundamental level of requirements definition, different design projects occur in different Environments of Design. It follows, therefore, that the design of a Continuous Performance Management organization occurs in an environment vastly different from that for the design of an Insider Threat Prevention Cyber Security organization.

Now add to this, the complexity of a more complex Environment of Design for a CPM-ITP Cyber Security unification design program in which a new organization design emerges derived from the previous designs of the two separate organizations. This is the challenges for organizations who wish to re-design themselves as Insider Threat Prevention Cyber Security Organizations who engage in profit or non-profit activities. Understanding this, we will review the Environments of Design.

Environment of the Dynamic Systems of Organizing Perspective

This environment consists of the ideas, aspirations, intentions, and problems that form the Unified Insider Threat Prevention Cyber Security Human Activity System. It serves as the conceptual space of the System of Problems and consists of the concrete, currently existing Continuous Performance Management Human Activity System with the Model of the Unified Insider Threat Prevention Cyber Security Human Activity System.

This environment further consists of models of the objectives and goals of the Unified CPM-ITP Cyber Security Human Activity System. Structural Models describe this HAS and the System of Intentions or Values (SIV). The SIV ignited the vision to:

(1) redesign the current CPM Human Activity System;

(2) implement a Unified ITP Cyber Security environment that concurrently;
(3) improves employee performance, and
(4) secures the enterprise against insider threats.

Environment of the Future System

This environment serves as a conceptual source of inputs for the Unified Insider Threat Prevention Cyber Security Human Activity System to be designed. This Environment contains the models of the future system and is the environment in which the Unified Insider Threat Prevention Cyber Security Human Activity System emerges. The Future System Design Environment consists of Enterprise-Wide ITP Cyber Security Sociotechnical System Unification Systems consisting of:

1. Design Teams Structure;
2. Rapid Response Team;
3. Long Term ITP Cyber Security Management Team concerned about Data Management/Metrics;
4. Continuous Monitoring System Implementation, and (5) Change Management Implementation.

Environment of the Design System

This environment delivers the matter, energy and information required for design. It contains the design Human Activity System and the models of the design system that becomes a concrete system during design. Our Design System Environment consists of the following activities See the Sample Design System Environment:

1.0 Design of Human Activity Systems Environment
1.1 Design Human Activity Systems
2.0 Design Situation Mitigation System
3.0 Design Mutual Support System
4.0 Design Coaching Process
4.1 Define Coaching Mastery
4.2 Develop Coaching Skills
4.3 Master Coaching Skills

4.4 Certify Coaching Skills

Knowledge Environment

The Knowledge Environment delivers the inputs that form the Knowledge Base System as an abstract system. This Environment is an abstract environment that contains the entire knowledge repository relevant to design as a disciplined inquiry. Our Knowledge Environment consists of:

Sample Knowledge Environment

1. Four books that clarify the wisdom involved in leading an Insider Threat Prevention Cyber Security Unification Program;
2. Forty Business Strategies for Leading an Insider Threat Prevention Cyber Security Unification Program.
3. Applied Intuitive Solutions(TM) Platform that Assists Teams with Solving a Large Range of CPM-ITP Cyber Security Unification Program Challenges.
4. Continuous Skills Development Program with 10 Online Courses Covering the Entire Territory of the Unification Program & Four Levels of Certification.
5. Train-the-Trainer Program for leading the Continuous Skills Development Program with 10 Online Courses.
6. Communication and Leadership Development Content.
7. Coaching Process Courses & Certifications.
8. Insider Threat Prevention Courses & Certifications.
9. Problem Based Learning Environment with 6,000+ Solution for Rapid Problem Solving During Continuous Performance Management-Insider Threat Prevention Cyber Security Unification Execution.
10. SEITPCS Certification.
11. Program Scenario History Management & Maintenance.

10: Classes of Systems

We can characterize systems in multiple ways. Several of the most useful characterizations follow below. The characterization we use often reveals something about the nature and functioning of the system, and perhaps our personal psychology.

Isolated, Open and Closed Systems

Systems are either closed or open. A closed system is one that does not need to interact with its environment to maintain its existence. Examples are atoms and molecules. Mechanical systems are closed systems. Open systems are organic and must interact with their environment in order to maintain their existence. People are open systems in that they must interact with their environment in order to take in food, water, and obtain shelter. People provide waste products to the environment in return. Poor environment.

The examples of the furnace, filling the water glass, adjusting the shower tap are all open systems as there are elements outside the system which are considered to have an impact yet are not elaborated. An open system may interact with its environment in a growth or balancing fashion. Often the time of influence of the open system on the environment or the environment on the system may be of such lengthy duration or of such minimal nature as to limit its need to be considered. In 1927 Ludwig von Bertalanffy first proposed that the human organism should be treated as an open system.

We can consider any system in a large enough context a closed system. It is often more appropriate to consider a system as a subsystem of some larger system with which it must interact in some way. Taking the larger system into account is unnecessary for understanding the operation of the subsystem. All systems are simultaneously subsystems of larger systems and larger systems composed of subsystems.

Boulding's Classification

Economist Kenneth Boulding, one of the founders of The Society for General Systems Theory, in his book, "The World as a Total System," defined five generalized classes of systems which encompasses all other systems. These systems provide a means of understanding some of the general characteristics of systems. Boulding arranged these systems in what is considered an evolutionary hierarchy.

Parasitic System

In the Parasitic System, a positive influence from one element to another provides a negative influence in return to the first element. I get positive things from you and provide you a negative return in response. Essentially, I subsist on you.

Prey/Predator System

In the Prey/Predator System, the elements are dependent on each other from the perspective that the quantity of one element determines the quantity of the other element. The Foxes/Rabbits example is a prey/predator system. Even though the fox may be detrimental to the continuation of an individual rabbit, the fox is instrumental in maintaining the health of the overall rabbit population. Foxes will feed upon Rabbits even though the Fox's existence is dependent upon the Rabbit's existence.

Threat System

In the Threat System, one element does not do something if the other element does not do something else. The U.S./Soviet Arms Race provides a specific example. This particular example ignited an escalation since each side inferred to the other: If you start a war, I will destroy you. Yet, to continue to validate the threat each side had to continue building arms. This is a powerful example of two countries racing to where neither of them wanted to be. If you do not do something I do not want you to do, then I will not do something you do not want me to do. This may also be framed as: If you do something I want you to do, then I will not do something you do not want me to.

Exchange System

In the Exchange System, the capitalist economy provides a very good example of an Exchange System. Elements of the system provide goods and services to other elements in exchange for money or other goods and services. If you do something I want you to do, then I will do something you want me to do. This may also be stated as: if I do something you want me to do then I expect you will do something I want you to do.

Our buy now pay later economy has a tendency to transform an Exchange System into a Threat System. Initially we purchase something and in exchange we provide a promise, a promise to pay more at a later time. Once we have received what we wanted, the system changes and the bank says if you pay your bills then I will not take the stuff away from you, which is essentially a Threat System.

Employer/Employee systems are often transformed from an Exchange System to a Threat System. The employee is hired under an exchange premise. I will pay you what you want if you do this work that I want you to do. Once the employee is hired the situation changes and becomes: if you do what I want, I will not fire you.

Integrative System

Examples of an Integrative System are charitable organizations or business endeavors where individuals ban together to accomplish some common desired objective or goal. Where you and I do something together because of what we both want to accomplish. The greatest leverage is found in Integrative Systems, where all the individuals are motivated by what they are endeavoring to create.

Generative System

During discussions on the Learning Organization in late 1995, Michael McMaster proposed another category beyond the Integrative System. He proposed a Generative System. This is represented by a situation where two people come together to create something neither of them had any idea of when they began. This is the Generative System.

Additional Systems Classification

The year 1995 was a quarter century ago. Strangely, 1995 seems only like last year; but it was 25 years ago. Not yesterday for sure. During this time systems science has not stood still. New theories and insights have occurred that have deepened our understanding of the systems perspective and how to master it. One of the great develops is our appreciation of the nature of systems, quasi-systems, and the systems classification that now follows.

Protection System

The Protection System acts when events occur. It is a reactive system that is after the fact. Cyber Security is heavily invested in the design and application of Protection Systems to defeat acts of Cyber Terrorists. Insider Threat Prevention Cyber Security requires protection Systems that actual "prevent" the malicious acts of insider actors.

Regulating System

The Regulating System behaves as a single loop system that continuously measures or samples control variables and compares these with pre-set desired values. This system responds by adjusting the environment accordingly to regulate control variables.

Optimizing System

The Optimizing System is a systemic, double loop system that regulates selected variables in accordance with desired values. It also ascertains what the desired values should be to satisfy pre-determined goals.

Adaptive System

The Adaptive System is a multi-loop/structural system that changes its internal structure to optimize its behavior in spite of continuous changes in the environment. This is an evolutionary system.

Systems Philosophy

Banathy argued that Systems Philosophy provides internal consistency to system theory and systems methodology and provides a general world view or way of thinking about reality. Systems Philosophy informs all philosophy with the systems view and brings forth an expansionist, dynamic (non-linear), synthetic, and holistic mode of thinking.

Systems Continuum

Systems Philosophy examines the classifications of systems such as those above and places them in a continuum that describes the relationship of one system to other systems and by categories of systems relationships running from mechanistic to closed systems. The Systems Continuum consists of the follow four systems relationships of systems:

From Mechanistic to Systemic

This system's relationship displays components which maintain a fixed relationship to each other and thus exist as stable peer systems, the Mechanistic, but also displays dynamic behavior among the system's components, the Systemic.

From Unitary to Pluralistic

This system's relationship displays systems imbued with singularity in goals, i.e., single goals integrated with a clearly defined purpose, the Unitary, but also displays significant diversity and conflict in purposes and goals, the Pluralistic.

From Restricted to Complex

The system's relationship displays systems with few decision-making levels and contains few clearly defined variables, the Restricted, but also displays a large number of variables with many decision-making levels, the Complex.

From Closed to Open

This system's relationship displays systems with limited interaction with its environment through rigidly controlled boundaries, the Closed, but also displays very flexible, fuzzy boundaries permitting considerable free interaction with the environment, the Open.

Contrived Systems

Human Activity Systems (HAS) are contrived systems in which the perceiver limits the system and sets its boundaries through the attribution process. After looking at the structure and functions of the Continuous Performance Management-Insider Threat Prevention Cyber Security Unification Human Activity System, we see that it fits the definition for a system in general and Human Activity System as derived from the general systems definition as a special class of systems, systems with human agents as components. Its systems nature is made evident by the processes of input, transformation, output, and feedback and adjustment, its nature, characteristics and human components.

Moreover, we can see from these characteristics at the subsystem level, that the Continuous Performance Management-Insider Threat Prevention Cyber Security Unification Human Activity System is a complex system embedded within an enterprise environment, one supporting an embedded hierarchy in itself. Additionally, depending on the nature of the project undertaken, the Continuous Performance Management-Insider Threat Prevention Cyber Security Unification Human Activity System is a system in which hard and soft thinking elements are present. We can see this in the system types below.

System Type A: Rigidly Controlled Systems

Summary Description: The Rigidly Controlled System is the least complex system type. It contains only a few elements with limited interactions controlled by the clearly defined goals of a single purpose. In this sense, then, Rigidly Controlled Systems behave mechanically. Highlights of Rigidly Controlled Systems include the following attributes:

- Static system states with little self-direction;

- Rigid structure as in man-machine systems, and
- Methods representative of Operations Research and Systems Engineering methods.

System Type B: Deterministic Systems

Summary Description: Deterministic systems are similar to Rigidly Controlled Systems. They are marked by a single-minded purpose driven by unitary goals and objectives. However, this system type, although functioning in a mechanistic mode, tends toward more open boundaries.

System Type C: Purposive Systems

Summary Description: From the perspective of system type, self-direction begins to emerge in full agreement with systems purpose and goals. Purposive systems exhibit operational freedom. Purposive Systems sit at the midpoint of the mechanistic-systemic & unitary-plural matrix. Other characteristics of this system type include:

- They are more complex than either System Type A and System B, and
- They are more open to the environment.

System Type D: Heuristic & Goal Formulating Systems

Summary Description: We characterize Heuristic & Goal Formulating Systems by noting considerable dynamic interaction that occurs among their components. While in previous system types, a controlled rigidity existed, in this system type, ambiguity, uncertainty, and emergence are more characteristic. Hence, these systems are more open to the environment and have the freedom to formulate their own goals in response to established policies.

System Type E: Purposeful-Indeterminate Systems

Summary Description: Purposeful-Indeterminate Systems are visionary systems. They are guided by images or visions of the future. They are complex and thus must be open to their environments. Since they are visionary systems, they shape their environments. They are, therefore, dynamically tuned to self-transcendence and reorganization at ever higher levels of complexity. Other characteristics of Systems Type E include:

- Self-Direction;

- Self-Regulation, and
- Self-Referencing.

CPM-ITP Cyber Security Unification Platform

An ideal CPM-ITP Cyber Security Unification Platform stores a multi-disciplinary soft and hard-skill Repository of problem-based content. The Platform rapidly delivers in-depth guidance in the form of evidence-based solutions to the challenges associated with delivering an Enterprise-wide-ITP Cyber Security Unification Program. The Repository consists of:

Example of CPM-ITP CS Unification Program Platform

1. Five Insider Threat Prevention Cyber Security Management Books
2. Forty Business Strategies for Leading a CPM-ITP Cyber Security Unification Program
3. Human Activity System Environment Design Guidelines for HAS Design
4. Design Specific Enterprise-Wide ITP CS Sociotechnical Systems Guidelines for Design Team Structure Model Guidelines including: (1) Rapid Response Team Guidelines; (2) Long Term ITP Cyber Security Management Team Guidelines
5. Communications Development Course
6. Leadership Development Course
7. Continuous Monitoring System Implementation Course
8. Situation Mitigation System Design Course
9. Mutual Support Systems Design Course
10. Change Management Implementation Course
11. Coaching Process Design Program including: (1) Coaching Mastery Definition Course: (2) Coach Skills Development Course; (3) Coaching Skills Mastery Course, and (4) Coaching Certification Course
12. Data Management/Metrics Course
13. Problem Based Learning Course
14. Applied Intuitive Solutions™ Platform
15. Continuous ITP Cyber Security Training & Development Course
16. Train-the Trainer Program

17. Strategies Ensuring Insider Threat Prevention Cyber Security (SEITPCS) Certification
18. Scenario History Management & Maintenance Handbook

11: On the Psychology of ITP Cyber Security

In this the fifth book in the series, Mastering Insider Threat Prevention Cyber Security, we examined the design systems and environments of Insider Threat Prevention Cyber Security. Here, we learned about the potency of Design Inquiry and how to engage in systems thinking to become a Consulting Specialist in this rare but critical discipline that will save many organizations in the coming years. We further described the unified enterprise-wide system's architecture from the systems perspective and discussed the corresponding environments components and behaviors that form the CPM-ITP Cyber Security unified model.

As a Consulting Specialist you will be expected to master the details of Insider Threat Prevention Cyber Security design. Clients, and their organizations, will depend on you to take the lead and provide a stabilizing force as the teams build the Insider Threat Prevention Cyber Security Unified Enterprise Architecture. You will also be expected to master the ins and outs of Insider Threat Prevention Cyber Security Leadership. This, of course, means that you will be quite adept as navigating the art of communicating for ITP Cyber Security effectiveness. Beyond this, as a Consulting Specialist you will find that you will take to the role of Trainor & Developer quite naturally as you guide teams through the responsibilities of Governance, Risk Management, Compliance, and ITP Cyber Security Process Control.

Obviously, you will have a full plate and many people will be leaning on you to get them through the pitfalls and tarpits of Insider Threat Prevention Cyber Security. Such an endeavor is a significantly complicated undertaking, so much so that you will "feel" a lot of eyes on you. What you say will matter immensely. As critical as all of these skills and expectations may be, they are not the most important determinants of success. The factor that trips up people the most with Insider Threat Prevention Cyber Security is not necessarily any of knowledge and skill challenges, difficult though they may be. It is the Psychology of Insider Threat Prevention Cyber Security. It is the problem of human behavior. What else would it be? No surprises here, I guess.

I have organized this series to get to this point. Throughout the series, beginning with Part One, I introduced a new model of workplace relationships and suggested a few pointers on how to navigate them. From there, I moved on to discuss Continuous Performance Management and possible strategies for unifying CPM with ITP Cyber Security to form an enterprise architecture that is fundamentally secure. From here, I discussed the role of systems thinking in establishing a unified CPM and ITP Cyber Security architecture. Finally, I discussed the nature and characteristics of systems and Human Activity Systems in particular. I discussed systems methodology, Design Inquiry, systems design, and the Systems Models Approach (SMA) to design relevant Human Activity Systems by constructing Environmental, Structural, and Behavioral Models.

The task now remains for systems designers to use the general models discussed throughout this series as a Framework for building the specific models of the unified architecture. These models are derived from the current enterprise model, for example Continuous Performance Management, and the current model of ITP Cyber Security currently used by the Cyber Security organization. As you make this leap, you will naturally move into the domain of human psychology and organization behavior. Obviously, a broader and deeper understanding of human behavior is the pressing concern as we begin to design the foundation for a unified CPM-ITP Cyber Security architecture. Doing this requires that we turn our attention to the task of understanding the purposeful person as a Purposeful System. This is actually the foundation of the unified CPM-ITP Cyber Security enterprise.

Foundation

As we once again focus our attention on the Behavioral Science dimension of CPM-ITP Cyber Security unification, we should accept that whatever methodology we design, whatever plan we prepare, what strategies we implement, the malicious insider will be doing the same. This person also will formulate a plan, implement some strategies, and design a methodology. Moreover, the malicious insider will enjoy a head-start, be an excellent cyber threat strategist, own a deeply thought-out plan, and, at the very least, be a master of the fundamentals.

The malicious insider will, without a doubt, be able to keep pace with the ITP Cyber Security organization step-by-step. The ITP Cyber Security response has to be superior along all fronts and developed in stealth mode. However, this will not always work because the perfect malicious insider will be the most accomplished ITP Cyber Security Specialist. After all, who knows your ITP Cyber Security Program the best? The answer is obvious, right? It is for this reason that so many Cyber Security experts disappear in Russia and China.

In cyber war, a strong defense calls for us to control those who most completely know our defensive strategies. However, since this is not usually possible, or even practical, we are forced to do the next best thing and change the way we look at the malicious insiders among us. Since these people are so insidious, and they are, we need see them as they really are, and that is as Purposeful Threat Agents. Then, we need to follow through and react to this insight in new and unexpected ways.

While the commonly adopted approach to ITP Cyber Security, where it exists, attempts to predict the behavior of malicious insiders and mitigate their actions, usually after the fact, the most resilient approach demands that we fully understand malicious insiders as Purposeful individuals and then leverage this insight in creative ways that eliminate their advantages. Organizations can do this, but ITP Cyber Security teams require a new kind of intellectual discipline, training, and deliberate will well beyond what is normally available.

For example, one problem is that successful malicious insiders often interrupt the Dynamic Equilibrium (Richard Scharch, 1954) of their organizations. This may become a fatal situation if management responds in an inappropriate manner or reacts by advocating a type of Structural Isomorphism, either Coercive, Normative, or Mimetic (Ludwig von Bertalanffy 1951 & 1968) that makes little sense.

Boundary Management

As the unified CPM-ITP Cyber Security organization is formed within an enterprise, the boundaries between the various business organizations, the enterprise subsystems, require alert management. In the unified CPM-ITP Cyber Security organization, boundary management is difficult due to the fluid structure of the enterprise. Katz and Kahn (1966) wrote that:

> Human organizations have unique properties, however, which distinguish them from other categories of open systems. Perhaps the most basic of these unique properties is the absence of structure in the usual sense of the term - an identifiable, enduring, physical

> anatomy which is observable at rest as in motion and which in motion generates and performs those activities which comprise the systemic function. (p. 14)

Since the unified enterprise is an open system, it requires boundaries that are open to the environment. Katz and Kahn (1966) distinguish open systems through "a recurrent pattern of events, differentiated from but dependent on the larger stream of life in which it occurs and recurs" (p. 13). When discussing openness, boundaries and Cyber Security, we can reason that openness is the most general systems concept that challenges our unification program. From Katz and Kahn (1966), we can see that openness concerns how broadly the unified organization will remain receptive to all types of input and under what constraints. Especially since every organization varies with respect to the general range of inputs that it can absorb and also to its openness to particular types of inputs.

For the ITP Cyber Security organization to remain viable, its boundaries must permit the flow of input and output between the itself and its enterprise, The Boundary Subsystem maintains the dynamic equilibrium of the ITP Cyber Security and manages a living system's negentropic functions, meaning, reverse entropy. For the ITP Cyber Security organization, the Boundary Subsystem is the mechanism which keeps the ITP Cyber Security organization separate from the corporate environment of other organization systems and determines to what extent the boundaries remain secure.

Using the Formal Systems Model (Checkland, 1981), we see that boundaries define the limits of the ITP Cyber Security Human Activity System in respect to its environment and the constraints and actors of the wider organization. The ITP Cyber Security HAS boundaries inform the enterprise that the ITP Cyber Security Human Activity System is chartered as a system by an enterprise or agency of the enterprise and consists of the appropriate human components of the ITP Cyber Security HAS and its facilities, hardware, software, physical space and other resources.

Holistic View

Meeting the enterprise challenge of effective Insider Threat Prevention Cyber Security, the ITP Cyber Security organization adopts a holistic view of human behavior and, hence, a necessarily functional, teleological or purposeful view. Moreover, adopting this view, a conceptual analysis of holistic experience becomes the starting point of a rigorous scientific disciplinary analysis of Objective Purposeful Behavior that includes the four pillars of:

1. life,
2. mind,
3. society, and
4. value.

Engaging our Conceptual Analysis of the ITP Cyber Security HAS, we define structure functionally and consider how goal directed behavior can become conceptually compatible with the common deterministic mechanical conception of nature that simply sees ITP Cyber Security as an objective ateleological mechanism.

Findings this incomplete or insufficient, we then proceed to understand why things behave the way they do. This leads us to the teleological perspective in which beliefs, attitudes, traits, instincts, and drives lie behind behavior. As such, they form a subjective teleology. But is this really correct? Do they concepts really cause the behavior they identify? Or, are beliefs, attitudes, and traits based on what people do that is observed?

Are not these concepts derived from the perceived regularities of human behavior under varied but specified conditions? Is it not more accurate to state that these concepts are rooted in observable behaviors? Are they not really an Objective Teleology? Through an Objective Teleology, we actually learn what is going on in the human mind by observation, not introspection. We guess less.

Through these observations, we build the idealized operational definitions that eventually become the standards describing how a concept ideally ought to be explained. From this perspective, and the potency of observation, we now characterize the malicious insider as a Purposeful individual whose behavior manifests an Objective rather than a Subjective Teleology. This is an important consideration for those charged with designing an effective ITP Cyber Security program.

Teleology of Decision Making

Since malicious insiders are Purposeful individuals, their decision-making process is likewise teleological. For Purposeful individuals, teleology influences decision-making even more so than the rational approaches of logic and disciplined reasoning or any of the other familiar decision-making procedures. Counter-intuitively, these processes commonly constrain decision-making as a function of personal choice. While common logic constrains personal choice, intuition significantly influences the outcomes of decision processes. Contrary to expectations, however, people most often make decisions that seem dull and repetitive whenever decision-makers apply the principles of general logic.

Ultimately, the commonly accepted decision-making processes deliver decisions that are rarely creative. Thus, for this reason teleological decisions are generally more creative than those that emerge from rigorous logical analysis. In an effort to better understand the constraints of logically informed decision-making. Wishing to enhance decision-making, ITP Cyber Security teams can build process models of the human behavior of Human Activity Systems. This enables ITP Cyber Security teams to better model the structure, function, and purpose of each malicious insider challenge confronting the ITP Cyber Security organization. In this way, ITP Cyber Security teams can better understand the individuality of psychological systems in respect to the personality of the malicious insider and the process of pursuing the purposes of the malicious insider.

These models are important because ITP Cyber Security teams gain much insight from them including the possible range of beliefs of the malicious insider and an evaluation of the feelings and attitudes of the malicious insider for any specific situation. Moreover, through the models, it may be possible to uncover the formulation and evaluation of the choices of the malicious insiders including the intuition, purposeful systems, and environments in which the malicious insiders succeed.

Paradigm for ITP Cyber Security Inquiry

Design Inquiry enables ITP Cyber Security teams to model the interactions of purposeful systems including the feelings, communications, signs, messages, and languages of the malicious insiders. Systems Thinking further enables ITP Cyber Security teams to build systems models of the communication processes and the conflicts, cooperation, and competition of social systems and social groups as Ideal-seeking systems. The psychological challenges of ITP Cyber Security organizations include: Choice, Communication, Conflict, Competition, Insensitivity, Platitudes, Tautology, Delusion of Precision, Inability to Distinguish Discovery, Simple-Minded Conclusions, and Confusion about Causal Sequences.

Obviously, the ITP Cyber Security organization needs a system of concepts and measures to guide it through one purposive state to another. In this sense, then, the various ITP Cyber Security teams have to employ concrete purposive behavior to anticipate the outcome or goal states of malicious insiders. Here, questions naturally emerge concerning the identity and objectives or the designer of the insider threat, the malicious insider. These questions are nontrivial and each deserves an answer. For example, consider the following ten questions:

1. Is the designer of the malicious threat the actual agent of the cyber-attack or is this attack agent collaborating as partner to the designer of the attack or still another malicious insider as yet unknown?
2. Are other potential malicious insiders waiting down line or are other cyber criminals waiting who possibly may come aboard for a second phase attack?
3. Do any accidental collaborators exist who are unaware of their involvement?
4. Can the ITP Cyber Security teams connect the dots between the malicious insider and the attack scenario or is an innocent bystander being set-up?
5. Do we know enough to calculate the probability of the attack occurring and being successful?
6. Have we identified the event or the structural class if we expect multiple events?
7. Beyond these issues, have we determined whether the malicious attack is to be executed directly by an individual or through a system or network?
8. Can we determine the action plan of the individual or system?
9. Can we anticipate the reaction of an individual end-user of the compromised system and the response of the individual or system executing the attack?

10. Do we understand the immediate outcome of the attack and the long term outcome?

12: Functional Maliciousness in ITP CS

When I speak of "Functional Maliciousness," I am referring to the structural situation in which multiple malicious insiders are simultaneous executing Cyber-Attacks using the same systems, strategies or networks with or without awareness of one another, and with or without coordination, cooperation, or collaboration. If malicious insiders are acting without awareness of one another, the malicious insiders are working together as co-actors indirectly and accidently without coordination, cooperation, or collaboration. If the malicious insiders are acting with awareness of one another, the malicious insiders are working together as co-actors directly and deliberately with coordination, cooperation, or collaboration.

Indirect Cyber-Attack Co-Actors

As we move from question to question to gain a broader understanding of the wider theatre of attack and its focused attack space, we eventually arrive at the Problem of Functional Maliciousness and the active versus potential threat space. Realistically, different individuals can launch a simultaneous cyber-attack without awareness of one another.

Each malicious insider can launch an attack on different systems in different organizations using different networks and different strategies simultaneously. Or each malicious insider can launch a cyber-attack on the same systems in the same organization using the same networks and the same strategies simultaneously. Or, malicious insiders can execute a sequence of random attacks without being aware or each other using vastly different strategies and technical and business environments. In these cases, the malicious insiders act as Indirect Co-Actors.

Direct Cyber-Attack Co-Actors

Most often, however, different individuals launch simultaneous cyber-attacks with the knowledge, cooperation, coordination, collaboration and participation of one another. In this case, each malicious insider can launch an attack on different systems in different organizations using different networks and different strategies simultaneously. Or each malicious insider can launch a cyber-attack on the same systems in the same organization using the same networks and the same strategies simultaneously.

Or, malicious insiders can execute a sequence of random attacks while being aware or each other using vastly different strategies and technical and business environments. In these cases, the malicious insiders act as Direct

Co-Actors. Beyond this, however, malicious insiders can plan each malicious attack together working as a single team that produces different results through different events.

Continua of Malicious Intrusions

Malicious intrusions range from the extraordinarily simple to the extremely complex. Malicious cyber-attacks can occur in different organization environments and form only a single attack profile. They can also occur in different environments and form more multiple differentiated attacks. Malicious intrusions can occur in different environments experiencing two or more attacks with at least two attacks occurring in a single environment.

Beyond this, malicious insiders can spread problems around an entire organization by using many environments to form a single coordinate and partitioned attack with each attack difficult to discover or track. If this is not enough, malicious insiders can also launch two or more attacks simultaneously with each attack in each environment being unique and difficult to resolve with each attack generating additional attacks and all attacks demanding ransom.

Technically, Cyber Terrorists enjoy a range of active and passive options that can exhaust all efforts to clear it. While some attacks are very simple and can only produce a single outcome, that outcome changes for each environment it affects. In other cases, an attacker can use the environment to co-produce the outcome and generate more complex outcomes beyond the control of the malicious attacker. In this case, a single attack produces two results, one directly produced by the attacker and the other produced by the environment.

In other cases, malicious insiders can launch attacks that react to changes within the environment. In this case, any attempt to clear the attack merely generates a more complex outcome. Some insider attacks create situations where any attempt to clear it increases the attack surface.

Insider intrusions often have goals that enable them to respond differently to different events to produce the desired goal or produce different outcomes in two or more different environments. Accomplished malicious insiders can produce the identical outcome in different environments. Occasionally, malicious insiders produce methods or instruments that produce the outcomes they desire within a targeted environment.

Purposeful Persons, HAS, & Purposeful Organizations

Insider Threats pose serious challenges to organizations everywhere. The hope is to find some way to prevent these threats from materializing. ITP Cyber Security generally is not very good at preventing most attacks because the criminal is generally a trusted employee. Insider Threat Prevention Cyber Security needs a systems theory that: (1) fits with a general behavioral theory (2) can be measured quantitatively, (3) has a methodology that is familiar to current research practice in Psychology, (4) and is supported by an experimental program. The definition of "Malicious Insider" needs a behavioral theory that:

- Captures the uniqueness of the individual
- Provides a general concept under which all other psychological concepts can be subsumed, and
- Locates personality in the responses of the individual to his environment.

Thus, the Insider must be a purposeful individual whose personality is found in the response of this individual to his or her environment. ITP Cyber Security works best when teams define the state of a purposeful individual or system using the following guideline. A Purposeful State consists of four components:

- Subject that displays choice;
- The choice environment;
- Available courses of action, and
- Outcomes possible in that environment.

We can specify the relevant relationships of these four components as three measures that identify the parameters of a purposeful state:

- Probability of Choice;
- Efficiency of a Course of Actions, and
- Relative Value of an Outcome to a Subject.

The probably of choice above refers to the probability that a malicious insider will produce a specified course of action in a targeted environment. Efficiency of a Course of Action refers to the probability that an intrusive course of action will produce a specified outcome in the targeted environment. Also, efficiency refers to the actions required to obtain a result delivered by specified actions. The malicious insider's available course of action in the targeted environment has a high probability of being chosen by the Insider Threat Prevention Cyber Security organization. The malicious insider's potential course of action in a targeted environment has a high probability of being chosen by the malicious insider. A potential course of action is always great than the available course of action.

Purposeful Individuals, both malicious actors and Insider Threat Prevention Cyber Security team members, make choices within the target environments. These choices reveal something about the personalities of malicious actors and ITP Cyber Security team members and suggest their courses of action. Choices actually involve the choice states of purposeful individuals and Human Activity Systems. Moreover, every person involved with an Insider Threat Prevention Cyber Security program is concerned with the Relative Value of the outcomes, from minimum to maximum. In conceptualizing a purposeful state, ITP Cyber Security teams can formulate the available courses of action and possible outcomes as exclusive and exhaustive sets of outcomes. Every outcome, actual, possible and potential, delivers a Relative Value. The malicious insider and the ITP Cyber Security organization are both in the process of pursuing purposes. Each has a purpose which opposed the other. It is a high stakes challenge. Both are Purposeful Systems and concern the extent to which their behavior:

- Is influenced by their immediate environment, and
- Affects that environment.

The Purposive State of a malicious insider emerges through choice and desire for a high Relative Value. Also, the malicious insider's individuality, meaning personality, derives from the way the probabilities of choice, efficiencies, and relative values depend on the properties of the situation. The courses of action and outcomes are functions of both the environment and the malicious insider.

Although the probabilities of choice, efficiencies, and relative values depend on the malicious insider, they are not independent of the situation. I do not conceive of Personality, individuality, here as an unobservable something that is asserted to explain the motive or agency of choice. Rather, personality refers to an observable, and quantifiable, function that describes how a malicious insider or Insider Threat Prevention Cyber Security team member transforms a choice situation into an expected relative value.

As the dependent variable, Probability of Choice refers to a familiarity with something. Moreover, the measures of familiarity emerge from the effect that different properties of courses of action have on probabilities of choice. However, this remains the case only if the displayed situations, with their selected courses of action, do not affect the outcome. Hence, in this case, they are Measures of Means Preferences. From this perspective, we refer to a Trait as a degree of familiarity with the course of action that is greater than any of the others. The intensity of the Trait emerges from the degree of familiarity associated with the course of action most often selected.

ITP Cyber Security and Insider Attacks are influenced by Perception, Consciousness and Memory. This means that both are influences by knowledge, understanding, intelligence, intention, and learning. We derived the Measure of Knowledge that concerns us in ITP Cyber Security from the effect of different efficiencies of choice on probabilities of choice for whose outcomes the relative values remain constant. Hence, they are measures of sensitivity to efficiency and reflect the Knowledge Situation, Degree of Knowledge, Knowledge Function, Generalized Knowledge Function, and the Knowledge Intelligence Function.

Knowledge refers to the awareness or possession of a fact or state of affairs. It is the possession of a practical skill. However, Understanding is much deeper than Knowledge. Understanding is a malicious insider's responsiveness to what he believes affects efficiency. Learning increases, in degree of effort, knowledge or understanding over time. Likewise, it is an ITP team's estimate of the degree of understanding, as intelligence, of the malicious insider's cognitive capacities. In this regard, understanding is an intelligence function. For the malicious insider, therefore, understanding reveals the personal capability of apprehending the meaning or significance of what they know about the attack target. The malicious insider's Efficiencies of Choice refers to knowledge they hold about the cyber-attack scenario. Learning: an increase in degree of knowledge or understanding over time.

Whenever the malicious insider reflects on the Relative Values of their planned attack, they are referring to their Efficiency of Choice and, therefore, the degree of intention. Both malicious actors and ITP Cyber Security teams Measures of Intent derive from the effect that differences in outcomes have on probabilities of choice where each available course of action can produce only one possible outcome and each possible outcome can actually be obtained. Hence, they are measures of ends preferences.

Moreover, a relationship exist between the Relative Value of the Cyber-Attack and the Intention of the attacker implicit in the Intention Situation, the Degree of the Intention, the Intention and Relative Value Function, and the Generalized Intention, Relative Value Function, and the Vacillation of Intention. Interestingly, both the malicious insider and the ITP Cyber Security organization define the same outcomes but with opposite results. They both desire an immediate intended outcome as an End, an intermediate intended outcome as a Goal, a long range intended outcome as an Objective, and an ultimate intended outcome as an Ideal. Also, each is in pursuit of a goal or an objective and in pursuit of an Ideal. And each is trying to defeat the other.

Connecting with the Insider Threat Environment

In the Continuous Performance Management environment, and other similar organization environments, management nurtures openness and trust among teams. As we learned earlier in this series, probably Part One, systems designers advocate a range of Hallmarks that characterize the behavior and structure of every enterprise. For the ITP Cyber Security organization, the behavioral Hallmarks include: Observation, Perception, Sensation, Awareness, and Consciousness. ITP Cyber Security teams have to be conscious, observant, perceptive, sensitive, and aware of everything happening in the enterprise that directly and indirectly impacts Insider Threat Prevention Cyber Security.

Consciousness in ITP Cyber Security

Perception validates Consciousness. A relationship exists between the Insider Threat Prevention Cyber Security Specialist and the malicious insider such that the depth of the self-awareness of the Specialist constrains the depth of the awareness that the Specialist can gain of the malicious insider. The Specialist is aware of malicious insider if he responds to the malicious insider. Naturally everything begins with Consciousness. An ITP Cyber Security Specialist has to become conscious of the malicious insider's mental state or at least any property of the mental state if possible. Hence, if the Specialist perceives any functional property of the malicious insider's purposeful behavior, the Specialist is conscious of that property of the mental state of the malicious insider.

Moreover, just as the ITP Cyber Security Specialist is self-conscious if he perceives one or more of his own mental states, so too is that Specialist conscious of the malicious insider by observing the properties of the malicious insider's mental state. Also, the Specialist will remain unconscious of the malicious insider's mental state if the Specialist perceives the malicious insider but not malicious insider's mental state.

If the Specialist perceives the malicious insider but not the malicious insider's perception of an attack strategy, the Specialist is then unconscious of the malicious insider's perception of the attack strategy. Fundamentally, though, the Specialist is nonconscious of the malicious insider if the Specialist does not perceive the malicious insider. Furthermore, the Specialist is unself-conscious of his own mental state if he perceives himself but not his mental state. Also, the Specialist is non-self-conscious if he does not perceive himself at all.

Memory in ITP Cyber Security

Memory is a cognitive process that exhibits intensity, durability, and correctness. Memory occurs whenever an ITP Cyber Security Specialist responds to a stimulus to which he reacted at an earlier time and still remembers the stimulus. The Intensity of a Memory refers to the intensity of the response that defines the memory. The Intensity of a Stimulus is a measure of a property of a stimulus that produces a result. The Intensity of a Response to a Stimulus refers to a measure of a property of a response that is produced by the stimulus of the response. Whereas the Durability of a Memory refers to the length of time over which it persists, the Correctness of a Memory refers to the efficiency of the memory response for the objective for which it is intended.

Since certainty is difficult to achieve with ITP Cyber Security threat analysis, the nature of reliability of Belief becomes a preeminent issue of decision-making in the practice of Insider Threat Prevention Cyber Security. For example, what is Belief and how is it related to the problem of Memory? Is Belief good enough to get the job done? What kind of knowledge does Belief deliver and does Belief ever deliver self-evident reasonableness?

As a purposeful individual, the ITP Cyber Security Specialist's relies on Belief as evidence from experience. Belief is not pulled out of thin air. Belief has a foundation and is formed in experience, and can be justified. The ITP Cyber Security Specialist accepts a model of a choice situation that consists of a set of structural and functional properties which the Specialist believes the choice situation to have. Moreover, the Specialist believes that these structural and functional properties affect his satisfaction and dissatisfaction with the situation. The Specialist believes this is the case because the set of structural properties of the stimulus he responds to constitute his image of the stimulus and the set of functional properties constitutes his conception of the stimulus.

It is worth noting that the Specialist cannot respond to a structural change without first reacting to that structural change through a sensation where sensation if defines as a response by the ITP Cyber Security Specialist to a change in one of the structural properties of the Specialist. Hence, we can define the mental state of an ITP Cyber Security Specialist as one or a combination of a number of functional properties of the purposeful behavior of the Specialist.

As we move beyond the concern over sensation, we address the meaning of the Degree of Sensitivity. Needing to know how the Specialist will react to a stimulus in a specific environment, we address the Sensitivity of a specified intensity existing in a structurally defined environment. Since we need to know how this Specialist will react to a stimulus in that environment, we relate the Sensitivity Function to the Degree of Sensitivity and a stimulus to its intensity and the structural properties of the environment. We do this because we realize that the Intensity of a reaction is a measure of a structural property of the reaction produced

The responsiveness of the Specialist to a change in at least one or more of his structural properties reveals the sensibility of the Specialist. Furthermore, the Degree of Sensibility of the Specialist to a change in one of his structural properties in a purposeful state is the probability that the Specialist will respond to the change in that state. Thus, the Degree of Sensibility is the probability that the Specialist will respond to that change. Moreover, the Sensibility Function of a Specialist to a change in one of his structural properties is the mathematical function that relates his Degree of Sensibility to the intensity of the change in his structural properties and the properties of his purposeful state.

Perception is a response to a stimulus that produces a change in at least one structural property of the ITP Cyber Security Specialist. Additionally, a reaction to a stimulus result in a change in one or more structural properties that are produced by another property. Also, an observation is a perception of a stimulus by an ITP Cyber Security Specialist who intended to perceive that stimulus. The Degree of Perceptiveness of a Specialist to a stimulus in a purposeful state is the probability that the Specialist will respond to a stimulus in that state.

The Perceptiveness function of a Specialist for a stimulus refers to a function that relates the Specialist's degree of perceptiveness of that stimulus to the intensity of the stimulus and the properties of the purposeful state of the Specialist. In this way, we say that the Degree of Perceptiveness of a Specialist is the product of the probability that the Specialist will react to the stimulus and the probability that he will respond if he reacts. The intensity of a perception is also a function of the intensities of reaction and response. Moreover, the intensity of perception of a stimulus by an ITP Cyber Security Specialist is the intensity of the Specialist's response to the reaction produced by the stimulus.

For Memory to function, a purposeful individual has to navigate purposeful states in environments of stimuli as an observer who perceives stimuli of various intensities to incite reactions that generate responses of differing sensitivities about functional and structural properties at different times and places through events under different probabilities of outcomes and choice strategies according to different efficiencies. Got it? This one sentence summarizes the last seven paragraphs. The interesting thing about this way of thinking is that once you learn to make sense of it you now know how the mind of the malicious insider and other Cyber Terrorist actually functions.

Remember this, as you learn to master this way of thinking, you are also learning to master how the malicious insider thinks, learns, plans, and behaves. If you actually put everything together from this series, you will be able to identify the vulnerabilities of your organization and anticipate the plans and devices of your malicious insiders. As you already know, the cyber terrorists are smart enough to know what you are doing. Mastering the preceding books enables you to anticipate how they know this and then you can beat them at their own game. Your organization, however, will need to change.

Belief in ITP Cyber Security

When I was a young Philosophy student in college in an earlier Century, a professor asked a classmate what she thought about Aristotle's argument on Hylomorphism, she began her reply with "I feel that Aristotle". Immediately, the professor interrupted her: "I did not ask you what you feel. I asked you what you thought." Interesting answer I thought. "Feel" and "Think" are not the same verb. The professor was correct; give him an A. This encounter in the classroom has stayed with me for many decades. It was indeed a great lesson if it stuck with me all these years.

Today, however, I can ask does not a relationship exist between feeling and thinking? It is common to experience feelings about the thoughts we are thinking when we think them. Indeed, when we tell people what we feel, we are also revealing something about what we think and also what we value and disvalue. In Cognitive Psychology, we can easily make the connection. Others do the same with "Rational-Emotive" Psycho-Therapy and Re-Decision Therapy, and many other schools of Psychology. Strictly speaking the professor was correct. We have to consider the context of the question. A though is not a feeling however connected they may or may not be.

This is the way it is when we ask people what they know about a specific situation. Invariably they tell us what they believe about that situation, if they answer at all. Think about your own experience. How much do you live in a world of Belief versus a world of Knowledge? Some people do not even know what they believe. Imagine the implications of this kind of conceptual confusion in a world of Cyber-Terror. In this war, and it is a war, we need to have our act together. You might think about it this way:

> We believe more than we know. We know more than we understand. We can use our experience to deepen the understanding of our lives and enhance what we know to center our beliefs.

Belief, knowledge and understanding form the experience of our lives. Lacking the capacity of Belief, we cannot implement ITP Cyber Security, anywhere, anytime in a potent way. Although "Belief" only contains six letters, it is a tremendous word that spans the Cosmos. We must first believe so that we can understand. The First Pre-supposition of Philosophy: Human beings have the capacity to know truth. We accept this statement on faith.

It is a fundamental Belief of our existence as human beings. We cannot prove this claim rationally. We must first believe so that we can know. We are creatures completely governed by faith in our power to know the truth of what is. We need to recognize this so that we can properly understand the central role of Belief in Insider Threat Prevention Cyber Security. At the very least, we require "smart guesses" about the design of our unified Continuous Performance Management-Insider Threat Prevention Cyber Security enterprise and the Insider Threat Prevention Cyber Security solutions we learn to initiate.

So, having said all of this, do you know how to describe Belief simply? Perhaps, we can say that Belief in the presence or absence of something in the mind representing internal and external reality. We can see, therefore, that beliefs have intensity and this intensity differs with each belief. Since a belief is a belief that we believe through intention it is not an absolute truth. As such, a belief always contains a specific amount of doubt about the presence or absence of whatever it is that the believer believes as existing or not existing. We can believe that something does not exist. Therefore, beliefs can recognize the existence and nonexistence of different belief targets.

Beliefs are vital to the success of Insider Threat Prevention Cyber Security. We can also believe in the existence or nonexistence as the presence or absence of something in another environment. We also can believe in the occurrence of a future event at a future time not yet defined. In this way, we experience expectation of things yet to come. Like, we can and do believe in past events. We call this history. Beliefs in past events can lead us to believe in future events. Belief especially enables ITP Cyber Security teams to rationally believe in an available course of action to prevent a malicious attack. You can be sure that the malicious intensively believes in his course of action.

For the ITP Cyber Security Specialist, Belief is a necessity. Do we not believe in necessity? We also believe in sufficiency and in the producer-product relationship as the foundation of ITP Cyber Security as a discipline. For example, some people intensively believe that they know they have experienced a Cyber Terror attack and further believe that they know several efficient methods to protect their organizations against it.

Thus, these people believe they know about an attack in the past but like believe they know about solutions for the future. Although they no doubt have some knowledge about what happened to them in the past, no one can predict the future. They only believe they can. However, this belief gives them then confidence they require to try to do something now that they can later demonstrate to be an efficient course of action in the future. In this regard, they are demonstrating that they are have committed themselves to accept believed outcomes.

This, of course, means that they have hypothesized specified outcomes derived from the assumptions mirror their belief about the situation. Since the ITP Cyber Security team is considering the relative values of outcomes based on the efficiencies of choice for purposeful systems derived from current knowledge about past outcomes that they believe to be true, the immediate challenge is avoiding all illusions nor pretend to deliver something they cannot when they know they cannot. Whether or not they initiate their ITP Cyber Security project depends, of course, on the intensity of belief they experience about their control of a property and the relevant uncontrolled properties of the choice situation.

The presence of Belief matters when learning to master the Insider Threat Prevention Cyber Security challenge. For example, the Degree of Belief in the Maximum Relative Efficiency (MRE) for the selected course of action has to be high enough while the Degree of Doubt of Maximum Relative Efficiency has to be low enough. Also, both the Degree of Knowledge and the Intensity of Belief in the MRE have to be high enough. Beyond this the Insider Threat Prevention Cyber Security team requires a reasonable Belief in the probability of the purposeful states.

When the Insider Threat Prevention Cyber Security teams design models of their choice situations to determine their relative efficiencies, they will find that they design a specific structure to adequately model the most essential characteristics of the choice situations. For example, to be effective, designers will be expected to build a set of models for change including process or behavior, environment, and structure models.

At a minimum, these human systems models describe the relationship between the value of the outcome to the Insider Threat Prevention Cyber Security organization, and the elements of the problem situation over which the Insider Threat Prevention Cyber Security Organization believes that it controls at least minimally and those elements over which the Insider Threat Prevention Cyber Security Organization believes that it does not control but, nevertheless, can influence the outcome.

One could refer to this realization as the Performance Function. Designers can focus on the relationships described in these models to estimate the believed efficiencies of the modelled courses of action defined by the Insider Threat Prevention Cyber Security Organization for the range of possible outcomes in the specific environmental conditions described in the models. In many situations, the Insider Threat Prevention Cyber Security Organization only has limited control over one or more of the "controllable variables".

13: Solving the ITP CS Problem

A problem is a challenge that people wish they did not have. Who needs more problems, right? Unfortunately, ITP Cyber Security is a challenge that exists specifically to conquer many challenges. ITP Cyber Security is a complex challenge. We can view it as a special kind of purposeful state that leaves a large number of purposeful individuals very miserable, that is, dissatisfied. ITP Cyber Security challenges managers because they are doubtful about which of the number of solutions plans available will actually produce a satisfactory result. As purposeful individuals, managers have three ways of disposing of a problem and ITP Cyber Security Problem:

- Dissolution,
- resolution, and
- solution. We now briefly consider each one.

Dissolution of a Problem

When we speak of the "Dissolution of an ITP Cyber Security Problem", we are speaking about the complete removal of an ITP Cyber Security Problem Situation by the ITP Cyber Security team. A positive way of looking at the plan to dissolve a problem situation is as the plan to implement a project to produce the subsequent absence of the problem. Here, we are interested in producing the absence of something. Interesting, right?

What we are saying is that the ITP Cyber Security team has changed its intentions about a person they now perceive to be a malicious insider. Or, the ITP Cyber Security organization is building the model because it has changed its intentions about how it wants to engage a person in the enterprise who may be a malicious insider. Or perhaps an individual somewhere in the enterprise has changed his intentions and the ITP Cyber Security organization sees this has a problem.

In addition to any of the preceding above, the ITP Cyber Security team can decide to make an arbitrary choice to dissolve a problem situation. In this case, the ITP Cyber Security team, as a purposeful Human Activity System, selects one from a set of available plans of action. Here, the team believes that each option delivers the same relative efficiency for removing the team's concerns. Since each choice available is the same in respect to relative efficiency, the team can safely make an arbitrary choice.

Resolution of a Problem

People generally believe that resolving a problem is the same as solving that problem. It is not. We can consider Problem Dissolution, Resolution and Solution as three choice situations. In an effort to select the right choice situation, that is, pick the most effective approach to resolving a problem, an ITP Cyber Security management team models the set of the structural and functional properties. Essentially, the management team believes that the set of properties delivers the most efficient outcome by building the team's satisfaction about the challenge of ITP Cyber Security. In this Model, the sets of structural and functional properties inform the team's image and conception of the problem as the stimulus. Problem Resolution refers to the use of an arbitrary choice by a purposeful ITP Cyber Security team to eliminate or remove a problem situation.

As a last resort, an individual can conduct an Inquiry to determine which plan of action of an available set of plans can do the job. When I speak of Inquiry, I am referring to a disciplined process that strengthens the belief of the ITP Cyber Security team in the efficiency of a plan of action, a choice situation, specific to an identified outcome or set of outcomes. In this case, the ITP Cyber Security team conducts the inquiry to:

- Dispel any lingering doubt the team may be experiencing about the most efficient choice of action, and
- Decide what choice will become a solution to the ITP Cyber Security problem.

Solution of a Problem

Technically, the Insider Threat Prevention Cyber Security team can solve a problem by selecting a single solution plan from a set of available solutions plans. Through the results of a Design Inquiry, the ITP Cyber Security team believes the choice situation is the most probable solution plan for delivering a state of satisfaction that does indeed produce a state of satisfaction in the ITP Cyber Security team. Solving a problem involves answering two questions:

1. What alternative solution plans are available, and
2. Which alternative is best or good enough to eliminate the state of

dissatisfaction?

An alternative solution plan that replaces dissatisfaction with satisfaction is a satisfying solution plan to the problem. A solution plan that produces as much or more satisfaction than any other solution plan not only satisfies the ITP Cyber Security team but optimizes the solution delivery process.

Identifying the possible courses of action is an essential task when constructing an ITP Cyber Security model of a choice situation. Through actual experience, the ITP Cyber Security team learns that the many problem-solving breakthroughs result from finding either (1) a new way of accomplishing old objectives, or (2) a new outcome obtainable by use of a familiar action plan as a course of action. The newness of these discovered alternatives implies that a creative act has occurred. In a sense, then, the ITP Cyber Security team actually examines creativity when formulating models of choice situations or efficient assumptions.

This approach takes a lot of Inference, Thought, or conscious inference, and Intuition, or unconscious inference. Intuition commonly produces a committed belief in the validity of the suggestions it yields. It also delivers new ways of thinking about a problem. An intuition takes some time to develop but comes to the surface at the speed of light. Intuitions are potent intellectual powers. They depend on the generation of an Inference that produces one or more beliefs or assumptions that were earlier produced by one or more other beliefs or assumptions. Rational cognitive capacities are complex processes that separate human beings from the instinctual processes of the brute animals.

Inference is an intelligent procedure that occurs as a set of beliefs or assumptions as premises, formation rules, and transformation rules that produce a subsequent set of beliefs or assumptions. A single Inference is responsible for several generals of beliefs or assumptions. Inferences become deductions when they move from the general case to the specific case. Inferences become inductions when they proceed from the specific case to the general case.

If you want to know how logical a person may be, examine that person's Inference-making process. An ITP Cyber Security team member's inferential process is his logic. How logical are you? How well to you process inferences? I have defined the components of an individual's logic so thoroughly that it is possible to study that person's logic behaviorally.

If a purposeful individual in a problem situation believes that none of the available courses of action that he knows about can work, that person still has two alternatives available to him. First, he can search for another alternative which is available but initially unknown to him. He can make a number of observations to become aware of a course of action that the observer was not aware of before making the observations. Secondly, he can develop a new instrument and a solution plan that is associated with it. This added task of developing an instrument to produce a solution plan is complex but necessary. However, the ITP Cyber Security team has the job of ensuring that the environment is capable of producing a solution plan that was not previously available in that environment.

14: Psychology of ITP Cybersecurity

Starting with Part One in this series, we began a discussion on The Psychology of Insider Threat Cyber Security with the introduction of a four-stage model of emotional development. Throughout the series, we discussed the concepts of Behavior Science that have some influence the design, implementation, and management of ITP Cyber Security. Here, we have discussed Belief, Consciousness, Memory, and Purposefulness. Each of these topics plays a part in the development of a potent Insider Threat Prevention Cyber Security discipline and the development of a malicious insider mindset.

As we learned in Part One, people move through several levels of emotional growth. While a number of people become fixated at their first level of emotional development, a few people spend their entire lifetimes as growth-oriented individuals experiencing four levels of growth. If they avoid fixation, people move from a self-centered focus at Level One to a Level of experience dedicated to spiritual growth.

Making this journey of emotional growth, people develop attitudes and experience feelings that are, of course, psychological, sociological, philosophical. After all, we are emotional beings with rational capacities. The interesting insight here is that malicious insiders are at different levels of emotional development than are those who prevent them from succeeding with their nefarious plans. Cyber Terrorist and the Specialist who overcome them function at opposite ends of the emotional development spectrum, although they experience their feelings differently and express radically different attitude about morals and ethics.

A sociopath and a saint are really different beings. This difference is not accidental. When you work with a sociopath and socialize with a saint, you may find both experiences challenging. While the former can be frightening, the latter will be uplifting. While both can become disappointed and even experience satisfaction, the drivers are never the same, and this is a rear occasion when I do mean never. Sociopaths and saints experience regret, hope and anxiety, but for difference reasons and in different ways.

Sociopaths become frustrated for reasons that make saints feel grateful. Another difference between the two, while sociopaths live in fear, saints live fearlessly. Also, while social manipulation inhibits the intentions of sociopaths, kindness inhibits the judgments of saints. Considering the foregoing, it is easy to see that sociopaths are dominated by their moods, but saints govern their moods. Much of it has to do with attitudes which also differ considerably from sociopath to saint, especially since attitudes are charged with affective or value properties in varying degrees.

Defined stimuli or stimulus situations elicit the attitudes (Sherif & Cantril, 1945). None of this would be obvious without feelings which are indicators of the attitudes and values people hold. To have a feeling is to be in a state of satisfaction or dissatisfaction. Whereas an emotion is a physical or structural response, a feeling is a functional property of an individual. It is an intention to change or retain something, an intention produced by that something.

For example, when people meet someone for the very first time they occasionally have a strong reaction to that person, either positive or negative. When pressed to explain their reaction they had to that person, they cannot put their finger on it. They simply do not understand why they felt the way they did. Without conscious awareness, they erupted in a strong emotional response. When you look at this situation carefully, you realize that a rapid value judgment has just occurred.

Without realizing it, these persons saw something in that person that they really valued or very much disvalued. The judgement was so automatic and so rapid that these people did not even reflect on it for a single minute. The stranger instantaneously triggered an alarm that challenged one or more important deeply held beliefs or values. In this case, the stranger affected the emotions and feelings, the psychology and the physiology of those meeting the stranger.

Each of these situations comes to the surface when developing an Insider Threat Prevention Cyber Security organization and uniting it with the enterprise. Good people are different from malicious criminals who would destroy an enterprise if left to their own devices. Success with ITP Cyber Security requires a new mindset and way of looking at the challenge of Cyber Security Prevention. Every word and every concept require a definition and a rationale when forming a coherent enterprise ITP Cyber Security program.

ITP Cyber Security success requires discipline, curiosity, focus and wisdom. Generally, the malicious insider is a step ahead of everyone in the enterprise. I wrote the series to change the equation and put the defenders in the lead for a change. A balanced is important and so is insight. Every ITP Cyber Security organization has to work hard to ensure that the balance is always on their side. This is the real problem. How do the ITP Cyber Security folks get ahead and stay there? This is the problem is it not? Prevention is unlike everything else in Cyber Security. The next chapter explores what I mean by problem and what can we do about it.

Observable Personality

Some people maintain that personality, as an implicit driver of behavior, is unobservable. Here, people infer personality. Personality is what some psychologist term an intervening variable. The explanation, of course, requires quite a bit of faith. It is a belief-centric argument that explains human behavior. For them, Personality is unknowable.

This view makes Insider Threat Prevention Cyber Security more of a "crap shoot" than an essential discipline for the modern world. Luckily, progress in Behavior Science did not stop there. Actually, we have a choice in how we can reasonably understand Personality as something not shrouded in mystery. We see Personality every day as a process that reveals the way people make decisions. Technically, we see how individuals convert choice situations into expected relative values for themselves. We see this in Insider Threat Prevention Cyber Security when teams affect their environment through environmental effectiveness and when their environment affects them through environmental responsiveness.

ITP Cyber Security Psychological Environment

ITP Cyber Security organizations and malicious insiders exist in a psychological environment. In an earlier book in this series, I explored the emotional development of individuals throughout their lives. I also discussed the different kinds of relationships people form that correspond to the different levels of emotional development they have attained. ITP Cyber Security teams and malicious insiders both experience life passing through these levels of development. During this process some people become ITP Cyber Security Specialists and others become Cyber Terrorists. Why the difference?

What else can we say about human psychology that enables us to better understand the behavior of human beings and the paths they carve out during their lifetimes? Reasonable answers to these questions require us to change tempo a bit and think about the dimensions of personality and unite these with the role played by Existential Hunger in developing human behavior. We will begin by addressing the environmental properties and the way we respond to them or attempt to change them. In this case, we are indeed interested in the probability of an Insider Threat Prevention Cyber Security Specialist responding to environmental properties or changes in them as a function of their intensity.

The more intense an environmental property becomes, the more probable it is that the ITP Cyber Security Specialist will respond to it. Also, the more intense an environmental property becomes, the more probable it is that the malicious insider will respond to it. Obviously, the intensity of an environmental property motivates bot the specialist and the malicious insider to respond. In what way though, will the malicious insider respond and how will the specialist meet this response? The answer to these questions, believe it or not, is simple. It depends on whether the specialist or the malicious insider is an Objectvert or Subjectvert and Externalizer or Internalizer.

An Objectivert is the extrovert among us. This person connects to the environment near and wide. A Subjectivert is the introvert among us, however, and is less concerned about the environment. Hence the Objectivert is extroverted. As such, the Objectvert is sensitive to the external world and is more easily influenced by it. The Subjectivert is more likely to be influenced by his or her own thoughts and feelings than by the environment. The Objectivert is an objective individual, one moved and motivated objectively. Whereas the Subjectivert looks internally to be moved and motivated. The Subjectivert is an introspective individual. This person is more likely to understand himself, but perhaps less likely to understand others.

If the ITP Cybrer Security Specialist is an Externalizer, the specialist will focus on the environment. As an Externalizer, the specialist will change the environment to remain comfortable. The specialist comes first. The positive aspect here is simple: The Externalizer does not welcome intruders. The specialist, if an Externalizer, will confront intruders and, if necessary, will stop them or at the least attempt to limit their access. An Externalizer is an organizer who will readily build a team to take action against an intruder if required. Externalizers make excellent Insider Threat Prevention Cyber Security Specialists. They will search out malicious insiders and when they get on their trail, they will go after them. They are disrupters.

An Internalizer behaves differently. This person more easily adapts to the environment. The Internalizer ignores intruders and responds to them by creating distance between the two. Internalizers are followers who prefer to fit in. Their motto: "No problems; bring me no problems". These individuals like to avoid discomfort. They are not to be confused with introverts. They are avoiders of conflict. Their preferred response to challenge is to avoid it unless they can deal with it on their own terms in their own way and in their own time.

Internalizers can become excellent counter-intuitive ITP Cyber Security team members. The greater the conflict, the greater they avoid the world around them. As followers, they will work hard to maintain their avoidance they desire. Since they do not like conflict, Internalizers are very good at recognizing who does not fit in or who should not be there. Managers can use the Internalizer's desire for avoidance as a measure of the integrity of the environment. They join teams; they do not lead them. They are not natural disrupters, but their avoidance and need to follow others can become very disruptive.

Internalizers and Externalizers and Objectiversion and Subjectiversion are not classifications of human beings. These four words describe a range of human behaviors that clarify commonly shared psychological tendencies. When we combine and organize these four classifications with the levels of Existential Hunger described earlier in Part One, we gain a rich picture of the different personality types including:

- Objective Internalizer;
- Objective Externalizer;
- Subjective Internalizer, and
- Subjective Externalizer

Interesting, Centraversion, a special case when no category dominates a person's behavior, signifies psychological maturity and strength. This also signifies human development at the fourth level of Existential Hunger. For an ITP Cyber Security team, Centraversion refers to a process of continuous adaptation that enables the Specialist to attain a state of balance that increases the efficiency of his behaviors. The process of adaptation occurs as a change in both the environment and the Specialist's internal state reduces his functional efficiency. Adaptation enables the Specialist to respond by changing his own state and perhaps that of his environment increase its functional efficiency.

An ITP Cyber Security team experiences Other-Other Adaptation whenever any team member reacts or responds to an external change by modifying the environment. Additionally, the ITP Cyber Security team experiences Other-Self Adaptation whenever any team member reacts or responds to an external change by modifying itself. Moreover, in Self-Other Adaptation the ITP Cyber Security Specialist reacts or responds to an internal change or imbalance by modifying his environment.

Beyond of these cases, there is still Self-Self Adaptation to assist us. In Self-Self Adaptation, the ITP Cyber Security Specialist reacts or responds to an internal change or imbalance by modifying oneself. Since Imbalance occurs whenever the Specialist experience internal or external changes in his environment as the difference in the distance from Centraversion, adaptation assists the Specialist with reducing moving the distance from Centraversion. In this sense, then, the distance from Centraversion is the distance from emotional maturity and psychological wholeness.

ITP Cyber Security & Malicious Insider

As we have seen every person shares the psychological characteristics identified above. We have seen the same characteristics in families and entire cultures in different parts of the world. Both ITP Cyber Security team members and malicious insiders can be Internalizers, Externalizers, Objectiverts or Subjectiverts. Also, both ITP Cyber Security team members and malicious insiders fall somewhere along the Existential Hunger Continuum. We have just described the different characteristics that form the four fundamental Personality Types. Now we discuss how these personality types match up when they conflict with each other. These insights will assist ITP Cyber Security teams with devising strategies to prevent malicious insider attacks.

We will adopt the following conventions for the following section: Objective Internalizer (OI); Objective Externalizer (OE); Subjective Externalizer (SE), and Subjective Internalizer (SI).

Malicious Insider (OI) Versus ITP CS Team (SE)

When a malicious insider (OI) initiates a threat against the ITP CS Team (SE), the OI will fully understand the impact of his attack on the (SE) while disregarding the risk to him or herself. The (SE) will be mindful of the situation and attempt to prevent the (OI) threat. If a change in the attack space is required, the (OI) will probably recognize this and work to defeat the (SE) thereby escalating the malicious attack.

Malicious Insider (SI) Versus ITP CS Team (OE)

When the malicious insider (SI) initiates a threat against the ITP Cyber Security Team (OE), the (OE) will immediately become aware of its effect on the attack plan of the (SI) action but not yet understand the danger of the attack on the (OE) organizations. The (SI) will rapidly recognize this situation and perceive what the (OE) perceives. The (SI) will then modify the attack to neutralize the defensive strategy of the (OE). However, the (OE) will work to modify the (SI) attack to dissolve the threat. The (SI) is likely to defeat this response of the (OE) but, nevertheless, change the attack strategy to maintain attack superiority and keep the (OE) guessing.

The (SI) will then permit the (OE) to secure the environment and subsequently use this act of the (OE) as leverage against the (OE). The common strategy employed by the (SI) in this case is to abandon the attack while encouraging the (OE) to continue the ITP Cyber Security campaign and waste more resources on the ITP process to compound the cost of the ITP Cyber Security operation and further compound the cost of the ITP Cyber Security effort. This is acceptable to the (SI) because it further erodes the security budget of the ITP Cyber Security organization. In this scenario both the (SI) and (OE) remain unstable players in an expensive game of malicious chess.

Malicious Insider (OE) Versus ITP CS Team (SE)

Both the (OE) and the (SE) are likely to be aware of the malicious insider attack threat against the (SE) as soon as it occurs. Also, both the (OE) and the (SE) are likely to takes actions to change the perception of the other to gain the advantage by gaining the upper-hand. However, only the (OE) is likely to be sensitive to such efforts and anticipate the actions of the (SE). Also, the (OE) will not become sufficiently sensitive to the efforts of the (SE). the

(OE) and (SE) each will then compete with each other to better align their strategies to their own environments but against the environment of the other as a problem-solving approach.

Both the (OE) and the (SE) will respond slowly throughout the attack and remain unadaptable in their environments. Both the (OE) and (SE) will merely appear to be aggressively oriented toward the attack and to others in it, but the (SE) will continue to go through the motions as the (OE) develops the fanatical drive to succeed.

Malicious Insider (OI) Versus ITP CS Team (SI)

Both the (OI) and the (SI) will become aware of the insider attack through its effects on the (SI). The (SI) will respond by improving its mitigation methods and the (OI) will try to modify his or her attack strategy to renew the attack. The malicious insider will be a dedicated criminal always willing to sacrifice whatever it takes to succeed. The ITP Cyber Security Team (SI) will, of course, work just as hard to defeat the (OI). Unfortunately, the SI team will not fully appreciate the effort required to defeat the malicious attacker. The (OI) and (SI) form a strange mixture of antagonism and attack, reground and retreat. For the (OI) and (SI), each lacks the ability to change the attack environment in meaningful or creative ways that can prevent the success of a malicious insider attack.

Malicious Insider (OI) Versus ITP CY Team (OE)

The (OI) and (OE) both will quickly recognize the effect of malicious insider attacks on the (OE) environment. The (OI) will react to the efforts of the (OE) with strategies that are designed to disrupt the best efforts of the ITP Cyber Security Team, the (OE). Also, the OE will try to neutralize the (OI) who will anticipate such strategies. Since the (OI) is a sensitive and malicious insider, he or she will respond to the strategies of the (OE). Here, the malicious insider and the (OE) will see the situation things differently because they see the Problem Situation from different perspectives in which the (OI) believes the (OE) deserves what it gets and the (OE) thinking the (OI) deserves what it gets.

Malicious Insider (SE) Versus ITP CS Team (SI)

The (SE) and the (SI) will harbor an indifferent reciprocity toward each other. The SE will engage in a range of malicious Cyber Attacks for personal gain even if they can possibly destroy the company. Unfortunately, the indifferent attitude of SI will disrupt the ITP Cyber Security process of the team. Depending on the intensity of the choice situation and the goals for the malicious attack, the malicious insider will gradually diminish the number of attacks each day as the (SE) and (SI) move further apart.

Malicious Insider (SE) Versus ITP CS Team (SE)

When a Subjective Externalizer launches a cyber-attack on another Subjective Externalizer, the malicious insider and the ITP Cyber Security Team will see how the malicious insider attack and the ITP Cyber Security efforts affect themselves. In response, the ITPCS Team will try to disempower the malicious insider while the malicious insider will continually try to initiate a successful attack. Both (SE) agents will behave very ruthless toward the other while remaining unaware of the severity of their intensity. The malicious insider will attempt to disrupt social situations through manipulation and misdirection while the ITP CS Team employs fear to recruit enterprise participation, regardless of the cost to the enterprise.

Malicious Insider (OI) Versus ITP CS Team (OI)

The malicious insider will see his or her cyber-attack through its effect on the enterprise. The ITP CS Team will see its prevention strategies through their effects on the malicious insider. AS Both the malicious insider and the ITP CS Team will try to adapt to the constantly changing situation to find a more potent attack strategy or a more potent prevention strategy. In proceeding this way, each (OI) will work independently through their own perceptions and efforts to succeed with their appointed tasks. As (OI) actors, each will see things unfold from one action to another but let things run their course as executed without intervention. In a sense, each (OI) actors lack the aggressiveness described in previous scenarios.

Malicious Insider (SI) Versus ITP CS Team (SI)

In this scenario, the malicious insider and the ITP CS Team will behave as if each actor does not exist. Even in situations where they work close together, they will rarely engage one another. The malicious insider will do everything that he or she can to avoid the ITP CS Team, and the ITP CS team will do all that it can to deny that the malicious insider actually exists. These (SI) actors lose contact with their environments and completely behave passively toward it.

Malicious Insider (OE) Versus ITP CS Team (OE)

Here, the malicious insider will do all that he or she can disrupt the enterprise to create terribly complicated Cyber Problems. In response, the ITP CS Team will mostly disregard the attack as long as the team can. However, when the ITP CS Team responds, the malicious insider will try hard to ignore the response. When they do finally respond, the malicious insider will change the attack plan and adopt new and more complex strategies while the ITP CS Team changes its prevention environment. Concurrently, each actor dedicates its attention to improving the attack platform and the Cyber Attack prevention system.

These eight scenarios describe the complexities of Human Behavior that influence the success of any Insider Threat Prevention Cyber Security Program. You can bet that it is not as simple as I make it look here. An ITP Cyber Security Specialist has to be well grounded in several disciplines. He or she requires psychological insight born of experience, emotional maturity, sound judgment, abundant resilience, and intellectual and emotional depth. He or she must also enjoy the hunt for the malicious insider who could be working nearly anywhere in the enterprise.

15: Some Final Thoughts

Throughout this series, I discussed definitive insights and themes in The Psychology of Insider Threat Prevention Cyber Security that can prepare the ITP CS Specialist to become more aware and cautious about the genius of the ordinary malicious insider. Malicious insiders are not often stupid. They are most often very smart people who do stupid things. The dangerous challenge occurs when brilliant people launch malicious insider attacks brilliantly. As we know by now, Insider Attacks can be fatal to an organization. We can never take cyber safety for granted.

ITP Cyber Security is all about a kind of interaction that is highly charged by a range of psychological elements such as feelings, models of communications, signs, messages, special purpose languages, the ITP 3Cs of Conflict, Cooperation, Competition, the behavior of social groups, Ideal-Seeking Systems Behavior, mastery of logical propositions, constraints of time, the problem of distortion and faulty observation, and the perfection of perception and identity.

These are all rich topics with a long history of development and clarification even before they were applied to Cyber Security. The challenge of working with people in your enterprise who may or may not be malicious insiders is one of the great challenges faced today by employees, managers, executives and the customers we all serve. Solutions, real solutions, the kind of solutions that prevent malicious insider cyber-attacks are difficult to discover, but you can discover them if you properly prepare yourself for a new kind of psychological warfare. .

Normally, special teams mitigate insider attacks after the attacks have occurred. Rarely does anyone actually prevent them. This is why I wrote this series. I know we can prevent them, I know how we can prevent them. I realize that management first designs an enterprise as a business entity. Sometime later, management then implements a Cyber Security organization to resolve insider threats. Today, this is a problem. You only need to think about Continuous Performance Management. It is wrought with risks the CPM people call Hallmarks.

In the near future, however, success will require an organization to be designed as a unified Business Process-Insider Threat Prevention Cyber Security enterprise that executes business transactions in a highly secure cyber driven environment. In closing this series, I want to leave you with a few clarifications that will mean a lot to you when your time comes.

In ITP Cyber Security, accuracy matters. Accuracy matters when we present the facts and assumptions of the cyber threat environment. Accuracy matters when we state the facts of the problem situation of insider threats. Accuracy matters when we define the terms and concepts of the cyber threat environment. Accuracy matters when we discuss the choice situations of the cyber threat environment.

Accuracy also matters when we describe Interpersonal Feelings in a highly rational and disciplined manner such as when we state that: Gratitude occurs when one individual (A) is grateful to another (B) for something (X) if A believes B intentionally produced X and A is satisfied with X. Or, when we say that Blame occurs when one individual (A) blames another (B) for something (X) if A believes B intentionally produced X and A is dissatisfied with X. (Ackoff & Emery, 1981, pg. 140).

Using this formal form in descriptions, we are able to more clearly measure the important elements of each formal description. Measures actually exist for blame and gratitude. These measures are the products of the measures of belief and satisfaction or dissatisfaction. Can you see how a single description establishes a series of descriptive relationships that are measurable and deliver deeper meaning of the concept?

This is the language we should use if describing any Insider Attack environment that emerges from one day to the next. Take a moment and reflect on the potent description of "a purposeful state of an individual":

1. The set of available courses of action, C;
2. The set of possible outcomes, O;
3. The environment, S;
4. The state of A;
5. The probabilities of A selecting each course of action, P;
6. The efficiencies of the courses of action for each objective, E;
7. The value of the outcomes to A, V.

Given the available courses of action and possible outcomes, the value of a purposeful state, V, must be some function of P, E, and V (Ackoff & Emery, 1981, pg. 143). Although this is a simply unambiguous way or presenting complicated concepts of ITP Cyber Security, it is not for everyone. It is, however, a wonderfully ingenious way of presenting the Modes and Measures of Communications in ITP Cyber Security including Information, Instruction, and Motivation.

Series Conclusion

Part One explored the Psychology of Insider Threat Prevention Cyber Terror by examining the impact of sociopathology on workplace relationships and the risk of malicious insiders. While introducing the Hallmarks of Continuous Performance Management (CPM), the author questioned Continuous Performance Management's resiliency in the face of the threat of Cyber Terror. It argued that Continuous Performance Management and Cyber Terror are both psychological phenomena coming from opposite ends of the behavioral spectrum.

Part Two in the series continued the theme of Continuous Performance Management-Insider Threat Prevention Cyber Security Unification by introducing the Newkirk Human Relationship Process Model as it begins to form the ITP Cyber Security strategies.

Part Three introduced the strategies and methods that enable organizations to secure their CPM environments through ITPCS Unification without disrupting business operations. Here this Series takes the challenge Insider Threat Prevention Cyber Terror head-on by introducing the vision of a Unified Continuous Performance Management and Insider Threat Prevention Cyber Security architecture derived from Behavioral Science.

Collectively, The Psychology of Insider Threat Prevention Cyber Security Series examines the behavioral, social, technical, philosophical, managerial, strategic and operational considerations of such a large-scale program. It addresses the challenge of building new workplace relationships in organizations designed to combat Cyber Terror by building Insider Threat Prevention Cyber Security effectiveness in any organization.

Part Four of the series, The Psychology of Insider Threat Prevention Cyber Security, we examined the wider environment of Insider Threat Prevention Cyber Security. Here, we will learn what it takes to become a Consulting

Specialist in this rare but critical discipline. We describe the unified enterprise-wide system's architecture and the corresponding components and processes that form the unified model of CPM-ITP Cyber Security unified environment.

Future Volumes in the series will examine the core components of an Insider Threat Prevention Cyber Security Unification Program including:

1. Building the Insider Threat Prevention Cyber Security Unified Enterprise Architecture
2. Mastering Insider Threat Prevention Cyber Security Leadership
3. The Art of Insider Threat Prevention Communication for Cyber Security Effectiveness
4. Training & Development for Insider Threat Prevention Cyber Security Success
5. Insider Threat Prevention Cyber Security Risk Management
6. Insider Threat Prevention Cyber Security Process Control.

"The Applied Intuitive Solutions™ environment forms a powerful mobile Platform that rapidly improves the performance of teams and individuals."

What Should We Remember

We store memories differently based on how they were experienced.

- Tip of the tongue effect
- Google effect
- Next-in-line effect
- Testing effect
- Absent-mindedness effect
- Levels of processing effect

We reduce events and list to their key elements:

- Suffix effect
- Serial position effect

- Part-list cueing effect
- Recency effect
- Primacy effect
- Memory Inhibition
- Modality effect
- Duration Neglect
- List-length effect
- Serial recall effect
- Misinformation effect
- Leveling and Sharpening
- Peal-end rule

We discard specifics to form generalities:

- Fading affect bias
- Negativity bias
- Prejudice
- Stereotypical bias
- Implicit Stereotypes
- Implicit associations

We edit and reinforce some memories after the fact:

- Spacing effect.
- Suggestable
- False Memory
- Cryptomnesia
- Source Confusion
- Misattribution of memory
- Too Much Information

We notice things already primed in memory or repeated often:

- Availability heuristic
- Attention bias

- Illusory truth effect
- Mere exposure effect
- Context effect
- Cue dependent forgetting
- Mood congruent memory bias
- Frequency Illusion
- Baader-Meinof Phenomenon
- Empathy gap
- Omission bias
- Base rate fallacy

Bizarre, funny, visually-striking, or anthropomorphic things stick out more than non-bizarre and unfunny things:

- Bizarreness effect
- Humor effect
- Von Restorff effect
- Picture Superiority effect
- Self-relevance effect
- Negativity bias

We notice when something has changed:

- Anchoring
- Conservatism
- Contrast effect
- Distinction bias
- Focusing effect
- Framing effect
- Money illusion
- Weber-Fechner Law

We are drawn to details that confirm our own existing beliefs:

- Confirmation bias

- Congruence bias
- Post-purchase rationalization
- Choice-supportive bias
- Selective perception
- Observer-expectancy effect
- Experimenter's bias
- Observer effect
- Expectation bias
- Ostrich effect
- Subjective validation
- Continued influence effect
- Semmelweis reflex

We notice flaws in others more easily than we notice flaws in ourselves:

- Bias blind spot
- Naïve cynicism
- Naïve realism

Not Enough Meaning so we tend to find stories and patterns even when looking at sparse data:

- Confabulation
- Clustering illusion
- Insensitivity to sample size
- Neglect of probability
- Anecdotal fallacy
- Illusion of validity
- Masked man fallacy
- Recency illusion
- Gambler's fallacy
- Hot-hand fallacy

- Illusory correlation
- Paredidolia

- Anthropomorphism

We fill in characteristics from stereotypes, generalities, and prior histories:

- Group attribution error
- Ultimate attribution error
- Stereotyping
- Essentialism
- Functional fixedness
- Moral credential effect
- Just-world hypothesis
- Argument from fallacy
- Authority bias
- Automation bias
- Bandwagon effect
- Placebo effect

We imagine things and people we are familiar with or found of as better:

- Out-group homogeneity bias
- Cross-race effect
- In-group bias
- Halo effect
- Cheerleader effect
- Positivity effect
- Not invented here
- Well-traveled road effect.

We simplify probabilities and numbers to make them easier to think about:

- Mental accounting
- Appeal to probability fallacy
- Normalcy bias
- Murphy's law
- Zero sum bias

- Survivorship bias
- Subadditivity effect
- Denomination effect
- Magic number 7+2
- We think we know what other people are thinking:
- Illusion of Transparency
- Curse of knowledge
- Spotlight effect
- Intrinsic incentive error
- Illusion of external agency
- Illusion of asymmetric insight

We project our current mindset and assumptions onto the past and future:

- Consistency bias
- Restraint bias
- Projection bias
- Pro-innovation basis
- Time-saving basis
- Planning fallacy
- Pessimism Bias
- Impact bias
- Declinism
- Moral luck
- Outcome bias
- Hindsight bias
- Rosy Retrospection
- Telescoping effect

We Need to Act Fast

- We favor simple looking options and complete information over complex, ambiguous options.
- Less-is-better effect
- Occam's Razor

- Conjunction fallacy
- Delmore effect
- Law of Triviality
- Bike-shedding effect
- Rhyme as reason effect
- Belief bias
- Information Bias
- Ambiguity bias

To avoid mistakes, we preserve autonomy, group status, and avoid irreversible decisions:

- Status quo bias
- Social comparison bias
- Decoy effect
- Reactance
- Reverse Psychology
- System justification

To get things done, we tend to complete things we have invested time & energy in:

- Backfire effect
- Endowment effect
- Processing difficulty effect
- Pseudocertainty effect
- Disposition effect
- Zero-risk bias
- Unit bias
- IKEA effect
- Loss aversion
- Generation effect
- Escalation of commitment
- Irrational escalation
- Sun Cost fallacy

To stay focused, we favor the immediate, relatable thing in front of us:

- Identifiable victim effect
- Appeal to novelty
- Hyperbolic discounting

To act, we must be confident we can make an impact and feel what we do is important.

- Peltzman effect
- Risk compensation
- Effort justification
- Trait ascription bias
- Defensive attribution
- Fundamental attribution error
- Illusory superiority
- Illusion of control
- Actor-observer bias
- Self-serving bias
- Barnum effect
- Forer effect
- Optimism bias
- Egocentric bias
- Dunning Kruger effect
- Lake Wobegone effect
- Hard-easy effect
- False consensus effect
- Third person effect
- Social desirability bias
- Overconfidence effect

Description of Terms

40 Inventive Principles: Refers to Altshuller's Collection of Principles derived from observation. People can employ the 40 Inventive Principles independently or with the Contradiction Matrix to solve problems creatively.

Abstract Term: Refers to a word or phrase that describes a generic feature, property or function that can identify an instant of one or more specific terms by adding or describing a relevant context. The same term can be specific in one case or abstract in another when used differently. For example, we can use the term "separate" abstractly one way while the term divide can be considered as specific another way.

Additional Function: Refers to a function that is not directly involved in delivering the main process but is merely associated with the main function or assists with achieving the main function.

Additional Inventive Principle: Refers to an Inventive Principle that people identified after Altshuller defines his collection of 40 First Principles. Today, researchers have identified 10 additional Inventive Principles.

Administrative Contradiction: Refers to the description of an undesired effect or the definition of an essential inventive action that improves a situation in which a problem solving method or a solution is unavailable.

Algorithm of Inventive Problem Solving (ARIZ): Refers to the most central analytical tool of Inventive Problem Solving, or TRIZ. As an algorithm, it consists of a specific sequence of logical processes, or steps, designed to analyze a vague or ill-defined problem and transform it as a distinct system conflict. Furthermore, analysis of the system conflict results in the formulation of the contradiction that ITP Cyber Security teams, using the separation principles and the enterprise's resources, must eliminate. This transformation is guided by the most fundamental concepts and methods of TRIZ including Ideal System, System Conflict, System Contradiction, the Su-Field analysis, the Inventive Standards and the Laws of Systems Evolution. Transformation occurs as the result of psychological and systemic operators.

Analogous Solution: Refers to a practice-based or inventive solution that emerges as teams resolve identical contradictions using the identical problem-solving process used in previous solutions. Analogous Problems might also be defined by employing the same SuField model or the same function.

Anticipatory Failure Determination (AFD): Refers to a method and technique that identifies potential problems, including failures, either within an enterprise, i.e. Human Activity System, or its super-system caused by the technical system. AFD includes Failure Analysis and Prediction Analysis.

Anticipatory Failure Determination Failure Analysis: Refers processes that reveal causes of negative or undesired effects.

Anticipatory Failure Determination Prediction Analysis: Refers to process that predict potential negative or undesired effects.

Anti-Function: Refers to a function that is always opposite to a given function such to become more agitated vs. to become less agitated.

Anti-Principle: Refers to an Inventive Principle that consists of a problem solving recommendation that is the opposite of a recommendation that delivers a known Inventive Principle. An anti-principle occurs such that the "Principle of Taking Away" becomes an anti-principle in relation to the "Principle of Adding to or Merging".

Anti-Process: Refers to a process that produces results that are opposite to another target process such as "agreeing" vs. "disagreeing", or "repairing" vs. "breaking". The anti-process" assists with formulating contradictions

Anti-System: Refers to a system that exists to oppose a function of another system. An anti-system may compete with the opposed system such that the closedness of an Insider Threat Prevention Cyber Security architecture may compete against the openness of a Continuous Performance Management.

Attribute: Refers to a fundamental quality of an architectural object that describes its interaction with other CPM and ITP CS objects. We associate attributes with types a range of values including Color, Weight, Complexity, and Phase state. The range of values may be linear, non-linear, or discrete. An attribute contains a parameter as subset of an attribute.

Auxiliary Function: Refers to a useful function of a component which behaves as a subsystem or a component of a system at a higher-level.

Base Technical System: Refers to a system that receives features from an alternative system. The base system is one of several systems selected for improvement.

Basic Function: Refers to a useful function targeted on an object of a system being analyzed.

Bell-Curve of Evolution: Refers to the cycles of growth or expansion and convolution or reduction.

Biological Effect (BE): Refers to an effect produced by a person or team that assists with the development of Inventive Problem Solving. The BE is at play whenever a team member leverages existing processes or actions present in the environment to improve Insider Threat Prevention Cyber Security. The team can collect these action steps to develop and execute Problem-Based Solutions.

Bi-System: Refers to systems that contain two or more identical, biased, or inverse components with functions or values of the same attributes that can be leveraged to create positive synergistic effects in which the results are more than the sum of their parts such that a considerable multiplication or decrease of a value of an attribute, or delivering a new property, or production of a new function.

Cardinal Virtues: Virtues are positive behaviors that become habits. The Cardinal Virtues include Justice, Fidelity, Self-Care, and Prudence. They are referred to as "Cardinal" because they are the hinges that lead to all the virtues.

Catalogue of Architecture Unification Effects: Refers to the CPM-ITPCS database of the Unification Program. The effects emerge from any involved discipline used in the Program. Designers organize the effects according to their generic functions. In each Program Catalogue, the effects are organized along different project groups. The following Catalogues of Program Effects are known: 1) Catalogue of Management Effects, 2) Catalogue of Network Effects, 3) Catalogue of Software Effects, 4) Catalogue of Social Effects, 5) Catalogue of Process Effects, 6) Catalogue of Cyber Security Effects, 7) Catalogues of Financial Effects, 8) Catalogues of Culture Effects, 9) Catalogue of Business Effects, 10) Catalogues of Training & Development Effects.

Cause Disadvantage: Refers to a disadvantage in the Unification Cause-Effect Chain that is a direct cause of a real versus apparent disadvantage.

Cause-Effect Chain: A visual model of a component of a Unification System being analyzed. The visual model maps the causes that directly or indirectly generate its disadvantage(s).

Cause-Effect Chains Analysis (CECA): Refers to an analytical process that identifies the principal disadvantages of the analyzed Unification system. We do this by building the cause-effect chains of disadvantages that link the disadvantages to their fundamental causes.

Computer Performance Evaluation (CPE): CPE is rigorous engineering experiment design to test the performance, reliability and capacity of an integrated computer system according to redefined external and internal acceptance criteria.

Design Inquiry: Iterative exploration of the systems, environments, spaces, dynamics, and models of design as the appropriate design inquiry architecture to produce a solution as a future system.

Existential Hunger: The innate and natural desire for union with other human beings. This refers to the human desire and capacity to form mutual relationships with human beings in a one-to-one and one-to-many correspondence, such as Social connectivity, peer acceptance, affirmation.

Five Functions of Cyber Security: Refers to the core functions of Cyber Security which collectively ensure the security of organizations and their information assets and systems against malicious or accidental intrusions. Customarily, these functions include Identify, Protect, Detect, Respond, and Recover. Prevention is notable by its absence. Protect and Prevent are not the same. Protect means to limit or contain. Prevent means to STOP an event completely so that an organization does not need to limit or contain an event.

Functional Relationship: Relationships in which human beings work together to achieve a mutual purpose or goal, as when sharing a social or professional project.

Human Activity System: A system in which the components are human beings engaging in processes of input, output, transformation, and feedback and adjustment.

Human Activity System Continua: The continuum of Human Activity Systems from open to closed, complex to simple (restricted), unitary to pluralist, and mechanistic to systemic.

Human Relationship Process Model: A relationships model that employs a Human Activity Systems view of transformation and growth.

Level One Existential Hunger: Fundamental human drive that leads to the formation of self-centered relationships.

Level Two Existential Hunger: Higher-level human drive to form relationships in which people may participate in attaining mutual goals.

Level Three Existential Hunger: Higher-Level human drive to form relationships in which the categories of love emerge as human beings become ends in themselves rather than means to ends.

Level Four Existential Hunger: Highest level of human relationship in which human beings seek out and pursue transformation of values and activities to experience deepest meanings of life, love, and relationships.

Manipulative Relationship: A relationship emerging from Type One Existential Hunger in which other people are seen as means to an end regardless of the personal cost involved.

Metamethodology: METAM is a methodology for designing methodologies; HAS engage a MetaM to design a methodology appropriate to the type of HAS that is to be designed as an Information Systems. The MetaM is beyond any methodology. Close ties exist between methodologies and MetaM. Both Banathy and Checkland offer examples of MetaM. While Banathy (1989a) discussed a strategy for Design Inquiry as the design of design, Checkland (1981) offers a system for generating methodologies.

Methodologies are valuable in that any advance in science is preceded by advances in methodology (Misiak & Sexton, 1966; Branden, 1974). However, "advances in methodology are preceded by advances in philosophy" (Newkirk, 1991, p. 34). For me, a MetaM is "a generalization of all methodologies as a second level abstraction to provide a MetaM of all methodologies" (Newkirk, 1991a, p. 28). Ontologically, as a second level abstraction, the metamethodology exists in the province of mathematics; retains intelligible matter; separates from common sensible matter; has the imagination as its end point; is a contingent system in that it cannot exist without individual sensible matter; and cannot be understood without intelligible matter (Hickey, 1976).

MetaM rest on the bedrock of philosophical exploration and development. MetaM are required to design methodologies appropriate to a given problem situation. They are based on theory and practice, enhance system's evolution, organize methodologies, facilitate embedded systems building and support multiple paradigms (Newkirk, 1991a).

Methodology: A methodology can be hard or soft. Banathy (1988a) writes that a methodology "is defined as a set of coherent, related, and internally consistent methods applicable to pursuing disciplined inquiry" (p. 27). Checkland (1981) viewing methodology praxiologically, argues that "a methodology will lack the precision of a technique but will be a firmer guide to action than a philosophy" (p. 162). Flood and Carson (1988) discuss hard and soft systems methodologies by arguing that hard methodologies "set out to select an efficient means of achieving a known and defined end" (p. 107).

Methodology building is a design situation. It requires a design system to function as a methodology generating system, a HAS that engages a METAM to conduct Design Inquiry. To design a methodology, the designer must employ a METAM.

Focusing on methodology and systems, Collen (1985) argues: "A systemic method is a formalized means of studying a system" (p. 536). He continues by arguing that "system methodology is the study of such methods, as well as the collective applications of such methods to the study of a human activity system" (p. 536). Dillon (1983) sees methodologies as imperfect. He argues that "Each is a product of the human mind and each is intended to bring some order out of the bewildering array of signals coming from the expanded sensory system. Each can form a mental image or model of the thing or event perceived, again it must be emphasized, from a particular perspective" (p. 11).

Newkirk Model of Employee Engagement: Refers to the programs, processes, and activities that collectively work together to consistently build the performance of employees.

Newkirk Model of Workplace Relationships: The Relationship Model of Dr. Raymond L. Newkirk that establishes Existential Hunger as the driving force energizing the formation of all human relationships from Type One to Type Four.

Newkirk Human Relationships Process Model: Refers the levels of Existential Hunger and the nature and characteristics of the relationships they form as Human Activity Systems.

Objective Relationship: A relationship derived from Type One Existential Hunger that depersonalized members in the relationship by using them as objectives for attainment of goals.

Objectivert: Refers to a person who responds to his or her environment.

Paradigm: Provides our perception of the world, how it works and what it contains in any given situation. We perceive the world within one world view or another which establishes any paradigm we may advocate for problem solving. Carrico (1989) describes a paradigm as a representation for the internal model that human beings employ to think about something. For Kuhn (1970), paradigms "define the legitimate problems and methods of a research field" (p. 10). Powers (1984), similar to Carrico above, argues that a paradigm "is a basic image which acts as an organizing and filtering agent, a socially accepted way of seeing, modelling, and communicating about reality" (p. 2).

Powers sees a paradigm as a larger system consisting of three crucial subsystems: ontological, methodological, and epistemological. As a systemist, I see a paradigm as a suprasystem consisting of ontological, epistemological, and psychological subsystems which together inform a metamethodology for making sense out of the world. Our paradigms influence our efforts at designing our own futures through design inquiry.

Carrico (1989) reasons that a paradigm serves as the representation for the internal model that we employ to think about something. Kuhn (1970) reasons that paradigms "define the legitimate problems and methods of a research field" (p. 10). Powers (1984) see a paradigm as a large philosophical system.

As a systemist, I see a paradigm as a suprasystem consisting of ontological, epistemological and psychological subsystems which together inform a metamethodology as a design inquiry for making sense out of the world. Our paradigm influences our efforts of designing on own future through design inquiry. Others see paradigms as metaphorical (Morgan, 1986).

Principles, Laws, Corollaries and Guidelines: The Systems Approach is operationalized through its various dictates, assumptions, pre-suppositions, and guiding notions as expressed in the form of principles, laws, corollaries and guidelines (Yourdon, 1989a). This "legal" and "disciplined" foundation derived from GST stresses the nature of the systems approach as an expanded encounter with the world being perceived in the form of dynamical systems in interaction and interdependence through the interconnectedness of subsystems rather than as a background of static, discrete and non-interrelated components in isolation (Yourdon, 1989a).

An important corollary of the system approach is that as systems thinkers, we come to appreciate the uniqueness of an entity as a member of any system. If it is correct that a system is changed whenever a component or subsystem enters the system or leaves it, the component must be unique (Mayon-White and Morris, 1982).

From the human science perspective studying both the expanded domain of HAS and the discrete organization structures and functions of traditional Organization Development, this corollary defends the uniqueness and indispensability of every person. Every human person brings something unique into their systems. This something unique makes the system other than what it previously was (Mayon-White & Morris, 1982). The axioms, propositions, principles, laws, corollaries, and guidelines of the system approach are derived from the basic definition of the concept system. Bertalanffy (1950), Ashby (1956), Miller (1956), Checkland (1981), Myon-White and Morris (1983), Bogdanov (1984), Christakis (1985) and Warfield (1987) have all made their contributions.

As the system movement evolves, the laws and principles developed within this perspective will gain increasing weight and influence. Although the dictates of the systems perspective lack empirical credibility, experience with them indicates that they contain logical content. Checkland (1981) reasons that: "As the use of systems concepts in problem-solving is developed we may expect a parallel emergence of laws deriving from the logic of the use of systems ideas" (p. 234). These systems ideas are derived from the various systems perspectives that are evolving as a new paradigm of disciplined inquiry. Systems principles are implicit in many new theories of corporate rebirth.

Rapid Solutions Mobile Platform (RSMP): Refers to the component of the AIS environment that delivers the rapid evidence-based solution to the end-users after a query.

Spiritual Personal Relationship: A high-order relationship derived from Type Four Existential Hunger that leads individuals to personal-spiritual transformation and the attainment of uniquely spiritual values.

Subjectivert refers to a person who ignores his or her environment.

System: Mayon-White and Morris (1982) argue that a system is an assembly of components of particular interest to someone that are connected in an organized way for doing something. The components are affected by being in the system in such a way that the system is changed if any component leaves it. Systems are classified as natural system, designed systems, human activity systems, and social systems.

Systems can be either hard or soft, designed physical systems or designed abstract systems. Some even authorities claim that systems exist which are beyond human knowledge; these are the transcendental systems (Checkland, 1981). In LST (Miller, 1988), systems consists of 19 subsystems.

Systems Design and Relevant Dynamics: Systems Design is a disciplined inquiry consisting of specialized techniques, general rules and universal principles. Banathy (1984) writes that "design is creative, disciplined, and decision-oriented inquiry carried out in iterative cycles. During these cycles, we develop design solutions by exploring three `spaces' that surround the design solution space: (a) the design knowledge space, (b) the design problem space, and (c) the design exploration space" (pp. 1-11). Design systems work within the spaces of design to produce a desired system.

Collen (1990) reasoned that "Systems design is an ongoing activity which requires the participation of all stakeholders if a HAS is to evolve" (p. 4). Collen refers to the systems design methodology as the "Systems Design Journey" (p. 4) to reflect the continuous or evolutionary nature of design as distinct from planning. The evolutionary nature of design flows from the dynamics occurring within the design experience. Two significant dynamics of design have been identified by Banathy (1984) as divergence and convergence. Design commences with an image of the future system and works to achieve it through iterations of divergence and convergence. The outcome of the design experience is a description of a new system to be implemented.

Systems Perspectives: The systems approach is engaged in a continuous debate. Debate rages over the very efficacy of the movement itself. Some fear that it may be just a new way of expressing old ideas. Others wonder if the systems approach is so general as to be vague, vacuous, and meaningless. Some argue over the best approach to systems. Just as the systems perspective is a way of perceiving the world, there exist several ways of perceiving systems.

Churchman (1979) reasoned that "the systems approach really consists of a continuing debate between various attitudes of mind with respect to society" (p. xi). He reasons that many systems debaters exist who fall into one of four classes of systems thinkers: (1) efficiency thinkers who study trouble spots; (2) science advocates who build objective models; (3) humanists who consider values while encouraging noninterference; (4) anti-planners who encourage experience at the expense of other rational approaches.

Theory of Creative Personality Development: Refers to the theory that investigates and examines the evolution of personal creative skills by analyzing and synthesizing the deep biographies of innovative and flexible thinkers and inventors. The examination particularly investigates how creative persons solve problems they encounter throughout their entire span of life. In effect, the Theory occurs as a longitudinal study of targeted biographies.

Theory of Technical Systems Evolution: Refers to the theory that emerged during evolution of TRIZ. The theory investigates the models of the evolution of technical systems and the laws, trends, and vectors, or lines, that identify the evolution of a specific technical system.

Virtual Expert Intelligence System (VEIS): Refers to the component of the Applied Intuitive Solutions environment that stores the problem generating content. It is the solutions repository.

Workplace Relationships: Refers to associations and relationships formed in the workplace to meet personal and professional goals derived from Type One to Type Four Existential Hunger.

References & Historical Bibliography

This section provides a historical Reference and Bibliography that takes you back to the beginning when visions like Networked Information Systems, Continuous Performance Management and Insider Threat Prevention Cyber Security first began to emerge and brings you up to today. It introduces many of the thinkers and their ideas and concepts that informed the emergence and subsequent evolution of Insider Threat Prevention Cyber Security (ITPCS). At its best, ITPCS is a difficult discipline that, fortunately for us, has amassed a wonderful volume of insight over the years.

Mastery of the Psychology of Insider Threat Prevention Cyber Security is not an overnight project. Although each company suffers its own ITPCS concerns, they all share common challenges that elicit shared strategies and responses. As we have seen in Part One, Continuous Performance Management shares several Hallmarks that make ITP Cyber Security more difficult to enforce such as trust and openness and minimal management. Other organization initiatives and architectures have issues that also complicate the enforcement of ITP Cyber Security.

Many, if not most, people today are unaware of the breadth and depth of the conceptual universe that can form a viable, potent, and successful Insider Threat Prevention Cyber Security Program. Actually, several dozen disciplines come together to form resilient ITP Cyber Security. These range from Software Development, Program and Project Management, Hardware Systems Engineering, Budgeting, Finance, Strategic Thinking, Operations Management, Network Management, Version Control, and Human Resource Management to Behavioral Science, Sociology, Theology, Forensic Psychology, Personality and Trait theories, Systems Thinking, Human Activity Systems Design, Philosophy, Physics, Mathematics, Management, Organization Design, Enterprise Architecture Planning, Critical Theory, Ideology Critique, Training and Development, Communications, Methodology Design, Product Development and several others. I am sure you get the idea.

ITP Cyber Security is a complex challenge that people generally under-conceptualize. Getting it right demands significant change throughout the enterprise. The key word here is "PREVENTION". I am not talking about repair, correction, or making something less painful which is common with mitigation strategies. Mitigation is the effort to reduce loss of life and property by lessening the impact of disasters. II am speaking of Insider Threat Prevention Cyber Security. I mean stopping it in its tracks before it happens. This is hard to do, but it can be done.

Insider Threat Prevention is essential because such malicious insider attacks can destroy an entire enterprise in a very, very short time. While external intrusions are dangerous, very expense, and threatening, they rarely destroy an entire enterprise. Organizations recover from them. ITP Cyber Security is far difference because an increasing percentage of them render their targets useless, forever. Executive shave to think differently about Insider Threats, and implement enterprise architecture that actually prevent them while concurrently enhancing business operations. Success in the ear of Cyber Terror is indeed the brave new world.

As you understand more clearly the danger of insider attacks, you will also begin to recognize how complex this problem really is. Many disciplines comes together to produce an Architecture that unifies enterprise models and Insider Threat Prevention Cyber Security models. An effective ITP Cyber Security solution presents a challenge of environmental unification that is well beyond the common practices of systems integration. This requires a knowledge base derived from the contribution of the thirty plus disciplines identified above.

Aamodt, Agnar: A Knowledge-Intensive, Integrated Approach to Problem Solving and Sustained Learning.

Ackoff, R. L. (1979, July). The Future of Operational Research is Past. In R. E. Cavallo (Ed.), Systems Research Movement: Characteristics, Accomplishments and Current Developments. Binghampton, NY: Society for General Systems Research.

Ackoff, R.L. (1981). Creating the Corporate Future. New York: John Wiley & Sons.

Ackoff, R. L. (1982). On the Hard Headedness and Soft Headedness of M. C. Jackson. Journal of Applied Systems Analysis, 9.

Ackoff, R. L. (1991). Ackoff's Fables: Irreverent Reflections on Business and Bureaucracy. New York: John Wiley & Sons, Inc.

Ackoff, R. L., & Emery, Fred E. (1972). On Purposeful Systems. Seaside, CA: Intersystems Publications.

Adam, Nabil R. & Wortmann, John C. (1989, December). Security-Control Methods for Statistical Analysis Databases: A Comparative Study. ACM Computing Surveys, 21(4), pp. 515-556.

Adams, Kevin: Towards a System of Systems Methodologies, Once Again. Old Dominion University.

Adams, Kevin (2012): Systems Theory: A Formal Construct for Understanding Systems. Old Dominion University.

Aligica Paul D. & Tarko,Vlad (2011). Polycentricity: From Polanyi to Ostrom, and Beyondgove 1550 237.262 © 2011 Wiley Periodicals, Inc.

Altshuller G.S. (1998). The Innovation Algorithm: TRIZ, Systematic Innovation, and Technical Creativity. Worcester, M A: Technical Innovation Center.

Altshuller G.S. (1994). Creativity as an Exact Science. New York, NY: Gordon & Breach.

Altshuller G.S. (2003). To find the Idea. 1st edition: Novosibirsk, Nauka, 1993, 2nd edution: Petrozavodsk, Scandinavia, 2003 (in Russian: Альтшуллер Г.С. Найти Идею, Новосибирск: Наука, 1-е издание, 1986; 2-е издание, 1991; 3-е изд., доп., Петрозаводск: Скандинавия,).

Altshuller G.S. (1989). Search for New Ideas: From Insight Towards Technology: Theory and Practice of Inventive Problem Solving. Kishinev, Karta Moldavenjaske, (In Russian: Альтшуллер Г.С., Злотин Б.Л., Зусман А.В. - Поиск новых идей: от озарения к технологии (теория и практика решения изобретательских задач). - Кишинев: Картя Молдовеняскэ.

Altshuller G.S. Vertkin I.M. (1994). How to Become a Genius: Life Strategy of Creative Personality. Minsk, Belarus, 1994 (In Russian: Альтшуллер Г.С., Верткин И.М. Как стать гением: Жизненная стратегия творческой личности. - Минск: Беларусь).

Altshuller G.S. (1982). Biological Effects as Analogy of Physical Effects, Baku, 1982 (In Russian: Альтшуллер Г.С. Биологические эффекты как аналогия физических эффектов, Баку.)

Altshuller, G.S. (2013). Altshullers's Foundation: Main Terms of TRIZ. Version 1.0 (In Russian: Фонд Альтшуллера: Основные термины ТРИЗ/ версия 1.0.

Amabile, Teresa M. (1983). The Social Psychology of Creativity. New York: Springer-Verlay

Andrews, Gregory R. (1991, March). Paradigms for Process Interaction in Distributed Programs. ACM Computing Surveys, 23 (1), pp. 49-90.

Andriole, Stephen J. (1985). Applications in Artificial Intelligence. Princeton: Petrocelli Books.

Andriole, Stephen J. (1986a). Microcomputer Decision Support Systems: Design, Implementation and Evaluation. Wellesley, MA: QED Information Sciences.

Andriole, Stephen J. (Ed.) (1986b). Software Validation, Verification, Testing and Documentation. Princeton: Petrocelli Books.

Annual Threat Report (2018). Produced by eSentire Threat Intelligence.

Anton, Corey (2015). A Heuristic Sketch of Lee Thayer's Systems Theory Orientation to Human Communication: Reflections on the Range of Open Systems. Grand Valley State University,

Aquinas, Thomas, Saint (1952). The Summa Theologica. Daniel J. Sullivan (Tr.). Chicago: The University of Chicago (The Great Books Edition), William Benton Publisher, Aquinas, Saint Thomas, De Veritate, Summa Theologiae, I, q. 14.

Aquinas, Thomas, St.: Summa Theologica, I, Q. 85. Art 7.

Argyris, C; Schön, Donald A. (1985) Strategy, Change and Defensive Routines. Ballinger: Cambridge, MA.

Argyris, Cris (1970). Intervention Theory and Method. Reading, MA: Addison-Wesley.

Argyris, Chris, et al., (1985). Action Science. San Francisco: Jossey-Bass.

Aristotle (1952). Works of Aristotle. W. D. Ross (Ed.), 12 Vols. Oxford: Clarendon, Press.

Armstrong, A. H. (1949). An Introduction to Ancient Philosophy. Chicago: Newman Press.

Arraj, James. Jungian Spirituality: The Question of Victor White, Spirituality Today, Autumn 1988, Vol. 40 No. 3, pp. 249-261.

Ashby, W.R. (1956). An Introduction to Cybernetics. London: Chapman and Hall.

Ashby, W.R. (1958). Requisite Variety and Its Implications for the Control of Complex Systems. Cybernetics, 1, pp. 1-17

Association For Computing Machinery. (1990, October). Proceedings of the Conference on Computer-Supported Cooperative Work, October 7-10, 1990 Los Angeles, CA. Sponsored by ACM SIGCHI & SIGOIS.

Augustine, of Hippo (1981). Basic Writings of St. Augustine. Oates & Whitney (Tr.). New York: Baker Books.

Auletta, Gennaro (2005). The Trialistic Structure in Physics, Spiritual Information: 100 Perspectives on Science and Religion, Charles L. Harper, Jr. ed. Philadelphia, PA: Templeton Foundation Press, 2005.

Austin, Charles F. (1966). Management's Self-Inflicted Wounds: A Formula for Managerial and Executive Self-Analysis. New York: Holt, Rinehart and Winston.

Ayer, Steve J. & Patrinostro, Frank S. (1992). Software Configuration Management Identification, Accounting, Control, & Management. New York: McGraw-Hill, Inc.

Baker, Richard H. (1985). The Computer Security Handbook. Blue Ridge Summit, PA: TAB Professional and Reference Books.

Banathy, Bela (1973). Developing a Systems View of Education. Seaside, CA: Intersystems Publications.

Banathy, Bela (1979). The Dynamics of Integrative Design. General Systems Research, a Science, a Methodology, a Technology. Louisville: Society for General Systems Research.

Banathy, Bela (1983). Systems Behavior. San Francisco: Saybrook Institute.

Banathy, Bela (1984). Systems Design in the Context of Human Activity Systems. San Francisco: International Systems Institute.

Banathy, B. H. & Mills, S. R. (1985). The Application of Living Systems Process Analysis in Education. ISI Monograph 85(7), pp. 1-16.

Banathy, Bela (1986a). The Design of Design Inquiry in the Context of Human Activity Systems. San Francisco: Far West laboratory for Educational Research and Development.

Banathy, Bela (1986b, October). A Systems View of Development. U.N. Educational, Scientific and Cultural Organization Symposium: Meeting of experts on goals of development. Budapest.

Banathy, Bela (1987a). The Design of Evolutionary Guidance Systems. San Francisco: Saybrook Institute

Banathy, Bela (1987b). The Characteristics and Acquisition of Evolutionary Competence. World Futures, 23, pp. 123-144.

Banathy, Bela (1987c). Choosing Design Methods. San Francisco: Far West Laboratory & Saybrook Graduate School.

Banathy, Bela, Ph.D. (1987). Design Inquiry, Vol.I, Edited by Bela Banathy, Ph.D. San Francisco, California: International Systems Institute.

Banathy, Bela (1987). Design Inquiry in the Context of Human Activity Systems: Design Systems and Systems Models. From Design Inquiry, Vol. I, edited by Bela Banathy, Ph.D. San Francisco, California: International Systems Institute.

Banathy, Bela (1988a). Matching Design Methods to System Type. San Francisco: Saybrook Institute.

Banathy, Bela (1988b). Goals of Development. Paris: U.N. Educational, Scientific and Cultural Organization.

Banathy, Bela (1989a). Design: A Journey to Create the Future, A Map of the Journey. Carmel: Far West Laboratory and Saybrook Institute.

Banathy, Bela (1989b). The Design of Evolutionary Guidance Systems. Systems Research, 4.

Banathy, Bela (1990). Design: A Journey to Create the Future, A Map of The Journey. R. Trappi (Ed.), Cybernetics and Systems, 1990: Proceedings of the Tenth European Meeting on Cybernetics and Systems Research. Singapore: World Scientific, pp. 197-204.

Banathy, Bela (1991). Systems Design of Education: A Journey to Create the Future. Englewood Cliffs: Educational Technology Publications.

Banathy, Bel (2010). Instructional Systems Design. Robert M. Gange (ED). Instructional Technology Foundations. Routledge Taylor & Francis Group. New Jersey.

Barr, Avron & Feigenbaum, Edward A. (1981). The Handbook of Artificial Intelligence, Volume 1. Los Altos, CA: William Kaufmann, Inc.

Barr, Avron & Feigenbaum, Edward A. (1982). The Handbook of Artificial Intelligence, Volume 2. Los Altos, CA: William Kaufmann, Inc.

Bateson, Gregory (1973). Steps to an Ecology of Mind. London: Paladin.

Bateson, Gregory (1979). Mind and Nature: A Necessary Unity. New York: E. P. Sutton.

Beckhard, Richard (1967). The Confrontation Meeting. Harvard Business Review, XLV(2), 149-153.

Beckhard, Richard (1969). Organization Development: Strategies and Models. Reading, MA: Addison-Wesley Publishing Company.

Beckhard, Richard & Harris, Reuben (1977). Organizational Transitions: Managing Complex Change. Reading, MA: Addison-Wesley Publishing Company.

Beckhard, Richard & Pritchard, Wendy (1992). Changing the Essence: The Art of Creating and Leading Fundamental Change in Organizations. San Francisco: Jossey Bass Publishers.

Beer, Stafford (1995). Diagnosing the System for Organizations. New York: Wiley.

Beer, Stafford (1995). Heart of the Enterprise. New York: Wiley.

Beer, Stafford (1994). Beyond Dispute: The Invention of Team Syntegrity. New York: John Wiley & Sons.

Beer, Stafford (1975). Platform for Change. New York: John Wiley & Sons.

Bellefontaine, Elizabeth. A Spirituality of Meaningful Experiences: Some Biblical Lesson, Spirituality Today, Autumn 1988, Vol. 40 No. 3, PP. 196-207.

Bennett, Roger (1989). Personal Effectiveness. London: Kogan Page Ltd.

Bennis, Warren (1969). Organization Development: Its Nature, Origins, and Prospects. Reading, MA: Addison-Wesley Publishing Company.

Bennis, Warren (1989a). Why Leaders Can't Lead: The Unconscious Conspiracy Continues. San Francisco: Jossey-Bass Publishers.

Bennis, Warren (1989b). On Becoming a Leader. Menlo Park: Addison-Wesley Publishing Company.

Bennis, Warren & Nanus, Burt (1985). Leaders The Strategies for Taking Charge. New York: Harper & Row, Publishers.

Bernstein, R. J. (1983) Beyond Objectivism and Relativism. Basil Blackwell: Oxford.

Bertalanffy, L. von (1950). The Theory of Open Systems in Physics and Biology. Emery (Ed.) (1969) Systems Thinking. Harmondsworth, England: Penguin.

Bertalanffy, L. von (1968). General Systems Theory. New York: Braziller.

Beruvides, Mario Ph.D. & Cantu, Jaime (2013). Isomorphological Analysis: The Theory of It All. Texas Tech University

Biggs et al. (2015). Strategies for Managing Complex Social-Ecological Systems in the Face of Uncertainty: Examples from South Africa and Beyond. Ecology & Society, Vol. 20, No.1, Art. 52

Boehm, B. A. (1981). Software Engineering Economics. Englewood Cliffs: Prentice-Hall, Inc.

Bogdanov, A. (1984). Essays in Tektology: The General Science of Organization. Seaside, CA: Intersystems Publications.

Boghossian, Paul A. (2007). Fear of Knowledge:Against Relativism and Constructivism. Oxford, England: Oxford University Press.

Boulding, Kenneth E. (1985). Human Betterment. Beverley Hills: Sage Publications.

Bowers, Todd, David. An Ontology for a Critical Systems Paradigm. Thesis submitted for the M.Phil./Ph.D. Upgrade. Centre for Systems Studies, Hull U. Business School. California State Polytechnic U. at Pomona January, 2009

Bowers, Todd D. (2008) An Ontology for a Critical Systems Paradigm. Ph.D. Upgrade. Hull University Business School, Unpublished.

Bowers, Todd D. (2011) Ontological Support for Multiparadigm Multimethodologies: Isomorphic Process–Structures and the Critical Moment. Proceedings of the 54th Meeting of the International Society for the Systems Sciences. Hull, U.K.

Bowers, Todd D. Ph.D. (2012) Towards a Framework for Multiparadigm Multimethodologies. Centre for Systems Studies, Hull University Business School, University of Hull: Hull.

Bowers, Todd David, Ph.D: Developments in Critical Systems Theory: On Paradigms and Incommensurability. Universidad del Norte – Barranquilla

Bowker, John W. (2005). God, Spiritual Information, and Downward Causation, Spiritual Information 100 Perspectives on Science and Religion, Charles L. Harper, Jr. (Ed.). Philadelphia, PA: Templeton Foundation Press. (pp. 479-483).

Boyd, Robert, D. & Myers, J. Gordon. Overcoming Leadership Scarcity: Discerning the Spiritual Journey, Spirituality Today, Autumn 1987, Vol. 39, pp. 225-240.

Branden, Nathaniel (1973). The Psychology of Self-Esteem. New York: Bantam Books.

British Telecommunications plc: How We Stay Ahead of a Changing Threat Landscape. (2018) Registered office: 81 Newgate Street, London EC1A 7AJ.

Bucker, Bill (2003). Spiritual Development and the Epistemology of Systems Theory, Journal of Psychology and Theology Vol. 31, 2003

Burrell, Gibson &Morgan, Gareth (1979) Sociological Paradigms and Organizational Analysis. Heinemann: London. Management Science, 17, B37–B53.

Capra, Fritjof (1982). The Turning Point. New York: Simon & Schuster

Capra, Fritjof (1991). The Tao of Physics, third edition. Boston: Shambhala.

Capra, Fritjof and Steindl-Rast (with Thomas Matus) (1991). Belonging to the Universe. San Francisco: Harper.

CERT National Insider Threat Center. Common Sense Guide to Mitigating Insider Threats, Sixth Edition. December 2018

Checkland, Peter B. (1981). Systems Thinking, Systems Practice. Wiley: Chichester.

Christakis, A. N. (1981). High Technology Participative Design: The Space Based Laser. Proceedings of the Annual Meeting, Society for General Systems Research. Louisville, KY.

Christakis, Alexander N. (1987). High Technoloqy Participative Desiqn: The Space Based Laser. From Design Inquiry, Vol.I., edited by Bela Banathy, Ph.D. San Francisco, California: International Systems Institute.

Churchman, C. West (1970). Operations Research as a Profession.

Churchman, C. W. (1971). The Design of Inquiring Systems. New York: John Wiley & Sons.

Churchman, C. W. (1979a). The Systems Approach and Its Enemies. New York: Basic Books. Churchman, C. W. (1979b). The Systems Approach. New York: Dell Publishing Company.

Churchman, C. W. (Ed.) (1989). The Well-Being of Organizations. Seaside, CA: Intersystems Publications.

Codd, E. F. (1990). The Relational Model for Database Management, Version 2. Menlo Park: Addison-Wesley Publishing Company.

Collen, Arne (1985). Experimental Method within Systems Methodology: The Case for and Against. Banathy, (Ed.). Proceedings of the Society for General Systems Research, 1, pp. 536-539.

Collen, Arne (1987, October). Living Systems Process Analysis for Program Evaluation. A paper presented at the annual meeting of the American Evaluation Association in Boston.

Collen, Arne (1988, May). Living Systems Methodology for Organizational Design and Redesign. Paper presented at the meetings of the International Society for General Systems Research, St. Louis, Missouri.

Collen, Arne (1990, April 10). Evolutionary Guidance Systems and Systems Design. A paper presented at the Tenth European Meeting on Cybernetics and Systems Research in Vienna.

Collen, Arne (1992). Methodological Perspectives on Human Systems, Design, and Learning for a More Global Ethic. San Francisco: Saybrook Institute.

Collen, Arne, Ph.D. & Newkirk, Raymond L. (1992). Cybernetics, Living Systems Theory, and Organizational Behavior. San Francisco & Concord, California: Saybrook Institute & Systems Management Institute (Paper for 13th international Congress on Cybernetics).

Collins, Robin A. (2005). Design and the Designer, Spiritual Information: 100 Perspectives on Science and Religion, Charles L. Harper, Jr. ed. Philadelphia, PA: Templeton Foundation Press.

Conrad, James W. (1988). Handbook of Communications Systems Management. Boston: Auerbach Publishers, Inc.

Conrad, James W. (1989). Handbook of Communications Systems Management, 1989 Yearbook. Boston: Auerbach Publishers, Inc.

Conrad, James W. (1990a). Handbook of Communications Systems Management, 1990-1991 Yearbook. Boston: Auerbach Publishers, Inc.

Conrad, James W. (1990b). Handbook of Communications Systems Management: Communications Standards. Boston: Auerbach Publishers, Inc.

Constantine, Larry (1995). Constantine on Peopleware, Yourdon Press.

Constantine, Larry & Ambler, Scott W. (2002). The Unified Process Transition and Production Phases Best Practices in Implementing the UP. CMP Books, Kansas

Craig & Houston-Ludlam (1989, May 25). A Psychological Framework for Testing. Sixth International Conference on Testing Computer Software, Ann Harbor, MI: Tec-Ed Technical Publications and Graphics Services.

Csanyi, Vilmos (1982). General Theory of Evolution. Budapest: Akademiai Kiado.

Davidow, William H. & Malone, Michael S. (1992). The Virtual Corporation: Structuring and Revitalizing the Corporation for the 21st Century. New York: Harper Collins Publishers.

Date, Christopher J. (1975). An Introduction to Database Systems. Addison-Wesley Publishing Company.

Date, Christopher J. (2001). The Database Relational Model: A Retrospective Review and Analysis: A Historical Account and Assessment of E.F. Codd's Contribution to the Field of Database Technology. Addison-Wesley.

Date, Christopher J. (2005). Database in Depth: Relational Theory for Practitioners. O'Reilly.

Date, Christopher J. (2006). The Relational Database Dictionary: A Comprehensive Glossary of Relational Terms and Concepts, with Illustrative Examples. O'Reilly.

Date, Christopher J. (2016). Type Inheritance and Relational Theory: Subtypes, Supertypes, and Substitutability. O'Reilly.

Date, Christopher J. (2009). SQL and Relational Theory: How to Write Accurate SQL Code. O'Reilly.

Davino, Louis. Francis of Assisi: Metaphor of Franciscan Maturity, Spirituality Today, Autumn 1987, Vol. 39, pp. 241-249.

Defense Systems Management College (1986a). Risk Management Concepts and Guidance. Fort Belvoir, VA: Defense Systems Management College.

Defense Systems Management College (1986b). Integrated Logistics Support Guide. Fort Belvoir, VA: Defense Systems Management College.

Defense Systems Management College (1987). Guide for the Management of Multinational Programs. Fort Belvoir, VA: Defense Systems Management College.

Defense Systems Management College (1988). Test and Evaluation Management Guide. Fort Belvoir, VA: Defense Systems Management College.

Defense Systems Management College (1989a). Defense Manufacturing Management: Guide for Program Managers Fort Belvoir, VA: Defense Systems Management College.

Defense Systems Management College (1989b). Systems Engineering Management Guide. Fort Belvoir, VA: Defense Systems Management College.

Defense Systems Management College (1990). Scheduling Guide for Program Managers. Fort Belvoir, VA: Defense Systems Management College.

DeMarco, Tom (1978). Structured Analysis and System Specification. Yourdon, New York.

DeMarco, Tom (1982). Controlling Software Projects, Yourdon Press.

DeMarco, Tom (1987). Peopleware: Productive Projects and Teams, Barnes & Noble.

DeMarco, Tom (2001). Slack: Getting Past Burnout, and the Myth of Total Efficiency. Broadway Books, New Your, New York.

DeMarco, Tom (2003). Waltzing with Bears: Managing Risks on Software Projects, Barnes & Noble

Denton, Michael, J. (2005). Henderson's Fine-Tuning Argument, Spiritual Information: 100 Perspectives on Science and Religion, Charles L. Harper, Jr. ed. Philadelphia, PA: Templeton Foundation Press, 2005.

Derek Melber, MVP (2020): Detecting Insider Threats and Attacks, Manage Engine Special Edition. John Wiley & Sons, New Jersey, 2020

Dickinson, Brian (1980). Developing Structured Systems: A Methodology Using Structured Techniques. New York: Yourdon Press.

Dickinson, Brian (1989). Developing Quality Systems: A Methodology Using Structured Techniques. New York: McGraw-Hill Book Company.

Dinsmore, Paul C. (1984). Human Factors in Project Management. New York: American Management Association Publications Group.

Domb, Ellen & Rantanen, Kalevi (2002): 40 Principles for Innovative Problem Solving. TRIZ, CRC Press.

Doohan, Leonard. Current Trends Scripture and Contemporary Spirituality, Spirituality Today, Spring 1990, Vol. 42 No. 1, pp. 62-74.

Downey, Michael. Current Trends Understanding Christian Spirituality: Dress Rehearsal for a Method, Spirituality Today, Fall 1991, Vol. 43 No. 3, pp. 271-280.

Drack, Manfred & Pouvreau, David (2006). On the History of Ludwig von Bertalanffy's "General Systemology", and on Its Relationship to Cybernetics Part I: Elements on the Origins and Genesis of Ludwig von Bertalanffy's "General Systemology." International Journal of General Systems, 44:5, 523-571,

Drack, Manfred & Pouvreau, David (2015). On the History of Ludwig Von Bertalanffy's "General Systemology", and on Its Relationship to Cybernetics – Part III: Convergences and Divergences. International Journal of General Systems, 44:5, 523-571, DOI:

Drucker, Peter (1989). The New Realities. New York: Harper & Row Publishers.

Drucker, Peter (1992). Managing for the Future: The 1990s and Beyond. New York: Truman Talley Books/Dutton.

Duffey, Michael K. Called to be Holy: The Reconvergence of Christian Morality and Spirituality, Spirituality Today, Winter 1986, Vol. 38, pp. 349-360.

Ellis, George, F.R. Progress in Scientific and Spiritual Understanding, Spiritual Information 100 Perspectives on Science and Religion, Charles L. Harper, Jr. ed. Philadelphia, PA: Templeton Foundation Press, 2005, pp. 130-131.

Emery, F. E. (1967). The Next Thirty Tears: Concepts, Methods and Anticipations. Human Relations 20(3), pp.199-237.

Emery, F. E. & Trist, E. L. (1960). Socio-Technical Systems. Management Science Models and Techniques, vol. 2. Churchman and Verhulst (Eds.). Oxford: Pergamon.

Emery, F. E. & Trist, E. L. (1973). Towards a Social Ecology: Appreciations of the Future in the Present. New York: Plenum.

Fals-Borda, O. Rahman, M.A. (1991) Action and Knowledge: Breaking the Monopoly with Participatory Action Research. Apex Press: New York.

Fensel, Dieter & Siorpaes, Katharina (2010): Intelligent Systems.

Fereidunian, Alireza e al: A Complex Adaptive System of Systems Approach to Human–Automation Interaction in Smart Grid. Smart Grid Lab, Faculty of Electrical Engineering, K. N. Toosi University of Technology,

Feyerabend, Paul (1993). Against Method, Third Edition. New York: Verso.

Flood, Robert L. (1989a). Archaeology of Systems Inquiry. Systems Practice., 2, 117-124.

Flood, Robert L. (1989b). Six Scenarios for the Future of Systems "Problem Solving". Systems Practice., 2, 75-99.

Flood, Robert L. (1990) Liberating Systems Theory. Plenum New York.

Flood, Robert L. (1993) Beyond TQM. Wiley:New York.

Flood, Robert L; Jackson, Michael C. (1991) Critical Systems Thinking: Directed Readings. Wiley: Chichester.

Flood, Robert L.; Romm, Norma R. A. (1995a). Diversity Management: Theory in Action. Systems Practice, 8(4), 469.

Flood, Robert L.; Romm, Norma R. A. (1995b) Enhancing the Process of Methodology Choice in Total Systems Intervention (TSI) and Improving Chances of Tackling Coercion. Systems Practice, 8(4), 377.

Flood, Robert L., Romm, Norma R. A. (1996): Critical Systems Thinking: Current Research and Practice. Plenum: New York London.

Florian, M. (1974). On the Teaching of Model Building: Mathematical Techniques and Data Analysis. B.A. Bayraktar, H. Muller-Merbach, J. E.

Folke, C. (2016). Resilience (Republished). Ecology and Society 21(4):44 https://doi.org/10.5751

Fricchione, Gregory L. (2005). Of Monocytes and the Spiritual Man, Spiritual Information: 100 Perspectves on Science and Religion, Charles L. Harper, Jr. ed. Philadelphia, PA: Templeton Foundation Press, 2005, pp. 400-405.

Gabriel, Henmar (1990). Tools and Techniques of Project Management. Tucson, AZ: Probity Corp.

Gadamer, Hans-Georg (1975). Truth and Method. London: Sheed and Ward.

Galbraith, Jay (1973). Designing Complex Organizations. Reading, MA: Addison-Wesley Publishing Company.

Gasparski, Wojciech (1984). Understanding Design: The Praxeological–Systemic Perspective. Seaside, CA: Intersystems Publications.

Georgiou, Ion (2007) Thinking Through Systems Thinking. Routledge: London.

Glasersfeld, Ernst von (1995) Radical Constructivism: A Way of Knowing and Learning. Falmer Press: London.

Gleiser, Marcelo (2005). Emergent Realities in the Cosmos, Spiritual Information: 100 Perspectives on Science and Religion, Charles L. Harper, Jr. ed. Philadelphia, PA: Templeton Foundation Press, 2005.

Goguen, Tad (1986). Designing Learning Systems for Anxiety Management in Clinical Training Systems. San Francisco: Saybrook Institute (Unpublished Essay).

Goodenough, Ursula (1998). The Sacred Depths of Nature, New York, New York: Oxford University Press.

Goodman, Nelson (1978). Ways of Worldmaking. Indianapolis, IN: Hackett Publishing

Gorin Yu. (1973). A Guide to Physical Effects for Solving Inventive Problems, Baku, (in Russian: Ю.Горин. Указатель Физических Эффектов для Решения Изобретательских Задач, Баку, 1973)

Green, Sara & Wolkenhauer, Olaf (2017). Tracing Organizing Principles: Learning from the History of Systems Biology. Stellenbosch Institute for Advanced Study (STIAS) Wallenberg Research Centre Stellenbosch University Marais Road, Stellenbosch, South Africa.

Gregory, Wendy J. Ph.D. (1992) Critical Systems Thinking and Pluralism: A New Constellation. Systems Science Department, The City University: London.

Gregory, Wendy J. (1996) Dealing with Diversity. In Flood, Robert L. and Romm, Norma R. A., eds. Critical Systems Thinking: Current Research and Practice. Plenum Press: New York, 37–61.

Gunderson and Holling (2002). Panarchy: Understanding Transformations in Human and Natural Systems. Environmental Management. Island Press.

Habermas, Jürgen (1981) The Theory of Communicative Action: Vol. One. Reason and the Rationalization of Society. Polity Press: Cambridge.

Hacking, Ian (1999). The Social Construction of What? Cambridge, Mass: Harvard University Press.

Haidar, Diana, et al. Any Threat: An Opportunistic Knowledge Discovery Approach to Insider Threat Detection. December 4, 2018.

Halkes, Catherina. Feminism and Spirituality, Spirituality Today, Autumn 1988, Vol. 40 No. 3, pp. 220-236.

Hardon, John A., S.J. Contemporary Spirituality, Father John A. Hardon Archives, Conference Transcription from a Retreat. (1988). Inter Mirifica. The Real Presence Association, Inc. 7030 West 63rd Street, Chicago: Ill.

Harper, Charles, Jr. (ED.) (2005). Spiritual Information. Templeton Foundation Press, Philadelphia.

Held, David (1980). Introduction to Critical Theory: Horkheimer to Habermas. Berkeley: University of California Press.

Hillman, James (1964). Emotions. Evanston, Ill.: Northwestern University Press.

Hodge, Richard. A Systems Approach to Strategy and Execution in National Security Enterprises. (PhD THESIS). Defense and Systems Institute, University of South Australia. 31 January 2010

Holling CS, Berkes F. & Folke C. (1998). Science, Sustainability and Resource Management. In: Berkes F. & Folke C. editors. Linking Social and Ecological Systems: Management Practices and Social Mechanisms for Building Resilience. Cambridge University Press, Cambridge.

Holt, Bradley P. (2005). Thirsty for God a Brief History of Christian Spirituality. Minneapolis, MINN: Fortress Press.

Hutchings, Alice, Clayton, Richard & Anderson, Ross: Taking Down Websites to Prevent Crime (2016). Computer Laboratory, University of Cambridge, Cambridge CB3 0FD

Huyssteen, J. Wentzel Van (2006). Alone in the World? Human Uniqueness in Science and Theology. William B. Eerdmans Publishing Company: Grand Rapids, Michigan.

Idinopulos, Thomas A. (1971). The Erosion of Faith an Inquiry into the Origins of the Contemporary Crisis in Religious Thought. Quadrangle Books Inc., Chicago, Ill.

Ingvar, David (1985). Memory of the Future:An Essay on the Temporal Organization of Conscious Awareness, Human Neurobiol, 1985; 4: 127-36.

Ivanov, Kristo (1989b). Computer Applications and Organizational Disease. The Well-Being of Organizations, C. West Churchman (Editor). pp. 283-312. Salinas, CA: Intersystems Publications.

Ivanov, Kristo (1989c). Information Systems Design through Creativity: A Tutorial Route Towards Aesthetics and Ethics. Umea, Sweden: University of Umea: Institute of Information Processing Department of Administrative Data Processing.

Ivanov, Kristo (1990). Hypersystems: A Base for Specification of Computer-Supported Self-Learning Social Systems. Umea, Sweden: University of Umea: Institute of Information Processing Administrative Data Processing.

Ivanov, Kristo (1991a). Computer-Supported Human Science or Humanistic Computing Science? Steps Toward the Evaluation of a Humanistic Computing Science. Umea, Sweden: University of Umea: Institute of Information Processing Administrative Data Processing.

Ivanov, Kristo (1991b). Computer-Human Interaction as Continuous System Reconstruction. Umea, Sweden: University of Umea, Institute of Information Processing Administrative Data Processing.

Ivanov, Kristo (1991c). Artificial Intelligence in the Context of Cultural Crisis. Umea, Sweden: University of Umea, Institute of Information Processing, Administrative Data Processing.

Ivanov, Kristo (1987). Rule of Law in Information Systems Research: The Role of Ethics in Knowledge-Building Procedures, Especially in the Updating of Inference Networks. Umea, Sweden: Umea University: Institute of Information Processing Administrative Data Processing.

Ivanov, Kristo (1989a). Ideas for Humanistic and Social Science Research about Consequences of the Increasing Use of Information Technology. Umea, Sweden: University of Umea: Institute of Information Processing.

Jackson,M. C.; Keys, P. (1984) Towards a System of Systems Methodologies. Operational Research Society, 35, 473-486.

Jackson, Michael C. (1985) Social Systems Theory and Practice: The Need for a Critical Approach. International Journal of General Systems.10, 135–151.

Jackson, Michael C. (1987). New Directions in Management Science. In Jackson, M. C. & Keys, P., eds. New Directions in Management Science. Gower: Aldershot, 133–164.

Jackson, Michael C. (1997) Pluralism in Systems Thinking and Practice. In Mingers, John C. & Gill, Anthony, eds. Multimethodology: The Theory and Practice of Combining Management Science Methodologies. John Wiley & Sons: Chichester, 347–37 8.

Jackson, Michael C. (1999) Towards Coherent Pluralism in Management Science. Journal of the Operational Research Society, 50, 12-22.

Jackson, Michael C. (2000) Systems Approaches to Management. Kluwer Academic/Plenum: New York, London.

Jaeger, Lydia (2005). Cosmic Order and Divine Word, Spiritual Information: 100 Perspectives on Science and Religion, Charles L. Harper, Jr. ed. Philadelphia, PA: Templeton Foundation Press, 2005.

Jantsch, E. (1976). Evolution and Consciousness. Reading, MA: Addison-Wesley.

Jantsch, E. (1981). The Evolutionary Vision. Boulder, CO: Westview Press.

Jantsch, E. & Waddington, C. H. (1976). Evolution and Consciousness: Human Systems in Transition. Reading, MA: Wiley.

Johnson-Laird, Philip N. (1988). The Computer and the Mind. Cambridge, MA: Harvard University Press.

Jones, Capers (1994). Assessment and Control of Software Risks. Yourdon Press.

Jones, Capers (2010). Software Engineering: Best Practices. McGraw-Hill.

Jones, Capers (2014). The Technical and Social History of Software Engineering. Addison-Wesley (Pearson Education).

Jones, Capers (2016). Software Methodologies, A Quantitative Guide. MathWorks, Inc.

Jones, Capers (2017). Quantifying Software: Global and Industry Perspectives. Auerbach Publications.

Jones, Peter H., PhD (2013). Social Systems. OCAD University, Toronto, Canada. Accepted chapter in: Social Systems and Design, Gary Metcalf (editor). Vol. 1 of the Translational Systems Science Series, Springer

Kallas, Endel. Spirituality on this Side of the Atlantic According to Alexis de Tocqueville, Spirituality Today, Winter 1985, Vol. 37, pp. 292-303.

Kaminsky, Donna Marie F. Secular Franciscans: Bearers of Peace, Messengers of Joy, Spirituality Today, Summer 1985, Vol. 37, pp. 120-129.

Kaplan S., Visnepolschi S., Zlotin B. & Zusman, A. (1999). New Tools for Failure and Risk Analysis: An Introduction to Anticipatory Failure Determination (AFD) and The Theory of Scenario Structuring, Ideation International Inc., 1999

Kennan, James, F., S.J. (2004). Moral Wisdom: Lessons and Texts from the Catholic Tradition, Claretian Publications, Quezon City, Philippines

Khomenko N. TRIZ as a General Theory of Powerful Thinking (OTSM), collection of articles, 1992-2003, http://www.trizminsk.org/e/prs/kho.htm Last seen: 01.12.2013.

Kilpatrick, William (2012). Christianity, Islam, and Atheism: The Struggle for the Soul of the West. Ignatius Press, San Francisco

Klir, G. (1985). Architecture of Systems Problem Solving. New York: Plenum Press.

Klubertanz, George P., S. J. (1953). The Philosophy of Human Nature. New York: Appleton-Century Crofts, Inc.

Klubertanz, George P., S. J. (1955). Introduction to the Philosophy of Being. Englewood Cliffs: Prentice-Hall, Inc.

Korolyov V.A. Glossary of TRIZ-OTSM Terms. (In Russian: Королёв В.А. Справочник терминов ТРИЗ-ОТСМ. 13 редакция.) http://www.triz.org.ua/enc/ Last seen: 01.12.2013.

Korzybski, Alfred, Science and Sanity: An introduction to Non-Aristotelian Systems and General Semantics, Institute of General Semantics, Lakeville, Conn, 1933.

Kotarbinski, T. (1966). Gnosiology: The Scientific Approach to the Theory of Knowledge. Oxford: Pergamon

Kremer, J. W. (1986). The Human Science Approach as Discourse. The Saybrook Review, 6(1). Spring, pp. 65-106.

Krippner, Stanley, et al. (1985). Toward the Application of General Systems Theory in Humanistic Psychology. Systems Research, 2(2), pp. 105-115. London: International Federation for Systems Research, Pergamon Press Ltd.

Kuhn, T. S. (1970). The Structure of Scientific Revolutions. Chicago: University of Chicago Press.

Kuong, Javier F. (1987). Computer Auditing, Security & Internal Control Manual. Englewood Cliffs: Prentice-Hall, Inc

Land, George & Jarman, Beth (1992). Breakpoint and Beyond: Mastering the Future - Today. New York: Harper Business.

Lane, Byron (1985). Managing People. Sunnyvale, CA: Oasis Press.

Langsam, Jude. The Discalced Carmelite Secular Order: One Member's View, Spirituality Today, Summer 1985, Vol. 37, pp. 130-139.

Lantz, Kenneth E. (1986). The Prototyping Methodology. Englewood Cliffs: Prentice-Hall

Laszlo, Ervin (1972a). Introduction to Systems Philosophy. New York: Gordon & Breach; Harper Torchbooks (2nd ed. 1973).

Laszlo, Ervin (1972b). The Systems View of the World. New York: George Braziller.

Lawler, Edward E. III & Rhode, John Grant (1976). Information and Control in Organizations. Pacific Palisades, CA: Goodyear Publishing Company, Inc.

Lecarme, Olivier & Gart, Mireille Pellissier (1986). Software Portability. New York: McGraw-Hill Book Company.

Lehman, M. M. (1980, September). Programs, Life Cycles, and Laws of Software Evolution. Proceedings of the IEEE, 68(9), pp. 1060-1076.

LeShan, Lawrence, Ph.D. (1990). The Dilemma of Psychology:A Psychologist Looks at His Troubled Profession. New York: Penguin Books.

Levenson, Edgar A. (1972). The Fallacy of Understanding: An Inquiry into the Changing Structure of Psychoanalysis. New York: Basic Books, Inc.

Levin, Ben: (2013) The Simple Art of Governing Complex Systems. University of Toronto.

Levinson, Harry (1972). Organizational Diagnosis. Cambridge: Harvard University Press.

Lewis, David & Greene, James (1982). Thinking Better. New York: Rawson, Wade Publishers.

Lewton, Joel, C. Reformed Spirituality: Towards the Development of a Transcendent Community, Spirituality Today, Autumn 1989, Vol. 41 No. 3, pp. 213-225.

Lightedge (2016): Cyberattack Threat and Prevention: Protecting Your Organization Can Be Easy for You.

Linde, Andrei (2005). Choose Your Own Universe, Spiritual Information 100 Perspectives on Science and Religion, Charles L.

Litterer, Joseph A. (1973). The Analysis of Organizations. New York: John Wiley & Sons.

Litvin S, A. Lyrbomirskiy A., Sigalovskaya I. G3:ID Method Glossary. (In Russian: С.Литвин, А.Любомирский, И.Сигаловская. Глоссарий к методике G3:ID.) http://gen3.ru/ru/3605/5453/. Last seen: 01.12.2013.

Litvin S., Lyobomirskiy A. Laws of Engineering Systems Evolution (In Russian: Законы развития технических систем. А.Любомирский, С.Литвин.)

Litvin S., Petrov V., Rubin M., (2007). TRIZ Body of Knowledge.

Lobel, Jerome (1986). Foiling the System Breakers: Computer Security and Access Control. New York: McGraw-Hill Book Company.

Lundell, Jay & Notess, Mark (1991). Human Factors in Software Development: Models, Techniques, and Outcomes. Human Factors in Computing Systems: Reaching through Technology, CHI '91 Conference Proceedings. Robertson, Scott P., Olson, Gary M., & Olson, Judith (Eds.). April-May, pp. 145-152. New Orleans, LA: ACM SIGCHI.

Lundy, James L. (1991). Lead, Follow, or Get Out of the Way: Invaluable Insights into Leadership Style. Quezon City, Philippines: Kadena Press, University of the Philippines.

Maccoby, Michael (1988). Why Work: Motivating and Leading the New Generation. New York: Simon & Schuster.

Mackintosh, Hugh Ross (1937). Types of Modern Theology. New York, New York: Scribner's.

MacIntyre, Alisdair (1966). A Short History of Ethics. A History of Moral Philosophy from the Homeric Age to the 20th Century. University of Notre Dame Press.

MacIntyre, Alisdair (1981). After Virtue, A Study in Moral Theory. Notre Dame University Press.

MacIntyre, Alisdair (1988). Whose Justice? Which Rationality? University of Notre Dame Press.

MacIntyre, Alisdair (2006). The Tasks of Philosophy. University of Notre Dame Press.

MacIntyre, Alisdair (2016). Ethics in the Conflicts of Modernity. An Essay on Desire, Practice Reasoning, and Narrative. Cambridge University Press.

Macnaughton, Ian (1987). Design in the Context of Human Activity Systems. San Francisco: Saybrook Institute (Unpublished Essay).

Madala, S. & Sinclair, J. B. (1991, January). Performance of Synchronous Parallel Algorithms with Regular Structures. IEEE Transactions on Parallel and Distributed Systems, 2(1). Washington, D.C: IEEE Computer Society.

Magnin, Thierry (2005). Quantum Logic and the God-World Relationship: A New Resource for Exploring Modern Christian Theology, Spiritual Information: 100 Perspectives on Science and Religion, Charles L. Harper, Jr. ed. Philadelphia, PA: Templeton Foundation Press.

Mair, William C., Wood, Donald R., & Davis, Keagle W. (1972). Computer Control & Audit. Wellesley, MA: Q.E.D. Information Sciences, Inc.

Management Research Group (1983). Management Effectiveness Analysis. Portland, ME: Management Research Group.

Management Research Group (1987). Leadership Effectiveness Analysis: An Introductory Guide. Portland, ME: Management Research Group.

Manzini, Andrew O. (1988). Organizational Diagnosis: A Practical Approach to Company Problem Solving and Growth. New York: American Management Association.

Manzini, Andrew O. & Gridley, John D. (1986). Integrating Human Resources and Strategic Business Planning. New York: American Management Association.

Maritain, Jacque (1952). Range of Reason. New York: Charles Scribner & Sons.

Martel, Leon (1986). Mastering Change: The Key to Business Success. London: Grafton Books.

Martin, James (1973). Security, Accuracy and Privacy in Computer Systems. Englewood Cliffs: Prentice-Hall, Inc.

Martin, James (1984). An Information Systems Manifesto. Englewood Cliffs: Prentice-Hall,

Martin, James (1985a). System Design from Provably Correct Constructs. Englewood Cliffs: Prentice-Hall, Inc.

Martin, James & McClure, Carma (1983). Software Maintenance: The Problem and Its Solutions. Englewood Cliffs: Prentice-Hall, Inc.

Martin, James & McClure, Carma (1988). Structured Techniques: The Basis of CASE. Englewood Cliffs: Prentice-Hall, Inc.

Martin, James & Oxman, Steven (1988). Building Expert Systems: A Tutorial. Englewood Cliffs: Prentice-Hall, Inc.

Marty, Martin E. If Theologians Do Not Measure, Can They Measure Up? Rules For Acquiring Spiritual Information, Spiritual Information 100 Perspectives on Science and Religion, Charles L. Harper, Jr. ed. Philadelphia, PA: Templeton Foundation Press, 2005, pp. 473-478.

Mattessich, Richard (1982). The Systems Approach: Its Variety of Aspects. Journal of the American Society for Information Science.

Maturana, Humberto R. (1988). Ontology of Observing: The Biological Foundations of Self-Consciousness.

Matvienko N.N. TRIZ Terms (Problem Collection). (In Russian: Матвиенко Н.Н. Термины ТРИЗ (проблемный сборник). http://www.metodolog.ru/node/689. Last seen: 01.12.2013.

Mayer, Michael (1984). The Mystery of Personal Identity. San Diego: ACS Publications, Inc.

McCabe, Thomas J. (1980). Software Quality Assurance: A Survey. Columbia, MD: McCabe & Associates.

McClelland, James L., Rumelhart, David E. & The PDP Research Group (1986). Parallel Distributed Processing: Explorations in the Microstructures of Cognition, Volume 2: Psychological and Biological Models. Cambridge, MA: The MIT Press.

McGinn, Bernard (2005). The Letter and the Spirit: Spirituality as an Academic Discipline, in Mind the Spirit: The Study of Christian Spirituality. Elizabeth A. Dreyer & Mark S. Burrows (Eds.). Baltimore, MD: The Johns Hopkins University Press. pp. 25-41.

McKie, James W. (Ed.) (1974). Social Responsibility and the Business Predicament. Washington, D.C: The Brookings Institution.

McLean (1976). The Human Side of Systems: The User's Perspective. Presented at the Western Systems Conference. Los Angeles.

McManus, Sonia, et al., (2017). Resilience Management: A Framework for Assessing and Improving the Resilience of Organizations. Resilient Organizations Research Report 2007/01 New Zealand

McMillan, Grant R., et al. (1989). Applications of Human Performance Models to System Design. New York: Plenum Press.

McNamara, Curt (1987). Designing The Future: The Possibility-Space and the Information Environment. From Design Inquiry, Vol. I. edited by Bela Banathy, Ph.D. San Francisco, California: International Systems Institute.

McNicholas, James B. III & Houssain Kettani (2019). Consideration of Insider Based

Collusion Attacks on Cyber Systems.

Mercer, Michael W. (1989). Turning Your Human Resources Department Into a Profit Center. New York: AMACOM.

Merker, S. L. (1985). Living Systems Theory: A Framework for Management. Behavioral Science, 30, pp. 187-194.

Merker, S. L. (1986). Living Systems Process Analysis in the Far-East: A Review of Two Studies. Proceedings of the Society for General Systems Research, 1, G., pp. 42-51.

Metzger, Philip W. (1987). Managing Programming People: A Personal View. Englewood Cliffs: Prentice-Hall, Inc

Midgley, Gerald (1989). Critical Systems: The Theory and Practice of Partitioning Methodologies. Proceedings of the 33rd Annual Meeting of the International Society for General Systems Research. Edinburgh.

Midgley, Gerald (1992). Pluralism and the Legitimation of Systems Science. Systems Practice, 5(2), 147-172.

Midgley, Gerald (1996). What Is This Thing Called CST? Flood, Robert. L. and Romm, N. R. A., eds. Critical Systems Thinking: Current Research and Practice. Plenum: New York, 11–24.

Midgley, Gerald (2000). Systemic Intervention: Philosophy, Methodology, and Practice. Kluwer Academic/Plenum: New York.

Midgley, Gerald (2011). Theoretical Pluralism in Systemic Action Research. Systems Practice and Action Research, 24(1), 1–15.

Miller, Eric (Ed.). (1991). Future Vision: The 189 Most Important Trends of the 1990s. Naperville, IL: Sourcebooks Trade.

Miller, G. A. (1978). The Magical Number Seven, Plus or Minus Two: Some Limits in Our Capacity for Processing Information. Psychology Review, 63(2), pp. 81-97.

Miller, J. G. (1978). Living Systems. New York: McGraw-Hill Book Company.

Miller, J. G. & Miller, J. L. (1980). The Family as a System. C. Hofling and J. Lewis (Eds.), The Family: Evaluation and Treatment, pp. 141-184, New York: Brunner/Mazel.

Miller, J. G. & Miller, J. L. (1989). A General Living Systems Analysis of Organizational Pathology. The Well-Being of Organizations, C. West Churchman (Ed.). Salinas, CA: Intersystems Publications.

Mills, D. Quinn (1991). Rebirth of the Corporation. New York: John Wiley & Sons, Inc.

Mingers, John C. (2000). The Contribution of Critical Realism as an Underpinning Philosophy for OR/MS and Systems. Journal of the Operational Research Society, 51(11), 12561270.

Mingers, John C. (2003). A Classification of the Philosophical Assumptions of Management Science Methods. Journal of the Operational Research Society, 54(6), 559-570 doi: 10.1057/palgrave.jors. 2601436|ISSN 0160-5682.

Mingers, John C. (2006). Realising Systems Thinking: Knowledge and Action in Management Science. Springer: New York.

Mishkoff, Henry C. (1985). Understanding Artificial Intelligence. Dallas: Texas Instruments.

Mitroff, I. I. & Kilmann, R. H. (1978). Methodological Approaches to Social Sciences. San Francisco: Jossey-Bass.

Mohrman, Susan Albers & Cummings, Thomas G. (1989). Self-Designing Organizations: Learning How to Create High Performance. Menlo Park, CA: Addison-Wesley Publishing Company.

Montalbano, Michael (1974). Decisions Tables. Chicago: Science Research Associates, Inc

Montazemi, Ali Reza & Gupta Kalyan Moy (2006): A Framework for Retrieval in Case-Based Reasoning Systems. School of Business, McMaster University, Hamilton, Ontario, Canada L8S 4M4

Montelibano, Joji & Andrew Moore (2012): Insider Threat Security Reference Architecture.

Morgan, Gareth (1986). Images of Organization. Sage: London.

Mowshowitz, A. (1976). The Conquest of Will: Information Processing in Human Affairs. Reading, MA: Addison-Wesley.

Muftic, Sead (1989). Security Mechanisms for Computer Networks. New York: Halstead Press, a Division of John Wiley & Sons.

Mulligan, Robert W., S. J. (1952). Truth: A Translation of Quaestiones Disputatae Deveritate, Questions I-IX of St.Thomas Aquinas. Chicago: Henry Regnery Company.

Murdoch, Iris (1992). Metaphysics as a Guide to Morals. New York, New York: The Penguin Press.

Murphy, Michael A. & Parker, Xenia Ley (1989). Handbook of EDP Auditing. Boston: Warren, Gorham & Lamont, Inc.

Murphy, Nancey, C. (2005). The Role of Discernment in Seeking Spiritual Knowledge, Spiritual Information: 100 Perspectives on Science and Religion, Charles L. Harper, Jr. ed. Philadelphia, PA: Templeton Foundation Press, 2005.

Musa, Iannino & Okumoto (1987). Software Reliability: Measurement, Prediction, and Application. New York: McGraw-Hill, Inc.

Myers, Glendord J. (1975). Reliable Software through Composite Design. New York: Van Nostrand Reinhold Company.

Myers, Glendord J. (1976). Software Reliability. New York: John Wiley & Sons.

Nadel, Robert B. (1987). Avoiding Micro-Computer Headaches: How to Control the Acquisition, Use, and Security Risks of Microcomputers. New York: McGraw-Hill Book Company.

Nadler, David A. (1977). Feedback and Organization Development: Using Data-Based Methods. Reading, MA: Addison-Wesley Publishing Company.

Nadler, Gerald (1967). Work Systems Design: The Ideals Concept. Homewood, IL: Richard D. Irwin, Inc.

Nadler, Gerald (1987). An Assessment of Systems Methodology and Design. B. H. Banathy (Ed.), Systems Inquiry, pp. 114-123. Louisville, KY: Society for General Systems Research.

Nadler, Gerald & Hibino, Shozo (1990). Breakthrough Thinking: Why We Must Change the Way We Solve Problems, and the Seven Principles to Achieve This. Rocklin, CA: Prima Publishing & Communications.

National Computer Security Center (1985). Personal Computer Security Considerations. Washington, D.C: National Computer Security Center.

National Computer Security Center (1988). Glossary of Computer Security Terms. Washington, D.C: National Computer Security Center.

Naughton, J. (1977). The Checkland Methodology: A Readers Guide, Second Edition. Milton Keynes: Open University Press.

Nemoto, Masao (1987). Total Quality Control for Management: Strategies and Techniques from Toyota and Toyoda Gosei. Englewood Cliffs: Prentice-Hall, Inc.

Newkirk, Raymond L. (1976). The Descent of Man. New York: NYIT.

Newkirk, Raymond L. (1979). Preliminary Phased Development Process Plan. Fort Lauderdale, FL: Systems Engineering Laboratories.

Newkirk, Raymond L. (1981a). Preliminary Phased Documentation: An Overview. Fort Lauderdale, FL: Systems Engineering Laboratories.

Newkirk, Raymond L. (1981b). Phased Documentation Process: An Overview. Fort Lauderdale, FL: Systems Engineering Laboratories.

Newkirk, Raymond L. (1982). The Chronicles of the Making of a Philosopher: Book I, What is Philosophy? Fort Lauderdale, FL: Columbia Pacific University, (Master Thesis).

Newkirk, Raymond L. (1982). The Chronicles of the Making of a Philosopher: Book II, Metaphysicas is Life in Motion. Fort Lauderdale, FL: Columbia Pacific University.

Newkirk, Raymond L. (1982). The Chronicles of the Making of a Philosopher: Book III, Theocity and the Human Spirit. Fort Lauderdale, FL: Columbia Pacific University,

Newkirk, Raymond L. (1982). The Chronicles of the Making of a Philosopher: Book IV, Mother Philosophy, Love of the Ages? Fort Lauderdale, FL: Columbia Pacific University,

Newkirk, Raymond L. (1982). The Chronicles of the Making of a Philosopher: Book V, Part 1, In Defense of Reason, Fort Lauderdale, FL: Columbia Pacific University.

Newkirk, Raymond L. (1982). The Chronicles of the Making of a Philosopher: Book V, Part II, In Defense of Reason, Fort Lauderdale, FL: Columbia Pacific University.

Newkirk, Raymond L. (1984a). Phased Development Process: An Overview. Jeddah, KSA: Royal Saudi Naval Forces.

Newkirk, Raymond L. (1984b). Project "A" Documentation Enhancement Plan. Jeddah, KSA: Royal Saudi Naval Forces (RSNF).

Newkirk, Raymond L. (1984c). The Process Philosophy of Project "A". Jeddah, KSA: RSNF.

Newkirk, Raymond L. & Reynolds, Michael L. (1984a). Phased Development Process: Project "A" Master Schedule. Jeddah, KSA: Royal Saudi Naval Forces.

Newkirk, Raymond L. & Reynolds, Michael L. (1984b). Phased Development Process: Project "A" Project Management Plan the Naval Supply Center Phased Automated Process. Jeddah, KSA: Royal Saudi Naval Forces.

Newkirk, Raymond L. & Reynolds, Michael L. (1984c). Phased Development Process: An Overview of the Project "A" Procedures Management Systems. Jeddah, KSA: RSNF.

Newkirk, Raymond L. & Reynolds, Michael L. (1984d). Phased Development Process: Project "A" Master Plan. Jeddah, KSA: Royal Saudi Naval Forces.

Newkirk, Raymond L. (1985a). Implementation Planning for Information Center Management, Vol.1. Quezon City, Philippine Islands: International Association for Information Management.

Newkirk, Raymond L. (1985b). Implementation Planning for Information Center Management, Vol. 2. Quezon City, Philippine Islands: International Association for Information Management.

Newkirk, Raymond L. (1985c). Phased Development Process Project "L" the Long-Range Plan for AFP: Automated Integrated Logistics Systems. Manila: IAIM.

Newkirk, Raymond L. (1986a). Post Implementation Review Handbook. Pleasant Hill, CA: (Pacific Bell MTS Project Document).

Newkirk, Raymond L. (1986b). Gestalt Training Process: Phased Training Plan Guidelines for Water and Sewer Customer Information and Billing System. San Francisco: IAIM.

Newkirk, Raymond L. (1987a). Post Implementation Review Handbook for Pacific Bell. San Ramon, CA: International Association of Information Management Press.

Newkirk, Raymond L. (1987b). A Systems Models Description of a Software Development System. San Francisco: Saybrook Institute.

Newkirk, Raymond L. (1988a). Operations Management in the 1990's. Pleasant Hill, CA: SMI.

Newkirk, Raymond L. (1988b). A Deductive Process Model of the Computer Software Development Human Activity System. Pleasant Hill, CA: Saybrook Institute.

Newkirk, Raymond L. (1988c). An LSPA Description of the Computer Software Development Human Activity System. San Francisco: Saybrook Institute.

Newkirk, Raymond L. (1988d). An Emerging Redesign of the Computer Software Development Human Activity System Using Living Systems Theory Guided by the Systems Models Approach. San Francisco: Saybrook Institute.

Newkirk, Raymond L. (1988e). Three Alternative Root Definitions of the Computer Software Development Human Activity System. San Francisco: Saybrook Institute

Newkirk, Raymond L. (1988f). A Conceptual Model of a Problem Situation Existing in the Software Development Human Activity System. San Francisco: Saybrook Institute

Newkirk, Raymond L. (1988g). A Project Proposal for the Design of a Computer Software Development Human Activity System. San Francisco: Saybrook Institute.

Newkirk, Raymond L. (1988h). The Nature and Characterization of Human Activity Systems in General and the Computer Software Development Human Activity System in Particular. San Francisco: Saybrook Institute.

Newkirk, Raymond L. (1988i). A Description of the Software Development Human Activity System. San Francisco: Saybrook Institute.

Newkirk, Raymond L. (1988j). A Comprehensive Characterization and Description of the Software Development Human Activity System. San Francisco: Saybrook Institute.

Newkirk, Raymond L. (1988k). Integrating Human Resource Planning with the Information Technology Business Plan: The Path to Contingency Planning. Pleasant Hill, CA: SMI.

Newkirk, Raymond L. (1989a). Capacity Management of the Corporate Computer System. Pleasant Hill, CA: Systems Management Institute Press.

Newkirk, Raymond L. (1989b). The Living Systems Approach: A New Software Design Paradigm for the 21st Century and Beyond. Pleasant Hill, CA: Saybrook Institute.

Newkirk, Raymond L. (1989c). Software Quality Assurance and Control. Pleasant-Hill, CA: Systems Management Institute.

Newkirk, Raymond L. (1989d). Design Operations and Tasks Leading to the Redesign of the Computer Software Development Human Activity System. San Francisco: Saybrook Institute.

Newkirk, Raymond L. (1989e). The Design System Supporting the Redesign of the Computer Software Development Human Activity System. San Francisco: Saybrook Institute.

Newkirk, Raymond L. (1989f). Developmental Objectives and Plans Supporting the Redesign of the Computer Software Development Human Activity System. San Francisco: Saybrook Inst.

Newkirk, Raymond L. (1989g). The Living Systems Approach a New Software Design Paradigm for the 21st Century and Beyond. San Francisco: Saybrook Institute.

Newkirk, Raymond L. (1989h). Revised Approach for the Design of the Software Development Human Activity System. San Francisco: Saybrook Institute.

Newkirk, Raymond L. (1989i). A Review of the Traditional Approach to Computer Software Development – An Ideology Critique. San Francisco: Saybrook Institute.

Newkirk, Raymond L. (1989j). The Creativity Myth: A New Software Design Paradigm for the 21st Century and Beyond. San Francisco: Saybrook Institute.

Newkirk, Raymond L. (1990a). SPAC Real Time Processing System Operational Evaluation Audit Handbook, Vol. I. Pleasant Hill, CA: Systems Management Institute Press.

Newkirk, Raymond L. (1990b). SPAC Real Time Processing System Operational Evaluation Audit Handbook, Vol.II. Pleasant Hill, CA: Systems Management Institute Press.

Newkirk, Raymond L. (1990c). Design Evaluation and Measurement: Evolutionary Guidance. System, San Francisco: Saybrook Institute.

Newkirk, Raymond L. (1990d). Executive Information Systems: Foundation for Tomorrow. Pleasant Hill, CA: Systems Management Institute.

Newkirk, Raymond L. (1990e). The Design of the Software Development Group as a Systems Issue. San Francisco: Saybrook Institute.

Newkirk, Raymond L. (1990f). A Research Proposal for the Redesign of the Software Quality and Control Group. San Francisco: Saybrook Institute.

Newkirk, Raymond L. (1991a). Metamethodology Design Foundation for Tomorrow. Pleasant Hill, CA: Systems Management Institute.

Newkirk, Raymond L. (1991b). Philosophical Foundation of a Metamethodology for Design Inquiry in Software Development Human Activity Systems. San Francisco, CA: Saybrook.

Newkirk, Raymond L. (1992). Using the Human Systems Methodology to Design the Strategic Organization. Concord, CA: Systems Management Institute (Seminar Presentation).

Newkirk, Raymond L. (1999). Beyond the Year 2000 Crisis, Systems Management Institute Press, Pleasant Hill, CA

Newkirk, Raymond L. (2006). Leading By Design. Booklocker, FL

Newkirk, Raymond L. (2019). The Benefits of Human-Centered Insider Threat Prevention. Systems Management Institute Press. Orlando. FL.

Niebling, Carl & Christie, Marian (1991). Competitive Behavior. Wassenaar, The Netherlands: Niebling Productions.

NIST (2018). Cybersecurity is Everyone's Job. Publication of the National Initiative for Cybersecurity Education Working Group: Subgroup on Workforce Management at the National Institute of Standards and Technology.

Norman, Maxwell H. (1974). Dimensions of the Future Alternatives for Tomorrow. New York: Holt, Rinehart and Winston, Inc.

O'Connell, Patrick, F. St Francis of Assisi: The Spirituality of Conformation, Spirituality Today, Winder 1986, Vol. 38, pp. 1-11.

Offerman, Lynn R. & Growing, Marilyn K. (1990, February). Organizations of the Future: Changes and Challenges. American Psychologist, 45(2), pp. 95-108.

Ohmae, Kenichi (1990). The Borderless World: Power and Strategy in the Interlinked Economy. New York: Harper Business, Harper Collins Publishers.

Oldham, John M., M.D. & Morris, Lois B. (1990). Personality Self-Portrait: Why You Think, Work, Love, and Act the Way You Do. New York: Bantam Books.

Olle, Hagelstein, et al. (1988). Information Systems Methodologies: A Framework for Understanding. Menlo Park, CA: Addison-Wesley Publishing Company.

Ormerod, R.J (2008). The Transformation Competence Perspective. University of Warwick, Coventry, UK

Orr, Ken (1977). Structured Systems Development. Yourdon Press.

Orr, Ken (1981). Structured Requirements Definition. Ken Orr, Publisher, Kansas

Orr, Ken (2984). The One Minute Methodology. Optima Inc.

Oskamp, Stuart (1990). Overconfidence in Case-Study Judgments. Judgment Under Uncertainty: Heuristics and Biases. Kahneman, Slovic & Tversky (Eds.), Cambridge, England: Cambridge University Press.

Ostrom, E. (2007). A Diagnostic Approach for Going beyond Panaceas. PNAS 104: 15181-15187.

Ouellette, L. Paul (1992). How to Market the I/S Department Internally: Gaining the Recognition & Strategic Position You Merit. New York: AMACOM.

Overton, Willis F. (1975). General Systems, Structure, and Development. Structure and Transformation: Developmental and Historical Aspects, Volume 3., Chapter 4. John Wiley & Sons., Inc.

Overton, Willis F. & Ennis, Michelle D. (2006). Cognitive-Developmental and Behavioral-Analytic Theories: Evolving into Complementarity. Journal of Human Development. Temple U.

Pagels, Heinz (1988). The Dreams of Reason: The Computer and the Rise of the Sciences of Complexity. New York: Simon and Schuster.

Pandikattu, Kuruvilla (2005). Spiritual Information for Integral Transformation, Spiritual Information 100 Perspectives on Science and Religion, Charles L. Harper, Jr. ed. Philadelphia, PA: Templeton Foundation Press.

Parberry, Ian (1987). Parallel Complexity Theory. New York: John Wiley & Sons.

Parentchik G.I., (2013). Terminological Aspect of TRIZ. (In Russian: Паренчик Г.И. Терминологический Аспект ТРИЗ). http://www.metodolog.ru/00252/00252.html Last seen: 01.12.2013.

Parikh, Girisj (1982). How to Measure Programmer Productivity. Wellesley, MA: Q.E.D. Information Sciences, Inc.

Parker, D. B. (1976). Crime by Computer. New York: Scribner's.

Parker, Nycum & Oura (1973). Computer Abuse. Washington, D. C: National Technical Information Service.

Pascale, Richard Tanner (1990). Managing on the Edge: How the Smartest Companies Use Conflict to Stay Ahead New York: Simon and Schuster.

Pasmore, William A. (1988). Designing Effective Organizations: The Sociotechnical Systems Perspective. New York: John Wiley & Sons.

Pava, C. (1983). Managing New Office Technology: An Organizational Strategy. New York: The Free Press.

Pelikan, Jaroslav, and Lehmann, Helmut T. eds. Luther's Works, 56 vols. St. Louis: Concordia Publishing House. Philadelphia: Fortress Press, 1955: 37:228.

Penzias, Arno (1989). IDEAS and Information. New York: Simon Schuster, Inc.

Perlmutter, H. (1965). Towards a Theory and Practice of Human Architecture. London: Tavistock.

Perls, Frederick S. (1971). Gestalt Therapy Verbatim. New York: Bantam Books.

Perry, D. E. & Kaiser, G. E. (1991, March). Models of Software Development Environments. IEEE Transactions on Software Engineering,17(3). College Park, MD: IEEE Computer Society.

Perry, William (1986). A Standard for Auditing Computer Applications: Selected Audit Areas. Pennsauken, NJ: Auerbach Publishers, Inc.

Perry, William (1986). A Standard for Auditing Computer Applications: Auditing Microcomputer Systems. Pennsauken, NJ: Auerbach Publishers, Inc.

Perry, William (1986). Cleaning Up a Computer Mess: A Guide to Diagnosing and Correcting Computer Problems. New York: Van Nostrand Reinhold Company.

Perry, William (1987). A Standard for Testing Applications Software: Testing Computer Security. Boston: Auerbach Publishers, Inc.

Peters, Tom (1987). Thriving on Chaos: The Handbook for a Management Revolution. New York: Alfred A. Knopf.

Peters, Tom (1993). Liberation Management. New York: Random House.

Peters, Tom & Waterman, Robert H., Jr. (1982). In Search of Excellence. New York: Alfred A. Knopf.

Peters, Tom & Austin, Nancy (1983). A Passion for Excellence. New York: Alfred A. Knopf.

Peterson, Richard B. & Tracy, Lane (1979). Systematic Management of Human Resources. Reading, MA: Addison-Wesley Publishing Company.

Petrie, H. G. (1968).The Strategy Sense of Methodology. Philosophy of Science, pp. 248-257.

Petrov V. (2006). Law – Antilaw. ETRIA TRIZ Futures Conference 2006. 5th ETRIA. 9-11 October 2006. Kortrijk, Belgium. pp. 133-140

Petrov V. (2006). History of Developing the Algorithm of Solving Inventive Problems: ARIZ, Tel-Aviv, 2006 (in Russan: В. Петров. История разработки Алгоритма Решения Изобретательских Задач. Тель Авив, 2006).

Petrov V. (2003). History of Developing Standards, Tel-Aviv, 2003 (In Russian: В. Петров. История Развития Стандартов. Тель-Авив, 2003)

Petrov V. (2001). Laws of Systems Evolution, Tel-Aviv, 2001 (In Russian: В. Петров. Законы Развития Систем. Тель-Авив, 2001)

http://www.trizland.ru/trizba/books/1759/

Petrov V. (2013). The Laws of System Evolution. Berlin: TriS Europe GmbH, 646 pages (in Russian: INNOVATOR (06) 01/2013, ISSN 1866-4180. Петров В. Законы развития систем. Монография. Тель-Авив, 2013 – 646 с.

Petrov V. (2002). Dictionary of TRIZ Terms, 2002.

Polinpapilinho, F. Katina & Ra'ed, M. Jaradat: A Three-Phase Framework for Elicitation of Infrastructure Requirements. International Journal Critical Infrastructures. Vol. 8, Nos. 2/3, 2012. National Centers for System of Systems Engineering, Norfolk, VA 23508, USA

Polinpapilinho F. Katina and Charles B. Keating. Metasystem Pathologies: Towards Discovering of Impediments to System Performance. The National Centers for System of Systems Engineering Department of Engineering Management and Systems Engineering. Old Dominion University, Norfolk, VA Proceedings of the 2016 Industrial and Systems Engineering Research Conference. H. Yang, Z. Kong, and MD Sarder, eds.

Polkinghorne, Donald (1983). Methodology for the Human Sciences: Systems of Inquiry. Albany: State University of New York Press.

Pontifex, Mark & Illtyd, Trethowan (1953). Meaning of Existence. London: Longmans, Green and Company

Posner, Michael I. (ED.) (1989). Foundations of Cognitive Science. Cambridge, MA: MIT Press.

Pouvreau, David (2009). The Dialectical Tragedy of the Concept of Wholeness: Ludwig von Bertalanffy's Biography Revisited. Exploring Unity through Diversity: Volume 1

Pouvreau, David (2013). The Project of "General Systemology" Instigated by Ludwig Von Bertalanffy Genealogy, Genesis, Reception and Advancement. Bertalanffy Center for the Study of Systems Science, Vienna, Austria.

Pouvreau, David (2014). On the History of Ludwig Von Bertalanffy's "General Systemology", and on Its Relationship to Cybernetics - Part II: Contexts and Developments of the Systemological Hermeneutics Instigated by Von Bertalanffy. International Journal of General Systems.

Prevention Committee President's Council on Integrity and Efficiency (1986). Computer: Crimes, Clues and Controls. Washington, D. C: Prevention Committee President's Council on Integrity and Efficiency.

Prigogine, I. (1976). Order through Fluctuation: Self-Organization and Social Systems. Jantsch, E. & Waddington, C. H. (Eds.). Evolution and Consciousness: Human Systems in Transitions. Reading, MA: Addison-Wesley Publishing Company.

Prince, Howard T., II (1985). (Ed.), Leadership in Organizations. West Point: Associates, The Department of Behavioral Science and Leadership, United States Military Academy

Probity, Inc. (1990). Tools and Techniques of Basic Project Management. Tucson: Probity.

Progoff, Ira (1990). Forward, in Mysticism: The Preeminent Study in the Nature and Development of Spiritual Consciousness. Twelfth Edition. Underhill, Evelyn (1990) New York, New York: Doubleday.

Prushinskiy V., Zainiev G. & Gerasimov V. (2005). Hybridization: The New Warfare in the Battle for the Market, Ideation International, Inc., 2005

Pugh, D. S., Hickson, D. J., & Hinings, C. R. (1964). Writers on Structure of Functioning of Management of People in Organizations in Society. New York: Penguin Books.

QED Information Sciences, Inc. (1985a). Security Evaluation for Small Computer Centers. Wellesley, MA: Q.E.D. Information Sciences, Inc.

QED Information Sciences, Inc. (1985b). Disaster Recovery: Contingency Planning and Program Evaluation. Wellesley, MA: Q.E.D. Information Sciences, Inc.

QED Information Sciences, Inc. (1985c). Personnel Productivity Management: Organization, Planning, Implementation and Control. Wellesley, MA: Q.E.D. Information Sciences, Inc.

Quick, James C. & Quick, Jonathan D. (1984). Organizational Stress and Preventive Management. New York: McGraw-Hill Book Company.

Quinlan et al. (2015). Quantifying Resilience: Measuring and Assessing Resilience: Broadening Understanding through Multiple Disciplinary Perspective. Journal of Applied Ecology.

Quinn, James Brian (1992). Intelligent Enterprises. New York: The Free Press.

Radner, Daisie & Radner, Michael (1982). Science and Unreason. Belmont, CA: Wadsworth Publishing Company.

Rado, Sandor (1969). Adaptational Psychodynamics: Motivation and Control. New York: Science House.

Rahman, M.A. (1993). People's Self-Development: Perspectives on Participatory Action Research: A Journey through Experience. Zed Books: London.

Ramirez, Rafael, Ph.D. (1991). The Beauty of Social Organization. Munich: ACCEDO

Verlagsgesellschaft mbH.

Ramamoorthy, C. V., et al. (1990). The Evolution Support Environment. IEEE

Transactions on Software Engineering,16 (11), pp. 1225-1235.

Rapoport, Vladimir S. (1987). Complex Relationships As a Subject-Matter Of Management Systems Analysis and Design. From Design Inquiry, Vol.I., edited by Bela Banathy, Ph.D. San Francisco, California: International Systems Institute.

Ray, Michael and Myers, Rochelle (1986). Creativity in Business. New York: Doubleday.

Reason, P. & Rowan, J. (1981). (Eds.) Human Inquiry: A Sourcebook of New Paradigm Research. Chichester, England: Wiley & Sons.

Reason, P. (ed.) (1988). Human Inquiry in Action: Developments in New Paradigm Research. Sage: London.

Reckmeyer, W. J. (1982). The Emerging Systems Paradigm: A Historical Perspective.

Washington, D. C: The American University (Unpublished Doctoral Dissertation).

Ritzer, G. (1977). Working: Conflict and Change. Englewood Cliffs: Prentice-Hall, Inc.

Robertson, Scott P., et al. (1991). Human Factors in Computing Systems: Reaching through Technology, CHI'91 Conference Proceedings. Sponsored by the ACM's SIG on Computer Human Interaction. New York: The Association for Computing Machinery

Robinson, Peter (1991). Real-Time Processing System Presentation. Los Angeles: Security Pacific Automation Company.

Roeber, Richard J. C. (1973). The Organization in a Changing Environment. Reading, MA: Addison- Wesley Publishing Company.

Roethlisberger, F. & Dickson, J. J. (1939). Management and the Worker. Cambridge, MA: Harvard University Press.

Rogers, Joyce. Mysticism as a Way of Spirituality, Spirituality Today, Summer 1988, Vol. 40 No. 2, pp. 100-108.

Rolheiser, Ronald (1999). The Holy Longing: The Search for a Christian Spirituality. Doubleday, New York, New York.

Rorty, Richard (1981). Philosophy and the Mirror of Nature. Princeton, New Jersey: Princeton University Press.

Rorty, Richard (1998). Truth and Progress, Philosophical Papers, Volume 3. New York: Cambridge University Press.

Rosen, Robert H., Ph.D. (1991). The Healthy Company: Eight Strategies to Develop People, Productivity, and Profits. Los Angeles: Jeremy P. Tarcher, Inc.

Rosenau, Pauline Marie (1992). Post-Modernism and the Social Sciences: Insights, Inroads, and Intrusions. Princeton, NJ: Princeton University Press.

Rosenbaum, Stephanie (1989). The Role of Human Factors and Usability Testing in the Software Testing Process. Sixth International Conference on Testing Computer Software, May 25, 1989. Ann Arbor, MI: Tec-Ed Technical Publications and Graphics Services.

Rosenbluth, Hal F. & Peters, Diane McFerrin (1992). The Customer Comes Second and Other Secrets of Exceptional Service. New York: William Morrow and Company, Inc.

Roy, Sonam (2016). Insiders and Insider Threats an Overview of Definitions and Mitigation Techniques. Indian Institute of Space Science and Technology, Thiruvananthapu.

RTPS Operational Evaluation Team (1991). Real Time Processing System (RTPS) Operational Evaluation Analysis. Los Angeles: Security Pacific Automation Company.

RTPS Project Team (1989). Security Pacific Automation Company Real Time Processing System Project High-Level Requirements Document. Los Angeles: SPAC

RTPS Project Team (1990). Security Pacific Automation Company Real Time Processing Project Supplementary. Systems Management Institute, Pleasant Hill, CA.

Ruchlis, Hy & Oddo, Sandra (1990). Clear Thinking: A Practical Introduction. Buffalo: Prometheus Books.

Runes, Dagobert D. (1967). The Treasury of Philosophy. Totowa, NJ: Littlefield, Adams & Company.

Ruscoe, G.C., Fell, R.L., et al. (1985). The Application of Living Systems Theory to 41 U.S. Army Battalions. Behavioral Science, 30, pp. 7-52.

Russell, Jeffrey Burton (2005). Historical Errors Impeding Progress in Science and Religion, Spiritual Information 100 Perspectives on Science and Religion. Charles L. Harper, Jr. (Ed.). Philadelphia, PA: Templeton Foundation Press. pp. 63-67.

Russell, P. (1983). The Global Brain. Los Angeles: J. P. Tarcher.

Russo, J. Edward & Schoemaker, Paul J. H. (1989). Decision Traps: The Ten Barriers to Brilliant Decision-Making and How to Overcome Them. New York: Simon & Schuster, Inc.

Sackman, Harold (1971). Mass Information Utilities and Social Excellence. New York: Auerbach Publishers.

Sakaiya, Taichi (1991). The Knowledge-Value Revolution or a History of the Future. New York: Kodansha International

Salk, Jonas (1983). Autonomy of Reality: Merging of Intuition and Reason. New York: Columbia University Press.

Salner, Marcia (1985). The Relationship of Naive Epistemology to Formal Epistemology: Implications for the Teaching of Human Science Methodology, Methods, Donald E. Polkinghorne (Ed.). San Francisco: Saybrook.

Sampson, Edward E. (1983). Justice and the Critique of Pure Psychology. New York: Plenum Press.

Salamatov Yu. (1999). TRIZ: The Right Solution at the Right Time. Insytec, The Netherlands,

Savary, Louis M., Berne, Patricia H., & Williams, Strephon Kaplan (1984). Dreams and Spiritual Growth: A Christian Approach to Dreamwork. Ramsey, N.J: Paulist Press.

Schank, Roger & Childers, Peter (1988). The Creative Attitude: Learning to Ask and Answer the Right Questions. New York: Macmillan Publishing Company.

Scharch, Richard, L. (1954). Dynamic Equilibrium.

Scharfstein, Ben-Ami, et al. (1978). Philosophy East Philosophy West: A Critical Comparison of Indian, Chinese, Islamic, and European Philosophy. Ben-Ami Scharfstein (Ed.). New York: Oxford University Press

Schloss, Jeffrey, (2005). Hath Darwin Suffered a Prophet's Scorn? Spiritual Information: 100 Perspectves on Science and Religion, Charles L. Harper, Jr. ed. Philadelphia, PA: Templeton Foundation Press, 2005.

Schneiders, Sandra, (2005). The Study of Christian Spirituality: Contours and Dynamics of a Discipline, Minding the Spirit: The Study of Christian Spirituality. Elizabeth A. Dreyer & Marki S. Burrows eds. Baltimore, MD: The Johns Hopkins University Press.

Schneiders, Sandra, (2005). A Hermeneutical Approach to the Study of Christian Spirituality, Minding The Spirit: The Study of Christian Spirituality. Elizabeth A. Dreyer & Marki S. Burrows eds. Baltimore, MD: The Johns Hopkins University Press.

Security Pacific Automation Company (1989a). ADS/Se Software Engineering Methodology. Los Angeles: Security Pacific Automation Company.

Security Pacific Automation Company (1989b). Real-Time Processing System Project High-Level Requirements Document. Los Angeles: Security Pacific Automation Company, RTPS Project Team.

Security Pacific Automation Company (1991). RTPS: Real Time Processing System Operational Evaluation Analysis. Los Angeles: Security Pacific Automation Company.

Semke, Jeannette & Nurius, Paula (1990, September). Information Structure, Information Technology and the Human Service Organizational Environment. Proceedings of the Conference on Computers and the Quality of Life CQL '90. Washington, D.C., The George Washington University: ACM Special Interest Group on Computers & Society and ACM Special Interest Group on Computers and the Physically Handicapped, p. 20.

Senge, Peter M. (1990). The Fifth Discipline: The Art & Practice of the Learning Organization. New York: Doubleday.

Shaeffer, Francis (1990). Escape from Reason, in the Francis A. Shaeffer Triology. Westchester, IL: Crossway.

Shannon, Claude (1948). A Mathematical Theory of Communication. Urbana, ILL: University of Illinois Press.

Sheldrake, Rupert (1981). A New Science of Life: The Hypothesis of Formative Causation. Los Angeles: Jeremy P. Tarcher, Inc.

Sherif,M., & M. Cantril (1945). "The Psychology of Attitudes". Psychological Review 52 301-4.

Shick, Deana & Kyle O'Meara (2016). A Unique Approach to Threat Analysis Mapping: A Malware-Centric Methodology for Better Understanding, the Adversary Landscape.

Shneiderman, Ben (1991, January). Human Values and the Future of Technology: A

Declaration of Responsibility. SIGCHI Bulletin, 23(1). New York: Association for Computing Machinery.

Silberstein, Michael (2005). On the Perennial Oneness of Being, Spiritual Information: 100 Perspectves on Science and Religion, Charles L. Harper, Jr. ed. Philadelphia, PA: Templeton Foundation Press, 2005.

Siler, Todd (1990). Breaking the Mind Barrier. New York: Simon & Schuster.

Silva, Michael & Sjogren, Bertil (1990). Europe 1992 & the New World Power Game. New York: John Wiley & Sons.

Silver, Susan (1989). Organized to Be the Best! Los Angeles: Adams-Hall Publishing.

Simon, Hebert A. (1964). The Architecture of Complexity. Readings in Managerial Psychology, Second Edition. Leavitt, Harold J. & Pondy, Louis R. (Eds.). Chicago: The University of Chicago Press.

Simon, Hebert A. (1969). The Sciences of the Artificial. Cambridge, MA: MIT Press.

Slawski, C. (1987). Causing Social Change. Proceedings of the Society for General Systems Research, Supplement, pp. 66-86.

Sloma, Richard S. (1977). No-Nonsense Management. New York: Bantam Books.

SMI (1990a). Systems Management Institute Audit Team Handbook for the RTPS Operational Evaluation and Performance Test Phase, Vol.1. Pleasant Hill, CA: Systems Management Institute Press.

SMI (1990a). Systems Management Institute Audit Team Handbook for the RTPS Operational Evaluation and Performance Test Phase, Vol. 2. Pleasant Hill, CA: Systems Management Institute Press.

SMI (1990a). Systems Management Institute Audit Team Handbook for the RTPS Operational Evaluation and Performance Test Phase, Vol. 3. Pleasant Hill, CA: SMI Press.

Smith, James K. A. (2006). Who's Afraid of Postmodernism Taking Derrida, Lyotard, and Foucault to Church. Grand Rapids, Michigan: Baker Academic.

Smolarski, Dennis C. (1988). The Spirituality of Computers, Spirituality Today, Winter 1988, Vol. 40 No. 4, pp. 292-307.

Sommer, R. (1974). Tight Spaces: Hard Architecture and How to Humanize It. Englewood Cliffs: Prentice-Hall, Inc

Souchkov V., Kucharavy D., Devoino I. (1991). Invention Machine Terms Dictionary, Invention Machine Labs, 1991.

Spirn, J. R. (1977). Program Behavior: Models and Measurements. New York: Elsevier

Stamps, Jeffrey S. (1980). Holonomy: A Human Systems Theory. Seaside, CA: Intersystems.

Stanat, Ruth (1990). The Intelligent Corporation: Creating a Shared Network for Information and Profit. New York: American Management Association.

Stannard, F. Russell (2005). Proof or Persuasion? Spiritual Information: 100 Perspectives on Science and Religion, Charles L. Harper, Jr. ed. Philadelphia, PA: Templeton Foundation Press, 2005.

Steers, R. M. (1977). Organizational Effectiveness: A Behavioral View. Santa Monica, CA: Goodyear.

Stern, Nancy & Stern, Robert A. (1983). Computers in Society. Englewood Cliffs: Prentice-Hall.

Sternberg, Robert J. (1988). The Triarchic Mind: A New Theory of Human Intelligence. New York: Penguin Books.

Stewart, Hugh B. (1989). Recollecting the Future: A View of Business, Technology, and Innovation in the Next 30 Years. Homewood, IL: Dow Jones-Irwin.

Stich, Stephen P. (Ed.) (1975). Innate Ideas. Berkeley, CA: University of California Press

Strauss, Danie (2016). The Tension between (Methodological) Individualism and Holism. Journal of Christian Scholarship.

Studenmund, A. H. (2013). Using Econometrics, Pearson

Suarez, Antoine (2005). Do Quantum Experiments Challenge Kant's Criticism of the Proofs for the Existence of God? Spiritual Information: 100 Perspectives on Science and Religion, Charles L. Harper, Jr. ed. Philadelphia, PA: Templeton Foundation Press, 2005.

Suarez, Francis (1947). On the Various Kinds of Distinctions. Translated by Cyril Vollert in the: Disputationes Metaphysicae, Disp. No. 7. Milwaukee, WI: Marquette University Press

Sutherland, J. W. (1973). A General Systems Philosophy for the Social and Behavioral Sciences. New York: George Braziller.

Taket, Ann & White, Leroy (1996). Pragmatic Pluralism, an Explication. Systems Practice, 9(6), 571-586.

Talbot, Michael (1991). The Holographic Universe. New York: Harper Collins Publishers.

Tapscott, Don & Caston, Art (1993). Paradign Shift the New Promise of Information Technology. New York: McGraw Hill, Inc.

Taylor, Charles (1989). Sources of the Self: The Making of the Modern Identity. Cambridge, MA: Harvard University Press.

Teilhard de Chardin, Pierre (1965). The Phenomenon of Man (2nd ed.). New Your York.

Terninko, John (2011): 40 Inventive Principles with Social Examples. Responsible Management 62 Case Rd. Nottingham, NH 03290-5507 USA

Thayer, Frederick (1972). General System(s) Theory: The Promise That Could Not Be Kept, Academy of Management Journal, XV (1972).

Thomas, Keith A. (1987). Building an Open System. New York: Van Nostrand Reinhold Company.

Thompson, James D. (1976). Organizations in Action. New York: McGraw-Hill Book Company.

Thompson, John B. (1984). Studies in the Theory of Ideology. Berkeley, CA: University of California Press.

Thomsett, Rob (1993). Third Wave Project Management: A Handbook for Managing the Complex Information Systems for the 1990s. Englewood Cliffs: Prentice Hall, Inc.

Tinbergen, Jan (1958). The Design of Development. The International Development Institute, International Bank for Reconstruction and Development. Baltimore, MD: The Johns Hopkins Press.

Todd, Mary Anne & Guitian, Constance (1989). Computer Security Training Guidelines. Washington, D.C: National Institute of Standards and Technology.

Toffler, A. (1971). Future Shock. New York: Bantam Books.

Toffler, A. (1980). The Third Wave. New York: Bantam Books.

Toffler, A. (1990). Power Shift: Knowledge, Wealth, and Violence at the Edge of the 21st Century. New York: Bantam Books.

Tosi, Henry L. & Hammer, W. Clay (Eds.) (1977). Organizational Behavior and Management: A Contingency Approach. Chicago: St. Clair Press.

Trist, E.L. (1978). Adapting to a Changing World. Readings in Quality of Working Life, George F. Sanderson, (Ed.). Ottawa: Labour Canada, pp. 10-20

Tschudin, Alain J-P. C. (2005). Preparing the Way for the lord: Evolution, Christianity, and the Dialog on Moral Freedom, Spiritual Information: 100 Perspectives on Science and Religion, Charles L. Harper, Jr. ed. Philadelphia, PA: Templeton Foundation Press, 2005.

Tsoukas, Haridimos; Papoulias, Demetrios B. (1996). Creativity in OR/MS: From Technique to Epistemology: Interfaces, 26(2), 73-79.

Turnage, Janet J. (1990, February). The Challenge of New Workplace Technology for Psychology. American Psychologist, 45(2), pp. 171-178.

Thurstone, L.L., & E.J. Chave (1929). The Measurement of Attitudes.Chicago: University of Chicago press.

Ulrich, Werner (1983). Critical Heuristics of Social Planing: A New Approach to Practical Philosophy. Wiley: Chichester.

Underhill, Evelyn (1990). Mysticism: The Preeminent Study in the Nature and Development of Spiritual Consciousness. Twelfth Edition. New York, New York: Doubleday.

Van Fleet, James K. (1983). 25 Steps to Power and Mastery over People. West Nyack, NY: Parker Publishing Company, Inc

Vam Kaam, Adrian, Fr. & Muto, Susan, Dr. (1978). Questions and Answers on Formative Spirituality: Am I Living a Spiritual Life? Dimension Books, New Jersey.

Vetter, Jennifer, (Ed.). (2016). Franciscan Virtues through the Year: 52 Steps to Conversion from St. Francis of Assisi. Written by Members of the Confraternity of Penitents.

Vikentiev I. (1987). A Spatial Geometrical Operator, Leningrad, 1987 (In Russian: И. Викентьев, Пространственный Геометрический Оператор. Ленинград, 1987).

Vost, Kevin (2018). How to Think Like Aquinas. Sophia Institute Press: Manchester, New Hampshire.

Wack, John P. & Carnahan, Lisa A. (1989). Computer Viruses and Related Threats: A Management Guide. Washington, D. C: National Institute of Standards and Technology.

Wadsworth (1973). The Human Side of Data Processing Management. Englewood Cliffs: Prentice-Hall, Inc.

Wagner, Clare (1985). Current Trends: Spirituality in a Dark Age: Some Reflections, Spirituality Today, Spring 1985, Vol. 37, pp. 59-71.

Wallace, Robert H., Stockenberg, John E., & Charette, Robert N. (1987). A Unified

Methodology for Developing Systems. New York: Intertext Publications, Inc., McGraw-Hill, Inc.

Walsh, Mike (1991). Productivity Sand Traps & Tar Pits: How to Detect and Avoid Them. New York: Dorset House Publishing.

Walsh, Myles E. (1981). Understanding Computers: What Managers and Users Need to Know. New York: John Wiley & Sons.

Walshe, T. J. (1933). Quest of Reality. Saint Louis, MO: B. Herder Book Company.

Warfield, J. N. (1987a). Education in Generic Design. Bela Banathy (Ed.). Design Inquiry, pp. 185-196. San Francisco: International Systems Institute & International Society for General Systems Research.

Warshaw, Leon J. (1979). Managing Stress. Reading, MA: Addison-Wesley Publishing Company.

Watkins, J. W. N. (1953). Ideal Types and Historical Explanation, in H. Feigl & M. Brodbeck (EDs.), Readings in the Philosophy of Science. New York.

Watkins, J. W. N. (1958). The Alleged Inadequacy of Methodological Individualism, Journal of Philosophy, LV (1958).

Watkins, J. W. N. (1959). Historical Explanation in the Social Sciences, in Patrick Gardiner (Ed.), Theories of History. New York.

Watson, Paul K. (2005). Living Purpose: The Study of Purpose in the Living World as a Sources of New Spiritual Information, Spiritual Information 100 Perspectives on Science and Religion, Charles L. Harper, Jr. (Ed.). Philadelphia, PA: Templeton Foundation Press. (p. 301).

Weber, Zach: Paradox and Foundation. Submitted in Total Fulfillment of the Requirements of the Degree of Doctor of Philosophy.May 2009

Website: Official G.S. Altshuller Foundation. http://www.altshuller.ru. Last seen: 01.12.2013.

Website: Ideation International Inc. http://www.ideationtriz.com. Last seen: 01.12.2013.

Website: http://www.metodolog.ru Last seen: 01.12.2013.

Website: Wikipedia: TRIZ. http://en.wikipedia.org/wiki/TRIZ. Last seen: 01.12.2013.

Weinberg, Gerald M. (1975). An Introduction to General Systems Thinking. New York: John Wiley & Sons.

Weinberg, Gerald M. (1982). Overstructured Management of Software Engineering. Proceedings, Sixth International Conference of Software Engineering. Washington, D.C: IEEE Computer Society. Pp.2-8.

Weinberg, Gerald M. (1986). Becoming a Technical Leader: An Organic Problem-Solving Approach. New York: Dorset House Publishing Company.

Weinberg, Gerald M. (1992). Quality Software Management Volume 1 Systems Thinking. New York: Dorset House Publishing.

Weinberg, Harry L. (1959) Levels of Knowing and Existence. Harper & Brothers, Publishers New York.

Weisbord, Marvin R. (1987). Productive Workplaces: Organizing and Managing for Dignity, Meaning, and Community. San Francisco: Jossey-Bass Publishers

Weiss, Paul (1967). The Living System: Determinism Stratified, in Koestler & Smythies, Beyond Reductionism. New York.

Weiss, Paul (1967). One Plus One Does Not Equal Two, in G. C. Quarton, T. Melnechuk, & F. O. Schmitt (EDs.), The Neurosciences: A Study Program. New York.

Wexley & Yukl (1977). Organizational Behavior and Personnel Psychology. Homewood, IL: Richard D. Irwin, Inc.

Wheatley, Edward W. (1976). Values in Conflict. Miami: Banyan Books.

Wheelwright, Steven C. & Makridakis, Spyros (1980). Forecasting Methods for Management, 3rd Ed. New York: John Wiley & Sons.

Whitaker, Randall, Essler, Ulf & Ostberg, Olov (1991). Participatory Business Modeling. Sweden: Lulea University, Research Report, Tulea 1991: 31.

Whitehead, Alfred N. (1929). Process and Reality. New York: The Free Press.

Whyte, W.F. (ed.) (1991) Participatory Action Research. Sage: London.

Wilber, Ken (2000). Integral Psychology: Consciousness, Spirit, Psychology, Therapy. Shambhala Publications House, Boston, MA.

Wildman, Wesley J. (2005). Global Spiritual Confusion and the Neglected Problem of Excess Spiritual Information, Spiritual Information 100 Perspectives on Science and Religion, Charles L. Harper, Jr. (Ed.). Philadelphia, PA: Templeton Foundation Press. (pp. 33-38).

Williams, Raymond (1989). The Politics of Moderism. New York: Verso.

Wilson, Anne. Holistic Spirituality, Spirituality Today, Autumn 1988, Vol. 40 No. 3, pp. 208-219.

Wiseman, James A. Teaching Spiritual Theology: Methodological Reflections, Spirituality Today, Summer 1989, Vol. 41 No. 2, pp. 143-159.

Wittgenstein, L. (1961). Tractatus Logico-Philosophicus. London: Routledge & Kegan Paul.

Wolman, Benjamin D. (Ed.). (1973). Handbook of General Psychology. Englewood Cliffs: Prentice-Hall, Inc.

Wood, C. C., et al. (1987). Computer Security: A Comprehensive Controls Checklist. New York: John Wiley & Sons.

Woodcock, Alexander & Davis, Monte (1978). Catastrophe Theory. New York: Penguin.

Woodson, Wesley E. (1987). Human Factors Reference Guide for Electronics and Computer Professionals. New York: McGraw-Hill Book Company.

Wooldridge, Susan, Corder, Colin, & Johnson, Calude (1973). Security Standards for Data Processing. New York: John Wiley $ Sons.

Wriston, Walter B. (1992). The Twilight of Sovereignty: How the Information Revolution is Transforming Our World. New York: Charles Scribner's Son's.

Yolles M. I. (1996): Critical Systems Thinking, Paradigms, and the Modelling Space. Systems Practice,

Yourdon, Edward (1975). Case Studies in Object Oriented Analysis and Design, Yourdon Press.

Yourdon, Edward (1975). Structured Design. Yourdon Press.

Yourdon, Edward (1989). Modern Structured Analysis. Englewood Cliffs, Yourdon Press.

Yourdon, Edward (1992). Decline & Fall of the American Programmer. Englewood Cliffs: Yourdon Press.

Yourdon, Edward (1994). Object Oriented Systems Design. Yourdon Press.

Yourdon, Edward, (1996). Rise and Resurrection of the American Programmer, Prentice Hall.

Yourdon, Edward (2002). Managing High Intensity Internet Projects, Yourdon Press.

Zandar, Alvin (1994). Making Groups Effective, 2nd Edition.Jossey Bass Publishers, San Francis co.

Zeben, Josephine van (2019). Polycentricity as a Theory of Governance from Part I University of Oxford, Ana Bobić Publisher: Cambridge University Press DOI: https://doi.org/10.1017/9781108528771.003, pp 9-27

Zedeck, Sheldon & Mosier, Kethleen (1990, February). Work in the Family and Employing Organization, American Psychologist. 45(2), pp. 24-251.

Zerzan, John & Carnes, Alice (1988). Questioning Technology. London: Freedom Press.

Zlotin B. & Litvin S. (1977). Creative Imagination Development, St. Petersburg, 1977 (in Russian: Злотин Б., Литвин С. Развитие Творческого Воображения. Ленинград, 1977)

Zlotin B., Zusman A., Altshuller G. & Philatov V. (1999). Tools of Classical TRIZ, Ideation International, 1999

Zlotin B. and Zusman A. (2001). Directed Evolution: Philosophy, Theory and Practice, Ideation International Inc., 2001

Zuboff, Shoshana (1984). In the Age of the Smart Machine: The Future of Work and Power. New York: Basic Books.

Zuker, Elaina (1991). The Seven Secrets of Influence. New York: McGraw-Hill, Inc.

Zvegintzov, N. (1982). What Life? What Cycle? Proceedings of the National Computer Conference. Reston, VA: AFIPS Press, pp. 563-568.

Zwart, Martin (1990). Constraint Driven Design/Engineering. Amsterdam: P.Q. Information Group, b.v., Mosselaan 57, 1934 PJ, Egmond a/d Hoef Netherlands.

Zwart, Martin (1991a). Integration of Workflow & EXTRA. Amsterdam: P.Q. Information Group, b. v.

Zwart, Martin (1991b). Object Documentation System. Amsterdam: P.Q. Information Group.

About the Author

Dr. Raymond Leslie Newkirk, Psy.D., Ph.D., Ph.D.
Founder, Entrepreneur, Product Architect, Inventive Problem Solver, Virtual-Learning Pioneer, Deep Technology Scientist, Thought Leader, Consultant, Mentor, Publisher Author, Speaker, Internationally Ranked Athlete.

Raymond L. Newkirk is an internationally respected consulting specialist having earned advanced degrees and certifications in several disciplines including Ph.Ds. in the Philosophy of Science and Behavioral Science, Psy.D. in Clinical Psychology, Th.C., in Theology and the Ph.D. with Distinction in Human Science. Dr. Newkirk originated the Ulthule™ approach to human performance and the Applied Intuitive Solutions™ Inventive Problem- Solving Knowledge Base System. His professional background includes a distinguished career in multicultural research, human system design, and executive development. He has presented the Keynote Address to global audiences.

He is the Founder & CEO of the Systems Management Institute, a firm that applies human systems design to the building of high-performance organizations. He was Founder and Chairman of Bay University, an innovative E-Learning Company. He has enjoyed a life-long interest in business and enterprise incubation. He founded his first company at the age of 16, a janitorial service with three employees, and has organized start-ups & joint ventures ever since.

Dr. Newkirk has served in diverse industries and executive capacities. He was a Senior Fellow of the Monterey Bay Management Group. He served as Chief Operating Officer of Mindmaker, Inc. of San Jose, California, an early A/I and neural net pioneer that won Best of Comdex two years consecutively during the dot.com revolution in Silicon Valley. He also served as President and Chief Operating Officer of P.Q. Information Group, b.v. the Netherlands, an innovative company that pioneered Business Rules processing software development, and Founder of the International Association of Information Management.

He led projects for the Minister of Defense and Aviation and the Royal Saudi Naval Forces for the Kingdom of Saudi Arabia and for the Office of the President, Republic of the Philippines. Dr. Newkirk has led industry-changing engagements for Southwest Bell, Bank of America, and Dell Computers. He was a VIP Priority Guest of the CNN World Business Development Congress. He was invited as a visiting Ambassador in Business Development and Technology Transfer to the Soviet Union and as an expert guest to development conferences in Cairo, Egypt and Oxford, England. He conducted seminars for Technology Transfer, Rome, I.B.C. London and Amsterdam and S.I.B.C. Jeddah, Kingdom of Saudi Arabia.

Dr. Newkirk never stops writing. A prolific writer, he has published more than 1,600 articles, monographs, books, e-learning courses, blogs, and guest columns for the San Francisco Examiner. His latest book, Navigating Sociopaths at Work, will be available early in 2020. His most recent book, Leading by Design, has become a widely sought collector's book that is available through the Systems Management Institute Press, Amazon, or Booklocker Press. His next book series, Ray Newkirk Tackles Workplace Relationships, advances a fresh look at leadership thinking and establishes the foundation for a new science of Leadership. He has authored works in English, Italian, Russian, Arabic, and Latin. He is the producer of the Ray Newkirk Library Series. He advocates the intellectual, physical, and spiritual development of the person. He studied philosophy as a Benedictine Monk in Italy and studied theology with the Franciscan Friars in Washington D.C. He participated for many years with the Amateur Athletic Union (AAU) both as a competitor and supporter.

Early in his athletic career, he attained international ranking in Olympic Weightlifting having won 12 championships and set 22 competitive records in the sport. He won Outstanding Weightlifter Award, Ohio State A.A.U. A few of his many records still stand today. Currently, he is in training to compete in the Masters World Championships and was the reigning Pacific Weightlifting Association Masters Champion where he is still in the business of chasing records.

As an amateur explorer, Ray went diving in the Red Sea, mountain climbing in Alaska, worked as a deck hand on Dutch freighter, sailed in the Bahamas, and enjoyed deep-sea fishing in the Caribbean, among other global adventures. Dr. Newkirk is an innovative social thinker. He is concerned about the problems facing the elderly in this technological and fast paced age. He has conducted workshops for senior citizens & executives on health, nutrition, and stress management. He established a health clinic and medical network for the elderly. He also contributed to the establishment of an orphanage in the Third World, funded fellowships for students in Eastern Europe to travel abroad and participate in seminars and professional training, and established a Southeast Asian International Fellowship. Dr. Newkirk's Guiding Perspective is:

Life, Love, Leadership, Growth, & Honor
"Live life fully. Love deeply with wisdom.
Lead others to great achievement.
Grow spiritually and intellectually.
Honor God in all I do."

SMI
Systems Management Institute

Visit www.smirsp.com[1]

or

email: rnewkirk@smilc.info

www.drraynewkirk.com[2]

1. http://www.smirsp.com

2. http://www.drraynewkirk.com

Don't miss out!

Visit the website below and you can sign up to receive emails whenever Dr. Raymond Leslie Newkirk publishes a new book. There's no charge and no obligation.

https://books2read.com/r/B-A-HJRKE-EPZMH

BOOKS 2 READ

Connecting independent readers to independent writers.

Did you love *Insider Threat Prevention Part 5*? Then you should read *21st Century Executive Life*[3] by Dr. Raymond Leslie Newkirk!

[4]

Adding people to an organization or transferring them out of an organization changes the culture of that organization. Imparting new knowledge changes culture. Changes in the structure, environment, or processes of a culture change that culture. Even the emotional transformation of a single member of a team changes the culture of that team. Change is everywhere. As the Greek philosopher Heraclitus (c. 500 BCE) told us more than 25 centuries ago, we cannot walk into the same river twice, change is every day. Change is continual. Just like that river of long ago, we cannot walk into the same organization twice. We and the world we live in, our reality, experience a continuous process of transformation. Change is inevitable. Even the people who do not like change, change. Learn to take charge of it.

---

3. https://books2read.com/u/47DAMj

4. https://books2read.com/u/47DAMj

The point here is that cultures are forever in flux. We cannot prevent a culture from evolving. However, we can guide the direction of such inevitable change. This is Evolutionary Leadership, or Leadership by Design. Functioning as an Evolutionary Guidance System, enterprise leadership can guide the evolutionary unfolding of an organization. In precisely this way, leaders guide the evolution of an organization from one state of culture to another. This is the best anyone can do. Think about it. As you do so, learn to leverage the power of change to defuse the treats of Cyber Terror. This will be one change that you can live with comfortably. Life is like a roller-coaster more often than we ever imagine.

Compelled by my driving interest in the success of other people, I am very much interested in the nature of Leadership and the leaders who attain the heights of Leadership success, something I call Ulthule™, my unique expression.

I think that it is interesting to note that over the years, I have found that the great majority of these leaders are unknown, unrecognized, and hidden behind the scene. For every great leader who is honored by peers and strangers alike, a dozen leaders carry him or her on their shoulders to savor the glory. This is no accident. For the hallmark of great Leadership is not fame, but it is actually evolutionary unfolding and design competence. This may not be where your prejudices lie, and it may be contrary to your opinions, common wisdom, or even your gut intuition. Nevertheless, it is the reality of leaders that they guide the evolutionary unfolding of their teams and organizations by unleashing the power of their design competence.

I have been deeply interested in people having a wonderful life for as long as I can remember. I like it a lot when things go well for others. What about you? I love the feeling of being around happy people, excited people, vibrantly joyful people, and involved people. I like to see people strive, grow, reach, yearn, and yes find satisfaction in the striving, growing, reaching, and yearning. Being part of a great experience like this is beyond mere satisfaction. And it is all the more exciting to see people achieve their dreams and become better for it. Life throws so much at us every day that it takes a lot of personal something for us to strive for achievement in spite of the obstacles that life brings our way. Think about it.

www.ingramcontent.com/pod-product-compliance
Lightning Source LLC
LaVergne TN
LVHW090316210926
848480LV00001B/268